The Many Careers of

D.D. KOSAMBI

The Many Careers of

D.D. KOSAMBI

Critical Essays

Edited by D.N. Jha

LeftWord

Offset edition first published in October 2011.
Digital print edition, January 2020.

LeftWord Books
2254/2A Shadi Khampur
New Ranjit Nagar
New Delhi 110008
INDIA

www.leftword.com

LeftWord Books is a division of
Naya Rasta Publishers Pvt. Ltd.

ISBN 978-93-80118-06-2

Contents

Preface

The birth centenary of Damodar Dharmanand Kosambi was celebrated in 2007 by several universities and other academic institutions in India. In the following year the *Economic and Political Weekly* brought out a special issue containing articles by scholars who attempted to asses Kosambi's work in different areas of Indology. But some of the assessments, far from being impartial and objective, were unduly critical and one of them bordered on vitriol and vituperation. The present volume, however, brings together articles by scholars who are neither allergic to nor adulatory about the work of Kosambi but seek to present a balanced and critical appraisal. Although they have focused on specific aspects of his work, a certain amount of overlap is unavoidable in a collection like this.

Of the eight essays included in this collection seven deal with his Indological writings and one discusses his engagement with science, and assesses his contribution to mathematics. The first two essays, written by me and Irfan Habib are revised versions of the papers originally published in the Kosambi Centenary issue of the *Marxist* (XXIV, 4, October-December, 2008). The paper by Prabhat Patnaik is a reprint from the same issue of the *Marxist* and the last essay, by C.K. Raju, has been reproduced from the *Economic and Political Weekly* of 16 May 2009 (XLIV, 20). The referencing style of the individual contributors has been retained as far as possible.

D.N. Jha

A Scholar Extraordinaire

D.N. Jha

I

Born on 31 July 1907 at Kosben in Goa, Damodar Dharmanand Kosambi was the son of Dharmanand Kosambi, the reputed Buddhist scholar who taught at Harvard for several years and from whom Damodar Kosambi, known as Baba to his friends, inherited his passion for learning, his sharp versatile intellect, and above all his humanism. After some schooling in Pune he accompanied his father to the United States and studied at the Cambridge Latin School until 1925. In 1929 he graduated with brilliant results from the Harvard University, where he showed special interest and proficiency in mathematics, history and several languages, especially Greek, Latin, German and French. During his stay at Harvard, Kosambi was in contact with distinguished mathematicians such as George Birkhoff and Norbert Wiener.

On his return to India in 1929 Kosambi joined the mathematics faculty of the Benares Hindu University. Before long he emerged a mathematician of outstanding ability and was invited by the Aligarh Muslim University, where he taught for a year. In 1932 he decided to settle down at Pune as professor of mathematics at the Fergusson College, where his father had taught Pali for several years before he went to Harvard. During the fourteen years that Kosambi taught at the Fergusson College he incessantly tried to master various fields of knowledge and established himself as a great scholar and thinker of modern India. In 1946 he was offered the chair of mathematics at the Tata Institute of Fundamental Research, Bombay, a position that he held till 1962. There he was able to interact with scholars of equal calibre from all over the world.

II

D.D. Kosambi specialized in and taught mathematics during most of his teaching career, and his contribution to this area has been acclaimed by many experts including the famous British scientist J. D. Bernal, who as much lauded his scientific works as his role in the world peace movement. The present writer is in no position to assess the importance of his researches in the sciences; but he certainly broke traditional disciplinary boundaries and made valuable, lasting and socially relevant contributions to genetics, statistics and other branches of knowledge. In genetics his work on chromosome mapping (1944) was believed to be an advance on the prevalent chromosome theory. In statistics he developed a technique called Proper Orthogonal Decomposition (POD) in 1943, before Karhunen (1945) and Loeve (1948) – a technique which was applied to such diverse fields as image processing, signal processing, data compression, oceanography, chemical engineering and fluid mechanics.

At the invitation of the Academia Sinica, he visited Beijing where, in his discussion with Kuo-Mo-Jo and Chou En-Lai, he suggested statistical methods for the forecasting of Chinese food crops and quality control in industry. At home, he forcefully argued against the arbitrary location and construction of dams and suggested statistical methods for the purpose. Similarly his study of the seasonal death rate proved that at least 500 lives could be saved annually in the city of Bombay alone by concentrating on anti-typhoid work about three weeks before the onset of the monsoon. He also suggested to the then Bombay government that a motorable all-weather road for Naneghat would be far more economical than the proposed expensive funicular. Kosambi was far from being an ivory tower scholar. His intellectual activity was deeply rooted in and greatly inspired by the needs of the people around him. Not surprisingly, he expressed himself fearlessly on issues of national and international importance. For example, more than half a century before the Indian government mortgaged its sovereignty to the USA by signing a nuclear agreement with it, he asserted that India 'is too poor a country to throw money away on costly fads like atomic energy merely because they look modern' and was passionately pleading for solar rays as an alternative source of energy.[1]

III

Often described as a man of truly 'Renaissance versatility' D.D. Kosambi applied his abstract mathematical methods to the study of various branches of social sciences. He thus extended the statistical method to the study of punch-marked coins and, by weighing nearly 12,000 coins (including 7,000 modern ones), he laid the foundation of scientific numismatics in India.[2] He established a link between the king-lists in the Pali Buddhist works on the one hand and the marks on the punch-marked coins on the other and ascribed them to the rulers of Magadha and Kosala. His method of dating the coins was seriously inhibited by his disregard for their archaeological stratigraphic context, but, proceeding on the assumption that every coin bears the signature of contemporary society, he tried to fix the chronology of punch-marked coins and postulated the relevance of the two famous Taxila coin hoards (dominated by the Magadhan issues) to the economic history of Taxila as well as Magadha.

Unlike the numismatists who wrote before and after him, Kosambi not only rescued numismatics from the coin collectors' purely antiquarian interest but also emphasized its importance for the reconstruction of the social and economic history of India. Accordingly he was the first to refer to the paucity of coinage and to its linkage with the decline of trade and the emergence of the self sufficient village economy in the post-Gupta period. The quantitative method which he applied to the study of the earliest Indian coins has not had any takers, but more or less at the same time as he published his paper on scientific numismatics, R.S. Sharma pointed to some of its limitations, made a strong case for the study of early Indian monetary history,[3] and himself undertook in-depth studies of the paucity of coinage, the decline of trade and urban centres, and the growth of the self-sufficient village economy, all these later becoming the building blocks of his model of 'Indian feudalism' and the characteristic features of what is now known as the early medieval period in Indian history.

IV

From the examination of ancient coin groups, Kosambi proceeded to ask who issued them. Struck by 'the shocking discordance' of the written sources (e.g., the Puranas, Buddhist and Jain records) which 'give different names for the same king', he decided to go to the original texts himself, for which he needed a mastery of Sanskrit. Despite his uncharacteristically modest statement that he 'absorbed Sanskrit only through the pores without a regular study',[4] he appears to have turned almost instinctively to his Sanskrit inheritance and acquired unquestionable proficiency in Sanskrit, Pali and Prakrit through having worked with his father, and in association with V.S. Sukthankar. His grasp over Sanskrit was indeed remarkable; it ranged from his interest in the search for manuscripts to their editing and publication. His critical editions of Bhartrihari's *Shatakatraya* (1942), *Chintamani-sharanika* of Dashabala (1949), Vidyakara's *Subhashitaratnakosha* (1957), as well as his writings on the *Parvasamgraha* of the *Mahabharata* (1946) and the text of the *Arthashastra* (1958) are lasting testimony to Kosambi's mastery of Sanskrit as well as his attainments in the field of text literary criticism. His translation (done jointly with J.L. Masson) of Bhasa's drama *Avimaraka* (1970) is also evidence of his linguistic competence in Sanskrit. In the later years of his life Kosambi was engaged in a standard translation of the *Arthashastra* of Kautilya, a project he could not complete on account of his sudden death on 29 June 1966.

Of the works examined and edited by D.D. Kosambi, the best known are Bhartrihari's *Shatakatraya* and Vidyakara's *Subhashitaratnakosha*. His critical edition of *Shatakatraya* is also a landmark in text criticism. On the basis of a comparative examination of 377 manuscripts out of the conservatively estimated total of 3,000 surviving manuscripts – 'undoubtedly a larger number than has ever been used for any single text in the history of Indian literary criticism'[5] – he identified 200 poems on which enough manuscripts agreed closely enough to be attributed to Bhartrihari.[6] Not surprisingly, his work has been hailed as 'a decided advance over anything his contemporaries had achieved' and 'will remain definitive for many, many more decades to come'.[7] Unlike the *Shatakatraya*, which had to be reconstructed from a large number of manuscripts, the restoration of the text of the *Subhashitaratnakosha*, an anthology prepared by Vidyakara, in a Buddhist monastery of the Pala period and dated to around AD 1100, had to be done on the basis of only three partial manuscripts, though many poems in it are drawn from other manuscripts and later anthologies.[8] The list of poets whose poems are included here numbers as many as 223; of them, Kosambi claims to have 'rescued over fifty poets from the total oblivion to which lovers of Sanskrit had consigned them'.[9] Although Daniel Ingalls, the translator of the anthology, was later to suggest more than 200 changes in the reconstructed text, according to Sheldon Pollock, Kosambi's *Subhashitaratnakosha* 'stands as one of the most valuable works in the history of Sanskrit philology.'[10]

Kosambi's analysis and understanding of Sanskrit literature was informed by his commitment to a social and political ideology rooted in Marxism. In his view, literature, like science, should be understood as a function of the age in which it is produced. He tells us: 'the great poet in a class society must not only express the position and aspirations of an important class, but must also transcend the class barriers, whether explicitly or implicitly' and, to be sure, his most provocative statements on Sanskrit language and literature were about its class character – statements he made in the context of the works of both Bhartrihari and Vidyakara. Writing about the former he asserts that 'the literary physiognomy' of Bhartrihari is that of 'a hungry Brahmin in distress', whose frustrations were shared by the 'the miserable class' of brahmanas. He is

> the poet of his class. But he is not a poet of the people. The Indian poets who made a real and lasting place for themselves in the hearts of the people came from the people themselves,

> and not from this narrow helpless substratum shut off from the masses by birth, training, occupation or the lack of it, language and culture. Those poets spoke the languages of the people, addressed themselves to the people and not to the court. Every child knows their names and every peasant their songs – Kabir, Tukarama, Tulasidasa: what portion of the country did not possess its poet of the sort?[11]

Kosambi's stress on the class character of Sanskrit literature is also evident from his introduction to the *Subhashitaratnakosha*:

> the average Sanskrit poet wrote for the patrician; we have to deal here with *class* literature. When drawing conclusions about life in ancient India from any such work as this, it must always be remembered that that life was not shared by most Indians of the poet's time or of any other time; in essence not even by the poet himself. The Sanskrit stanza implies mind and memory not otherwise preoccupied, simple leisure to work out its double and triple meanings, mythological allusions, complicated figures of speech – apart from the long training needed to write even the simplest bit of Sanskrit. The Brahmin class is primarily responsible for keeping both ritual and language alive while regarding itself as superior to the rest of the people.[12]

One may, however, find it difficult to accept that Sanskrit literature was wholly the creation of brahmanas or remained solely in their possession. The earliest known mention of the great poet Bhartrihari is by the Jaina Somadevasuri in his *Yashastilaka-champu* (AD 959); the oldest reference to any specific work by him, Kosambi himself tells us, is in the *Prabandhachintamani* (AD 1306) of the famous Jaina Acharya Merutunga; and the first commentary on Bhartrihari's *Shatakatraya*, so ably edited by Kosambi, was written by a Jaina called Dhanasara in around 1478 at Jaipur. Similarly, the author of the anthology *Subhashita-ratnakosha*, whose text was reconstructed by Kosambi, was

Vidyakara, an abbot of the Buddhist monastery at Jaggadala during the Pala period. Even the author of the astrological text *Chintamanisharanika* was a Buddhist called Dashabala. All this shows that Sanskrit was not the monopoly of the brahmanas and that it was very much the idiom used by Buddhists and Jainas. But this does not contradict Kosambi's basic assertion about the class character of Sanskrit literature; for the Jaina and Buddhist authors writing in Sanskrit were neither indigent nor were they totally deprived of patronage: the Jaina Acharya Hemachandra (eleventh-twelfth century) is a case in point. There is thus much truth in the view that classical Sanskrit literature was the literature of the upper class, though it is not hard to find the description of poverty and misery in it. Vidyakara, verse 1318, for example, reads: 'Naked as I am my skin must play the cloak, a cloak well furred with gooseflesh raised by the cold wind'.[13]

The use of historical materialism in reading literature and analysing it from the class perspective is also seen in Kosambi's study of the working class in the *Amarakosha*. Its author Amarasimha was 'mnemonically superior' to other lexicographers because 'he gave more attention to objective reality than to ideal categories' and so gives a good idea of social divisions. Kosambi therefore undertakes an elaborate analysis of terms in the text that are related to the working class, which leads him to state that 'the *Amarakosha* was written in feudal times', although he is conscious that 'the evidence is poor.'[14] Another important example of Kosambi's interpretation of literature against its changing social contexts is his essay on the Urvashi-Pururvas story which travels a long distance in time from its earliest occurrences in the *Rigveda* and *Shatapatha Brahmana* to become the theme of the five-act drama *Vikramorvashiyam* written by Kalidasa. Kosambi analyses the original version of the myth as well as its variations found in various literary texts over time, and argues how Kalidasa's retelling of it 'reflects the difference between the Vedic society and the Gupta period, being in fact a transition from ritual to drama.'[15] Kosambi applies a similar approach to the *Bhagvadgita*. 'The song divine', he tells us, 'is sung for the upper classes by the Brahmins, and only through them for others'. He also links the *bhakti* doctrine enunciated in the *Gita* with the rise of feudalism and asserts that to hold a feudal society and state together, 'the best religion is one which emphasizes the role of *bhakti*, personal faith, even though the object of devotion may have clearly visible flaws.'[16] Examples of similar studies by Kosambi may be multiplied further and, even if one may differ on details, it is difficult to reject his perception of the inherent linkage between the material conditions of society and the historical prevalence of specific literary and aesthetic forms.[17]

V

While D.D. Kosambi underscored the importance of scientific numismatic studies and class analysis of literature, he was equally aware of the utility of archaeology for the reconstruction of the Indian past and did much valuable archaeological work himself.

He discovered megaliths in the Poona district, collected a huge amount of microliths and, on the basis of his finds, tried to explain the movements of ancient peoples and establish prehistoric links between the Deccan and central India. His field work led also to the discovery of ancient trade routes, Buddhist caves at Kuda, and some ancient inscriptions which he published along with his own comments. Kosambi undertook archaeological explorations more than half a century ago and, not surprisingly, some of his conclusions appear dated, flawed and unacceptable now, but trashing his archaeology by Shereen Ratnagar,[18] a reputed Indian archaeologist, on the ground that he did not publish his findings in the bulletins of the Archaeological Survey of India (e.g. *Indian Archaeology: A Review* and *Ancient India)* and in any peer reviewed journal is an amusing academic trivia – that his writings appeared in the *Man,* published by the Royal Anthropological Institute of England and Ireland is of no consequence to her! She has also pointed out that by the 1960s the faculty of the Deccan College, Poona (of which her mentor H.D. Sankalia was the director) had excavated several sites from Rajasthan to northern Karnataka, but Kosambi willfully ignored the data available from them.[19]

While one may find fault with both Sankalia and Kosambi in their soured personal relationship which prevented any fruitful academic interaction between them, one cannot ignore the fact that Indian archaeologists (Sankalia included) have not been forthcoming in sharing their data with the scholarly community outside their respective caucuses; and, suffering from an antiquity frenzy as they do, they have generally shied away from thinking of larger issues of social and cultural transformation. Nor can one disregard the fact that several reports of the sites excavated by the Deccan College were published only a few months before Kosambi's demise so that he could not possibly have seen them. One of them saw the light of day no less than three years after his death. It is preposterous therefore to allege that Kosambi disregarded the data available in his time. His review of Sankalia's *Prehistory and Protohistory in India and Pakistan* (Bombay, 1962-63), which incorporated data from all the sites excavated by Sankalia and his colleagues, albeit harsh and unkind, does take notice of what could have been the latest excavated material available at the time.[20]

Also, it is necessary to bear in mind that Kosambi shared neither the obsessive antiquarianism of the Indian archaeologists nor their rigid adherence to Mortimer Wheeler's perception that the sole purpose of archaeology was to identify stratigraphies, which could serve as chronometer of culture sequences but could not address Kosambi's concern with larger historical issues and with factors of social, economic and cultural change – a concern that did not find place in the agenda of the so-called 'trained' archaeologists at all and even today gets limited attention from them. In his view, Indian archaeology had 'achieved nothing of correlative historical value'[21] and was not 'advanced enough to solve the really important questions, not even to ask some of them'.[22] He asserted that a meaningful use of archaeological material was possible only if it was correlated not just with the traditional written records but also with ethnographic data which offers a detailed analysis of phenomena roughly comparable to those which the historians are reconstructing with a good deal less evidence. This meant extensive field work and collection of anthropological data including folklore, oral traditions and myths which furnish clues to aspects of human life forgotten over time. He himself undertook field studies with 'critical insight, taking nothing for granted or on faith,' and gathered substantial evidence to support his archaeological data, to confirm the historical process of mutual acculturation between tribal and caste-based agrarian societies, as well as to trace the tribal origins of many Hindu deities, religious beliefs and practices, thereby demystifying Indian history and philosophy.

The archaeological method of Kosambi was vastly enriched by ethnographic material whose neglect, he tells us, 'leads to a ridiculous distortion of Indian history and to a misunderstanding of Indian culture, not compensated by subtle theology or the boasts of having risen above crass materialism'.[23] His archaeology, despite its limitations, may be the precursor of what is nowadays fashionably called ethnoarchaeology just as his historical work introduced into Indian historiography an interdisciplinary approach[24] which is nowadays more often talked about than practised.

VI

Combining his understanding of historical materialism with an interdisciplinary method, D.D. Kosambi undertook extensive researches on various aspects of Indian history and culture,[25] which appeared in the form of more than a hundred articles from the early 1940s onwards. He later wove his major findings into the three books: *Introduction to the Study of Indian History* (1956), *Myth and Reality* (1962) and *Culture and Civilisation of Ancient India in Historical Outline* (1965). Written in a highly effective style, with occasional acerbity, his works were a strong antidote to the colonial pontification about and the nationalist glorification of the Indian past; and stirred the stagnant and turgid waters of contemporary Indian historiography.

That Kosambi made use of Marxism in his researches on Indian history is clear from his oft quoted statement: 'History is the presentation in chronological order of successive changes in the means and relations of production'. However, he disapproved of the application of 'a mechanical determinism, particularly in dealing with India'.[26] Marxism, he said, is 'far from the economic determinism which its opponents so often take it to be.'[27] It 'cannot be reduced to a rigid formalism like mathematics' and 'cannot be treated as a standard technique such as an automobile lathe'. It was for him a method, 'a tool of analysis', and not 'a substitute for thinking'. Accordingly Kosambi did not hesitate even to reject some of the formulations of Marx and Engels if they did not fit facts. In his view the history of India could not be straightjacketed into the slavery-feudalism-capitalism scheme of periodisation.[28] Not surprisingly, he asserts that ancient Indian society, unlike the Greek and the Roman, was not based on the slave mode of production. Although some people were not free from earliest times to the present century, he holds that the importance of chattel slavery in the relations of productions as a supply of labour for economic production was negligible in ancient India. The place of the slave whose surplus could be appropriated was taken by the lowest caste, that of the shudras, whom he equated with the helots of Sparta.[29]

Kosambi's statement is true of the Vedic period, when slaves were few in number and could not have engaged in productive activities like their Homeric counterparts. The Vedic passages referring to the gift of slaves to priests invariably speak of women slaves, who may have worked as domestic slaves and whose participation in economic production may have been inhibited largely by the incipient nature of the agricultural economy during a major part of the Vedic period. But during the period 400-100 BC, represented by the early Pali texts and the *Arthashastra* of Kautilya, which make copious references to slaves – the latter even laying down detailed rules about them – slavery emerged as a factor in production. The Pali works, the oldest of which cannot be taken beyond 400 BC, indicate that in north-eastern India slaves (*dasas*) and hired labourers (*karmakaras*) were employed in cultivation, especially in large-sized fields ranging from 500 to

1000 *karisas*. This is confirmed by Kautilya, who enjoins the superintendent of agriculture to requisition the services of *dasas* and *karmakaras* for working on state farms. Thus there is little doubt that slaves participated in the community's productive activities during the post-Vedic and Maurya times. But even if the state and some members of society owned slaves who were made to work in the agricultural sector, it is difficult to characterize Indian society as a slave society in the absence of any quantitative data about their numerical strength. The numbers of slaves have been worked out for some other countries (e.g., classical Athens, Roman Italy, the West Indian Islands and southern states of the USA),[30] but this has not been done for India. Kosambi thus seems to have a point when he rejects the concept of a slave mode of production as being applicable to India.[31]

Kosambi is also critical of the Marxian notion of the Asiatic mode of production.[32] Never clearly defined by Marx and often put to highly tendentious use by Western scholars (e.g., Karl Wittfogel), his idea of the Asiatic system of production is based on the concept of a society characterized by tribal communal ownership of land and a self-sustaining economy based on a 'combination of manufacture and agriculture within the small community'. Connected with this is the view of both Marx and Engels about the slow-moving character of Oriental society, as can be inferred from the former's prominent reference to its 'stagnatory and vegetative life' and the latter's remarks on its 'tremendous staying power'.

Kosambi made a departure from this orthodox Marxist notion of 'the unchangeableness of Asiatic societies'. After all, the very formation of the village economy with the plough used on a fixed plot of land implied a tremendous advance in the means of production. Self-sufficiency, which, according to the founders of Marxism, is the hallmark of Asiatic societies, was not possible in the strict sense of the term. For, as Kosambi rightly tells us, most of the Indian villages produce neither salt nor metals, the two essentials that had to be obtained by exchange. In the years before and after his death, other historians (notably R.S. Sharma) have also questioned the supposed stagnant nature of Indian society and have drawn attention to the dispersal of agriculture, technological changes, stages in the growth of urbanization and trade and to the formation of the state from the later Vedic period down to the time of the Gupta rulers.[33] Nevertheless, it does remain true, according to Kosambi, that the Indian village tended to become nearly self-contained from the Gupta period onwards owing mainly to the decline of trade and urban centres. This led to the break-up of the guilds of merchants and artisans, who migrated to villages where they eked out a living by catering to the needs of the people and altered the rural social structure, especially through the formation of new castes. In view of the fact that Kosambi referred to some of the features of the major social transformation in early India, he does not seem to have accepted the idea of the Asiatic mode unreservedly.[34]

VII

Although Kosambi does not accept the notions of the slave and the Asiatic modes of production, he does make use of the concept of feudalism in the context of pre-colonial India. But here also he differs from the Marxist position in that he postulates two stages in the development of feudalism in India – feudalism from above and feudalism from below. The first is a 'state wherein an emperor or powerful king levied tribute from subordinates who still ruled in their own right and did what they liked within their own territories – as long as they paid the paramount ruler.' These subordinate rulers might even be tribal chiefs, and they seem in general to have ruled the land by direct administration, without the intermediacy of a class which was in effect a land-owning stratum. By feudalism from below is meant the next stage, where 'a class of landowners developed within the village, between the state and the peasantry, gradually to wield armed power over the local population.'

Such two-stage feudalism has nowhere been visualized in the writings of Marx and Engels, and it has been questioned by several scholars.[35] R.S. Sharma, for example, presented overwhelming empirical data in his comprehensive work on Indian feudalism which contradicts Kosambi's model.[36] While Sharma's own work has generated animated academic debate, Kosambi's two-stage theory of feudalism has not received the attention it deserves. Be that as it may, the major weakness of the models of Indian feudalism delineated by both Kosambi and Sharma, lies in the fact that they explain feudal developments in terms of the decline of trade which depended on external factors. Essentially Pirennian[37] in nature, this explanation would in fact imply that the early Indian society did not possess any built-in potential for change – a position implicit in the theory of the Asiatic mode. But this does not go well with Kosambi's own view of caste as a class, albeit 'at a primitive level of production'; for a class society is bound to have its own contradictions which will usher in a new mode of production – in the present case, the feudal mode.

In an assessment of Kosambi's contributions to Indology, especially his views on the Indian version of feudalism, Romila Thapar has asserted that he was not familiar with the writings of Marc Bloch and Fernand Braudel, who were the founder and a prominent exponent, respectively, of the Annales school of historiography. Nor was Kosambi, it is further alleged, familiar with the works of Karl Polanyi.[38] The implication of her argument is that had he been *au fait* with the works of these scholars, he would either have viewed the feudal phenomenon differently or would not have posited its existence at all. But the criticism is unfounded. Marc Bloch's *Feudal Society* first appeared in French in 1939 and its English version appeared as late as 1961, five years after Kosambi published his *Introduction to the Study of Indian History.* Braudel's famous work on the Mediterranean world was published in French in 1949 and its English version came out in 1972, more than a decade and a half after Kosambi's *Introduction.* Similarly, of the two works of Polanyi, the one which could have had some bearing on Kosambi's study of early medieval society was *Trade and Markets in Early Empires*, which was first published in 1957, a year later than Kosambi's work. Chronology thus goes against Thapar. The English versions of the French works came out after Kosambi published his own work in 1956; and one of them, by Braudel, saw the light of day more than half a decade after Kosambi's death.

One may argue, as Thapar has done, that Kosambi could have read them in the original, given the fact that he had a good command over several European languages including French. But how do we know he didn't? Maybe he read them all and remained uninfluenced by them! Thapar may even charge Kosambi of being ignorant of the writings and ideas emanating from the Frankfurt School, which was gaining ground at the same time as the Annales and, in a similar vein, she may ridicule him for being unfamiliar with the writings of the Italian communist Antonio Gramsci (d.1937), who made significant departures from classical Marxism! Although similar captious criticisms can be multiplied to almost any length, a fair assessment of D.D. Kosambi should be made against the background of the thought currents which influenced him and not against those that passed him by. The finest Indian historians of today have remained uninfluenced by post-modernist thought, but does that minimize the importance of their contribution?

VIII

For all his rejection of some of the familiar formulations of Marx and Engels, Kosambi remained a Marxist and used their historical materialist method without showing a Procrustean adherence to it. He was unsparing in his denunciation of those who blindly repeated the conclusions of Marx and Engels all the time. His censorious verdict on S.A. Dange's *India from Primitive Communism to Slavery* (1949) is a case in point.[39]

Kosambi's history did not flourish 'under the aegis of the muse Clio who has an abacus to determine chronology' and 'a trumpet to celebrate the victories of kings and generals'. He rescued history from the chroniclers of 'personal', 'episodic' and drum-and-trumpet history of India, which 'should be enjoyed as a romantic fiction' or 'some Indian railway time table', and focused on the history of the people.[40] The more important question, according to him, is not who was king or whether a given region had a king, but whether its people used a plough, light or heavy, at the time. He thus highlighted the important role of technology and economic production, the productive forces which catalysed major social and political change. He spoke of the transforming role of iron in the context of the Ganga valley during the post Vedic period, which saw the dispersal of agriculture, availability of economic surplus, growth of urban centres and the formation of states in the region. In one of her recent writings Romila Thapar concedes that the 'crucial questions in Kosambi's argument are still relevant', but she underplays the role of technology by arguing that the archaeological presence of iron at the Megalithic sites in peninsular India was not accompanied by the kind of developments seen in north India, and thus lends colour to the assertions of those who deny the role of technology, especially the use of iron in early north India. Admittedly, the study of social change through the prism of technological and economic developments is complex and gives rise to problems.

For example, Kosambi's view that Buddhism declined in India with the decline of trade and the emergence of closed village economic units when the vast Buddhist monastic foundations became a drain on the economy is too simplistic to be convincing, especially when judged in the context of the Hindu temples. They acquired fabulous wealth through generous gifts and donations in the early medieval period, and used it for extending agriculture and augmenting agrarian production: but in course of time they became repositories of vast amounts of unproductive wealth and thus turned into a drain on the economy. If we go by Kosambi's explanation of Buddhism's decline, all famous Hindu temples should have decayed and dwindled from sheer neglect. However, Kosambi himself, being aware of the complexities in and limitations of the materialist approach, would not offer economic explanations for all historical developments. He therefore asserted that mere 'economic determinism will not do'[41] and that 'ideas (including superstition) become a force, once they have gripped the masses'.[42]

D.D. Kosambi's opposition to the colonial view of India as

stagnant and having no history was vehement and forceful; and so was his antagonism to revivalism and obscurantism [43] as is borne out by some of his mordant and pungent statements about the popular religious dogmas and stereotypes. 'A modern orthodox Hindu', he thus tells us, 'would place beef-eating on the same level as cannibalism, whereas Vedic Brahmins had fattened upon a steady diet of sacrificed beef.'[44] 'The Gita with its brilliant Sanskrit and superb inconsistency', we are told, 'is a book that allows the reader to justify any action while shrugging off the consequences. The many-faceted god [Krishna] is likewise inconsistent, though all things to all men and everything to most women.'[45] He also says of the Gita: 'This divine but rather scrambled message with its command of expository Sanskrit is characteristically Indian in attempting to reconcile the irreconcilable, in its power of gulping down sharp contradictions painlessly'.[46] And this is what he has to say about the much cherished notion of the 'golden age' of the Guptas, whom orthodox historians have credited with 'a revival of nationalism': 'Far from the Guptas reviving nationalism, it is nationalism that revived the Guptas'.[47] Such statements as these are unpalatable to the orthodox historians whose favourite pastime has been to gild the lily at the cost of writing a serious history of the people. It would appear that the entire body of his research was intended to undermine the traditional bourgeois perception of the past, as is evident from the following:

> The principal aim of history, as hitherto written, has been the presentation of great events in a chronological sequence. However, the relative importance of events rarely appears the same to the people of another time, place, civilisation, class bias, so that a mere chronicle does not suffice. The course of social development, the inner causes which ultimately manifest themselves in the striking events, the driving forces which underlie great movements, have to be made clear before any work can be dignified by the name of serious history. Yet this type of analysis is not always welcome to some historiographers. They, or the people who really

> condition their version of history, are unwilling to face the inevitable consequences of the procedure. For the implication is necessarily that all history can be so analysed, hence current events too; but if so, it follows that the course of events can be influenced by deliberate action, that history has hereafter to be consciously made by those that live it, not merely set down after a safe interval of time by the professional historian. This is clearly dangerous to those who would suffer by the change, usually those in power. Thus such historical writing is labelled subversive. History then remains a means of escape, a romantic pastime, a profession, or a method of inducing submissiveness; it cannot become a scientific pursuit.[48]

Kosambi's writings were subversive for both traditional historiography, and its patron, the Indian bourgeoisie. He succeeded in overthrowing the former insofar as much of the historical discourse veers round his ideas even several decades after his death. The Indian bourgeoisie, however, has gained strength and is more prosperous now than it ever was. The paradigm shift in historiography was not accompanied by a power shift in politics. But that is a different matter.

NOTES

1 See C.K. Raju, 'Kosambi the Mathematician' in the present volume.

2 'Scientific Numismatics', *Scientific American* (February 1966), pp. 102-111. Between 1940 and 1966 he wrote no less than a dozen articles on punch-marked coins, the earliest coinage of India, which were published under the sponsorship of the Indian Council of Historical Research (ICHR), New Delhi, under the title *Indian Numismatics*, Orient Longman, New Delhi, 1981. Another collection of 51 articles (excluding the numismatic studies) called *Historical Diversities* was submitted by me to the Indian Council of Historical Research in 1978. While its fate remains unknown to me, a similar volume of Kosambi's papers was published by the Oxford University Press, New Delhi, in 2002. In the present essay I refer to the books and journals where Kosambi's writings were originally published.

3 R.S. Sharma, 'Coins and Problems of Early Economic History', *Journal of the Numismatic Society of India*, XXXI (1969), pp. 1-8. The original version of this paper was presented at a seminar held at Patna University in 1967.

4 D.D. Kosambi, 'Steps in Science', *Science and Progress: Prof. D.D. Kosambi*

Commemoration Volume, Bombay, 1974.

[5] Sheldon Pollock, 'Towards a Political Philology: D.D. Kosambi and Sanskrit', *Economic and Political Weekly* (hereafter *EPW*), July 26, 2008, p. 53.

[6] Ibid., pp. 52-53.

[7] Albrecht Wezler, 'Preface', *The Epigrams Attributed to Bhartrhari edited by D.D. Kosambi*, Delhi, 2000, p. ix.

[8] The *Subhashitaratnakosha* compiled by Vidyakara, edited by D.D. Kosambi and V.V. Gokhale, Harvard University, 1957, Introduction.

[9] D.D. Kosambi, 'Steps in Science', p. 200.

[10] Pollock, 'Towards a Political Philology', p. 54.

[11] Kosambi, *Exasperating Essays*, Pepole's Publishing House, New Delhi, 1957, p. 70.

[12] *Subhashitaratnakosha*, Introduction, pp. xlv-lvii.

[13] The scholars who have given a great éclat to Kosambi for his work in the field of literary text criticism are also the ones who have fiercely contested his views on the class character of Sanskrit poetry. For example, Pollock ('Towards a Political Philology', p. 54) has drawn attention to a thirteenth century literary anthology which praises the Sanskrit poetry of a simple potter named Ghrona and that of a Candala named Divakara.

[14] Kosambi, 'The Working Class in the Amarakosa', *Journal of Oriental Research*, xxiv (1954-5), pp. 57-59.

[15] Kosambi, *Myth and Reality*, Popular Prakashan, Bombay, 1962, p. 42.

[16] Ibid., pp. 15, 32.

[17] Kosambi's approach to the study of the classical Sanskrit literature reminds us of his contemporaries in the West: Christopher Caudwell, whose posthumous publications on Marxist literary criticism (*Illusion and Reality*, *Studies and Further Studies in a Dying Culture*, etc.), George Thompson, whose study of the social context of the origins of Greek drama (*Aeschylus and Athens* and *Marxism and Poetry*), and Arnold Hauser, whose *Social History of Art* were major influences on the English educated youth of our generation.

[18] For a prejudiced view of Kosambi's archaeology see Shereen Ratnagar, 'Kosambi's Archaeology', *EPW*, pp. 71-77.

[19] Ibid. p. 71.

[20] *The Times of India*, 13 October 1964.

[21] *An Introduction to the Study of Indian History* (hereafter *Introduction*), Bombay, 1956, p. 5.

[22] *Culture and Civilisation of Ancient India in Historical Outline* (hereafter *Culture*), Routledge, London, 1965, p. 13.

[23] *Myth and Reality*, p. 2.

[24] Kosambi expounded his research methodology in the following two articles: 'Combined Methods in Indology', *Indo-Iranian Journal*, vol. VI (1963), pp. 177-202; 'Living Prehistory in India', *Scientific American* (February 1967).

[25] 'Combined Methods in Indology', *Indo-Iranian Journal*, VI.

[26] *Culture*, p. 12.

[27] *Introduction*, p. 10.

[28] *Culture*, p. 23-25.

[29] Ibid., p. 21-22.

[30] Keith Hopkins, *Conquerors and Slaves*, Cambridge, 1978.

[31] D.N. Jha, 'A Marxist View of Ancient Indian History', in Mohit Sen and M.B. Rao (eds.), *Das Kapital Centenary Volume*, People's Publishing House, New Delhi, 1967. Also see 'D.D. Kosambi', in S.P. Sen (ed.), *Historians and Historiography in Modern India*, Institute of Historical Studies, Calcutta, 1973, pp. 121-132.

[32] Ibid.

[33] R.S. Sharma, *Aspects of Political Ideas and Institutions in Ancient India*, Third Edition, Delhi, 1991, chapter VI. For a detailed criticism of the application of the concept of Asiatic Mode of Production to the Indian situation, see Brendan O'Leary, *The Asiatic Mode of Production*, London, 1989, chapter 7. The only Indian Marxist historian to have defended the concept and justified its application to India is Diptendra Banerjee. See his following two articles: 'In Search of a Theory of Pre-Capitalist Mode of Production' and 'Marx and the "Original" Form of India's Village Community' in Diptendra Banerjee (ed.), *Marxian Theory and the Third World*, New Delhi, 1985.

[34] There is considerable ambiguity in Kosambi's position on the Asiatic Mode. In *Introduction* (pp. 15-16, note 14) he says: 'India showed a series of parallel forms which cannot be put into the precise categories.' But in an article published in the *Journal of the Indo-Soviet Cultural Society* (vol.1, 1954) he states that 'it is clear that an Asiatic mode did exist – at least the term is applicable to India, whatever the case elsewhere'. In a private conversation he told me that the editors of the journal had 'mutilated' his article beyond recognition.

[35] Irfan Habib (*Seminar, Past and Present*, No.39, 1962) and R. S. Sharma (*Journal of the Economic and Social History of the Orient*, 1958).

[36] R.S. Sharma, *Indian Feudalism*, Calcutta, 1965.

[37] In the context of European feudalism the Belgian historian Henri Pirenne, writing between the two Wars, argued that the classical world was founded on the unity of the Mediterranean Sea and the flourishing trade which this unity made possible. In the seventh century, however, the Arab followers of Muhammad disturbed this trade, as a result of which Europe was thrown back on its own agrarian resources. In the new situation where money revenues were absent, Charlemagne began the practice of supporting his soldiers through grants of land, thus creating the new feudal state and society and giving birth to the Middle Ages (*Economic and Social History of Medieval Europe*, London, 1936; *Mohammed and Charlemagne*, London, 1939).

[38] Romila Thapar, *Interpreting Early India*, Delhi, 1992, pp. 110-11.

[39] *Annals of the Bhandarkar Oriental Research Institute*, vol.29 (1948), pp. 221-27.

[40] According to a recent suggestion, Kosambi's emphasis on people's history was inspired by Rabindranath Tagore; though Leo Tolstoy had advocated as early as 1869 that 'historians should concern themselves not with heroes and battles but

with the life of the people' in his *War and Peace*. See Vanina's paper in this volume.

41 *Culture*, p. 12.

42 *Introduction*, p. 10.

43 Although Kosambi did not write on medieval India (often described as 'Muslim' India by most historians), his attitude to the communal perception of the past can be gauged by his gibe at R.C. Majumdar and K.M. Munshi who 'dismiss with contempt the nomenclature of the "so-called Muslim Period".' He says: 'the proposal [to dismiss the Muslim period] is surpassingly incongruous when made by two Hindus with good Muslim professional names, Munshi and Majumdar'. See *Annals of the Bhandarkar Oriental Research Institute*, vol. 35 (1955), pp. 194-201.

44 *Culture*, p. 102.

45 Ibid., p. 114.

46 Ibid., p. 207.

47 *Introduction*, p. 313

48 'The Study of Ancient Indian Tradition', *Indica*, The Indian Historical Research Institute Silver Jubilee Commemoration Volume, Bombay, 1953.

What Kosambi has Given Us

Irfan Habib

For understanding the intellectual and cultural environment in which Damodar Dharmanand Kosambi's ideas were formed, it will perhaps not be out of place to remind oneself that he was the son of Dharmanand Kosambi (1876-1947), a remarkable figure for his time: a Sanskrit scholar, a practicing Buddhist, thrice holding assignments at Harvard, the first to introduce Marxism to the Marathi reading public as early as 1912, and a participant in the Civil Disobedience Movement, breathing his last in Gandhiji's ashram at Wardha.[1] The son, D.D. Kosambi, first chose a very different sphere for himself. He graduated in mathematics from Harvard with distinction, and returned to India in 1929 to embark on a conventional teaching-and-research career. He carved a place for himself by his contributions to his field in mathematics; but in the late 1930s some of his father's major concerns seem to have beckoned to him and the direction of his studies began fundamentally to change as he turned to Marxism and History.

By this time (the mid-thirties) the ideas of Marxism and socialism had come to exercise considerable influence in the ranks of the National Movement. The anti-colonial struggle began to be seen more and more as part of an international struggle for revolution and liberation. The elected Provincial governments of 1937 relaxed the rigid ban on Marxist literature, and the first selection of Marx's articles on India was now published from Allahabad. A reading of this volume led to an innocently titled article ('The Emergence of National Characteristics Among three Indo-European Peoples') from Kosambi's pen, published in an eminently academic journal of Pune, in 1939. This was in effect an announcement of Kosambi's adoption of Marxism as his basic intellectual standpoint. The class struggle, he here asserted, was as much a feature of Indian history as of other civilizations. In a trenchant sentence he displayed his equal hostility to the exploitation of oppressed classes in India's past and the current despotism of British rule:

> *The caste system corresponds to our modern censorship and the Indian Arms Act together* (italics in the original).[2]

For Kosambi history in its essential features appeared to be as universal as was now the struggle for liberation and socialism. He was a consistent opponent of colonial rule before 1947. Greatly shocked by America's dropping of atomic bombs on Japan in 1945 and the subsequent imperialist drive towards war, he became a notable figure in the World Peace Movement. We must always remind ourselves that the conditions of the world that made Kosambi turn to Marxism as the great ideology of international solidarity have not changed; only perhaps, the current terrain of imperialist military concentration has shifted from East Asia to the Middle East.

It is, therefore, all the more necessary to underline Kosambi's basic starting point (from 1939 onwards), namely, the acceptance of the universality of class struggle. To him the broad picture of historical change, with succeeding modes of production that Marx drew in his Preface to *A Contribution to the Critique of Political Economy* (1859), represented the core of Marxist historiography, and it naturally became a favourite point of reference with him.[3] Today many academics seek to dilute the theme of class struggle in past societies by laying the entire emphasis on issues of multi-class 'subaltern' communities, or 'marginal' groups, or different value systems of various cultures. Louis Dumont, in his *Homo Hierarchicus* (1970) has been an eminent exponent of the last view. This amounts in essence to a recycling of hoary assertions such as the one by Karl Wittfogel in the 1950s that 'class-struggle far from being a chronic disease of mankind is the luxury of multi-centred and open [i.e. Western] societies.'[4] This tendency, in turn, goes back to the pre-World War I theorists of 'Social Imperialism' who used Marx's reference to the 'unchangeableness' of Asiatic societies to justify a long period of control over them by the Western colonial powers. As against this, the Leningrad discussions of 1931, which endorsed the universality of a unilinear scheme of Primitive Communism–Slavery–Feudalism–Capitalism, represented a challenge to the Euro-centred view of historical development, since it took class-struggle to be an equally universal phenomenon.[5] The rigid scheme, however, put Marxist historiography in such a straitjacket that it became in time a fetter on its development.

The break that Kosambi made with the understanding of the mainstream Marxist historians of the time stemmed from his insistence that while the principles that Marx put forth were fully valid, they did not justify such an inevitable four-stage succession of modes of production. His opening salvoes on this came in his 1949 criticism of S.A. Dange's *India from Primitive Communism to Slavery*, Bombay, 1949.[6] Here and in his *An Introduction to the Study of Indian History*, Bombay, 1956, Kosambi emphasizes that Marxist historical interpretation must be based on very detailed and critical study of the evidence and not take the form of an inflexible preconceived framework imposed by a selective or casual use (or misuse) of historical material.

The universal scheme of periodization we have just mentioned naturally excluded in time the 'Asiatic' from the recognized succession of modes of production in mainstream Marxist discourse. Kosambi spotted this change when he found that the term 'Asiatic' was omitted in Stalin's essay on 'Dialectical and Historical Materialism', published in 1938, which contained an enumeration of 'the main types of relations of production' successively found in human society.[7] It would seem, as is apparent from Kosambi's own refutation of Wittfogel's effort to build a theory of Asiatic despotism on the basis of certain remarks by Marx, that Kosambi was not attracted by the identification of the Asiatic mode with any form of political despotism; rather, he saw it as a recognition that forms of class societies different from those established for Europe could well be found in Asia (and, indeed in other parts of the world).

Once this freedom from a fixed scheme was attained, one would not need to ride roughshod over historical or philological facts as Dange had done in his *India from Primitive Communism to Slavery*. It was essential to study the evidence available rigorously and in diverse, but always objective and critical ways. Here Kosambi took a firm position on academic rigour. This is manifested in all of Kosambi's work, but he explicitly spelt out the essentials of his own approach to historical evidence in his paper, 'Combined Methods in Indology', published in 1963.[8] He had himself years earlier prepared well for such investigation by his painstaking work on the editions of the compositions of the Sanskrit poet and grammarian, Bhartrihari, which he published in 1945-48 and 1957. He set new standards for manuscript collation, commentary and interpretation in the editing of Sanskrit texts. He believed that endless details had to be accounted for before one could attempt a plausible historical generalization.

Kosambi clearly recognized that in the path of research one had to utilize and sharpen tools of study and criticism which had been developed in the West, and had duly influenced oriental scholarship. He acknowledged that 'most of our source-material was first collected, analysed and arranged by foreign scholars', though it was also a fact that the historical writings of British scholars had been coloured by their 'national and class prejudices'.[9] He clearly differentiated between the factual knowledge gained, and its interpretation, though the former was bound to modify or refine the latter. In ascertaining facts, the scientific and objective methods must be the same for all cultures, and it was in this context that he saw Marxism as a universally applicable mode of interpreting social facts. But, to him Marxism was 'a tool of analysis', not a 'substitute for thinking'.[10]

Kosambi's position, both explicit and implicit, on the universality of research methods and standards of interpretation, has come under severe attack during the last three decades and more from several quarters, now gathered into a practically single stream. The kind of research that Kosambi and the Orientalists in general had undertaken was heavily censured by Edward Said in his very popular work *Orientalism*, published in 1978. He argued that 'the work of innumerable devoted scholars, who edited texts and translated them, codified grammars, wrote dictionaries, reconstructed dead epochs [and] produced positivistically verifiable learning', had merely served as a tool in a huge intellectual conspiracy of the West to misrepresent the Orient, for 'the truths' the 'devoted scholars' find are put in a language that contains assumptions misperceiving and concealing the 'real' Orient.[11] This meant that the Orient cannot be studied by the scientific and critical tools and with the rational values developed in the West (including, of course, Marxism). Such an argument suited well the approach already adopted by Louis Dumont in his *Homo Hierarchicus* (1970), in which he had proclaimed that the value systems of India and the West were so different that there can be no history of India of the kind that historians explore in the West (India is supposed to have had no economic history, for example).[12]

In 1982 Ranajit Guha (an NRI academic) took the process of cultural fragmentation still further with his coinage of the 'subaltern' communities, to whom incredibly radical autonomies of ideology were assigned so that they became the only genuine actors of history: on the other hand, colonialism, its nationalist opponents and the organized working class were all put in the same undesirable 'elite' basket.[13] All these theories have found a common umbrella under post-modernism, as enunciated particularly by Michel Foucault with his belief in varieties of truths corresponding to different cultures.[14]

Whatever be the intentions of the individual practitioners of these obscurantist crafts, the sum total of their enterprise is the assertion that non-Western societies cannot be studied with the same critical and rational methods of research as are applicable to Western societies, and that, indeed, even any two among those non-Western cultures cannot be studied with identical intellectual tools. Just when, on the one hand, globalization is being forced upon the Third World, the latter is, on the other hand, sought to be intellectually broken up into culturally isolated fragments. All 'metanarrative', principally Marxism, is required to be abandoned in favour of the pursuit of utter trivia or half-lit bylanes leading nowhere.

It was inevitable that under the influence of such a flood of verbiage, fairly warmly received, if not entirely nurtured, in Western academic institutions, Kosambi's commitment to scientific rigour and Marxism would be duly called in question as an obsolete form of universalism. Sheldon Pollock explicitly demands that Kosambi should have anticipated the work of Foucault and his admirers and not used the critical and logical apparatus that Kosambi's own work as a scientist had made him so profoundly familiar with.[15]

If we see – as we ought to see – the entire offensive on rationality and universal values as objectively an attempt at the intellectual disarmament and fragmentation of peoples of the non-Western world, then there is all the more reason to defend without reservation the general validity of Kosambi's method. A re-reading of his *Introduction to the Study of Indian History* always proves to be an experience, an encounter with not only so much brilliance but also such defiant assertion of rationality.

One would surely notice from such reading, a further fundamental element in Kosambi, which pervades all genuinely Marxist efforts to read history: a linking of the past with the present (and future) by a basic commitment to the liberation of the oppressed and the exploited. Kosambi began his writing when India was still under the throes of colonial rule. We have already mentioned how in 1938-39 he put the caste system with its repressive elements at par with the violent, despotic methods of British rule. The sense of sympathy with the uprooted communities, however primitive, is palpable when he carefully describes their ways of life and customs after they settle in dire poverty in a modern city. This needs to be underlined in view of Shereen Ratnagar's attack on Kosambi's attitude towards the tribes, on the ground that he had called the Veddars 'primitive' and had remarked in passing that their settlements' degeneration into slums posed 'a problem for the Poona municipality, *complicated by the lack of employment*.' (Ratnagar omits from her quote the words here italicized). Kosambi is also taken to task for his statement in the report of his fieldwork on the Pardhis that as they became 'regular members' of society, it was 'expected that the change may even lead to their use of soap'. Kosambi was reporting an actual process; and it is difficult to see what attitude of condescension is implied in the use of words like 'primitive' or 'uplift'. One cannot close one's eyes to dire poverty and its baneful consequences. If there is any influence of 'urban middle class culture' (Ratnagar's words), then surely it is to be found in one who feels contented that the poor remain as poor as they were and be content to be in their (original) state. To Kosambi, who saw their misery and primitiveness as survivals of the past, it was inconceivable that this should be allowed to continue or, indeed, preserved so as to keep them as museum pieces for the satisfaction of 'the middle classes'.[16]

Kosambi's *Introduction to the Study of Indian History* (1956) climaxed a number of successive papers and reviews that he had begun writing in 1938-39. From the beginning Kosambi was struck, on the one hand, by the attraction of the Marxist historical framework and, on the other, by the uniqueness and strength of the caste system that necessarily called for a modification, in India's case, of the fixed scheme of successive modes of production. In an article which he contributed to the journal of the Indo-Soviet Cultural Society in 1954, he gave the following definition of caste:

> Caste is *class* at a primitive level of production, a *religious* method of forming social consciousness in such a manner that the *primary producer* is deprived of his surplus with the minimum *coercion*. (Italics ours.)[17]

This definition is important in that Kosambi sees the caste as fundamentally a mechanism helping to maintain a system of class-exploitation, with the primary producer as the principal victim at the end of a chain of surplus-extractors. Religion, 'the opium of the people',[18] is always a pillar of support for the reigning exploitative system, but with caste this role is magnified in that a rigid social organization is created, the hereditary members of whose separate units (castes) consider it religiously obligatory to carry out their fixed duties, submit to their fixed betters and suppress their own ambitions for improvement. Here, therefore, more than in any other religiously oriented society, religion and society are integrated to a very high degree. The submission of the primary producers so gained reduces the threat of class struggle in direct and open forms and so greatly brings down the costs of coercion for the ruling classes.

Kosambi suggested that the caste system itself probably originated with the enslavement of the non-Aryan *Dasas* or *Dasyus*, treated first as common tribal property and then assigned to tribal sub-groups.[19] It also grew subsequently by 'tribal elements being fused into a general society'.[20] The whole process was aided by brahmana priests, whose own caste created a model for the whole society.[21] Once the caste system was constructed, Indian ruling classes did not need slavery on any large scale in order to control primary production for the simple reason that caste-bound labour was available to them at such low cost. To Kosambi it seemed that this was one 'Asiatic' form of class-society that could be categorized as neither that of slavery nor of serfdom. Feudalism itself he found to be of later growth in India, and again, with its own specific features.

Kosambi's major thesis on caste is strongly argued, with a large array of evidence. And yet, while conceding to him the substance about caste as a factor of social control with a religious veneer, it may still be asked if the system was really originally an entirely brahmanical construction. Could it be that as a system it arose out of a normal process of class-differentiation within the society of Magadha and Kosala where Jainism and Buddhism were born, and then spread under the religious sanction of not only the brahmanas, but also of the Buddhists and Jains, who, with their emphasis on transmigration of souls, offered for it the most persuasive religious justification?[22] Even so, the fact would remain that it was Brahmanism, with its huge corpus of *dharmashastra* texts that sanctified the caste system most whole-heartedly and uncompromisingly. This could, then, partly explain the ultimate triumph of Brahmanism. Even in this version of events, however, Kosambi's point about caste-consciousness deriving its strength from religion would remain valid, because that is what did come about at the end of a doubtless complex process.

Kosambi's views about 'Indian feudalism' bore marks of his constant disinclination to apply the European model to India. In developing his own views, he had other important points to make as well. Unlike Marx, he would not trace the historical Indian village community back to primitive pre-class origins. He asserted that 'the villages did not exist "from times immemorial". The advance of plough-using agrarian economy over tribal India is a great historical achievement by itself.'[23] He himself dated the 'growth of virtually self-contained villages' to as late as Gupta times (fourth and fifth centuries AD).[24] He saw what he called 'Indian feudalism' as a process of ruralization, a matter on which he and R.S. Sharma, the leading Marxist scholar on Indian feudalism, are both agreed.[25] But unlike Sharma, Kosambi also insisted that no identifiable traces of serfdom or manorial economy were to be found in India.[26] The possibility that a form of 'Asiatic Despotism', where, as Marx said, 'rents and taxes coincide',[27] could exist in medieval India has not been considered by either Kosambi or Sharma, although it is not perhaps as unrealistic a depiction of the Mughal Empire, as was once thought.[28] On his part, Kosambi believed that Muslims, partly by force, increased commodity production in India,[29] but this important fact also seems to have been tucked away somewhere under his thesis of 'Feudalism from Above'.[30]

Kosambi developed his thoughts carefully, pursuing research in all kinds of ways, textual studies, sociological field work, philological analysis, numismatic and archaeological work, etc. He opened doors for many of us to new ideas and new questions, and, after 1957, especially, we looked forward to any article or book that might come from his pen. There were themes he had left unexamined or only partly explored (his pages on the British colonial regime in the *Introduction to the Study of Indian History* were, for instance, far too few and, perhaps, even hurried),[31] and it was natural to hope all the time for fresh word on such matters from him. D.D. Kosambi seemed to be in full vigour, and in command of all his powers, when death took him away so suddenly in June 1966, when he was not yet sixty.[32] Our loss was great, but he will ever remain a source of inspiration.

NOTES

[1] The main facts of the life of Dharmanand Kosambi will be found in Professor Meera Kosambi's Introduction to *Dharmanand Kosambi: The Essential Writings,* translated and edited by her, Ranikhet, 2010.

[2] D.D. Kosambi, *Combined Methods in Indology and Other Writings* (henceforth *CMI),* ed. Brajadulal Chattopadhyaya, New Delhi, 2002, p. 759. The original article, 'The Emergence of National Characteristics Among Three Indo-European Peoples', appeared in the *Annals of the Bhandarkar Oriental Research Institute,* Vol. 20 (1938-39), pp. 195-206.

[3] Kosambi quotes the passage *in extenso* in his *An Introduction to the Study of Indian History* (henceforth *Introduction*), Bombay, 1956, p. 9.

[4] Karl A. Wittfogel, *Oriental Despotism: A Comparative Study of Total Power,* Yale, 1957, p. 329.

[5] In English these discussions are best known from a very biased source: Wittfogel, *Oriental Despotism,* pp. 402-04. Kosambi wrote a hostile review of this work (*CMI,* pp. 797-801), but did not consider Wittfogel's report on the Leningrad Discussions worth commenting on.

[6] Review reprinted in *CMI,* pp. 784-89

[7] This essay was contributed as part of the *History of CPSU(B) – Short Course,* but was also published separately, as in J. Stalin, *Problems of Leninism,* Moscow, 1953, pp. 731-45. Kosambi's comment is to be found in *Introduction,* p.15 (f.n. 13).

[8] Originally published in *Indo-Iranian Journal,* Vol.6 (1963), reprinted in *CMI,* pp. 3-29.

[9] A statement made in 1949: see *CMI,* p. 785.

[10] In a review contributed in 1949, *CMI,* p. 789.

[11] See Edward W. Said, *Orientalism: Western Conceptions of the Orient,* New York, 1978, p. 203.

[12] Louis Dumont, *Homo Hierarchicus: The Caste System and its Implications,* Chicago, 1970 (revised English ed., New Delhi, 1998). The point about economic history is made on p. 209 and about history in general on p. 212.

[13] This is the title of the series which Ranajit Guha initiated with an essay on 'the Historiography of Colonial India' where he spelt out the essentials of his cult. Though he borrows Gramsci's terminology here without a word of

acknowledgement, he does not even recognize Marxism as a historiographic trend (*Subaltern Studies-1*, Delhi, 1982, pp. 1-8).

14 See Aijaz Ahmad, 'Postmodernism in History', in K.N. Panikkar *et al*, *The Making of History*, New Delhi, 2000, pp. 440-77.

15 See S. Pollock, 'Towards a Political Philology: D.D. Kosambi and Sanskrit', in *Economic and Political Weekly* (henceforth *EPW*), July 26, 2008, p. 58.

16 Kosambi's statements occur in *Introduction*, pp. 30-31 (not pp. 32-33 as mentioned by Ratnagar). Ratnagar's criticism is to be found in *EPW*, pp.75-76. I cannot trace the passage where, according to Ratnagar, Kosambi is supposed to have mentioned the tribesmen's 'body odour'; it is neither on the page she specifies nor thereabouts.

17 *CMI*, p.59. The original article titled 'Stages of Indian History', appeared in *ISCUS*, I (1), January 1954.

18 Karl Marx, 'Contribution to the Critique of Hegel's *Philosophy of Right*' (1844), in Karl Marx and Frederick Engels, *On Religion*, Moscow, 1957, p. 42.

19 *Introduction*, pp. 92-93.

20 Ibid., p. 25.

21 See Kosambi, 'On the Origin of Brahmin Gotras' (1950) in *CMI*, pp. 98-166.

22 I have raised this question in Irfan Habib (ed.), *Religion in Indian History*, New Delhi, 2007, pp. xviii-xxiii.

23 *Introduction*, p.11.

24 Ibid., pp. 280-81.

25 After his seminal work, *Indian Feudalism*, Calcutta, 1965 (first ed.), R.S. Sharma has reinforced the theory of ruralization in his *Urban Decay in India (c.300-c.1000)*, New Delhi, 1987.

26 *Introduction*, pp. 326-27.

27 Karl Marx, *Capital*, III, Moscow, 1959, pp. 771-72.

28 See the statements of Marx collected together in my Introduction ('Marx's Perception of India') in Iqbal Husain (ed.), *Karl Marx on India*, Aligarh, 2006, pp. xxv-xxxv.

29 'The problem of increasing commodity production was solved in part by force, in the feudal period – Islam's chief contribution to India – which promoted trade in the expropriated surplus and connected India more tightly with a much larger international market' (from a review penned in 1995: *CMI*, p. 796).

30 *Introduction*, pp. 344-46.

31 Ibid., pp. 365-70.

32 As I write these lines, I recall my own reading of Kosambi's writings in the fifties and early sixties. I was privileged to see him at Poona in December 1963 and then not long afterward at Aligarh. These meetings all the more deepened the sense of loss at his passing away. Meera Kosambi provides an excellent sketch of her father, 'D.D. Kosambi: the Scholar and the Man', in *EPW*, pp. 34-42.

Kosambi and the Frontiers of Historican Materialism

Prabhat Patnaik

D.D. Kosambi's interpretation of Indian history from a Marxist perspective was path-breaking in a dual sense. It not only sought to provide an analysis of Indian history *as a process*, as distinct from a mere litany of names and dates, and thus to open up an entire 'continent' for scientific exploration (to borrow Althusser's phrase), but also, in doing so, contributed to an expansion of the frontiers of historical materialism itself. His contribution to the understanding of Indian history and to its being opened up for scientific analysis has been discussed extensively by historians. But his contribution to historical materialism has hitherto received scant attention. The present paper attempts in a small way to redress this balance, by focusing on only two aspects of his work, namely his account of the Magadhan State, and his theory of 'acculturation'.

I

Usually in Marxist analysis, the State, which is an instrument of class rule, is seen to rest upon a class structure that has both ontological and epistemological priority. The usual pattern, both in history and therefore in Marxist theory, can be described as follows: the dynamics of social life bring about changes over time in the class structure and the balance of class strengths within any particular mode of production; the new class, as distinct from the extant dominant class, that progressively gains ascendancy within this mode of production, rallies other classes under its banner, and succeeds eventually in bringing about a change in the nature of the State; having acquired control over State power it then sets about establishing the sway of a new mode of production in which it is the dominant class.

In this entire story, the formation, the consolidation, and the gradual ascendancy of what eventually becomes the ruling class, occurs prior to, and independently of, its becoming the ruling class. Because of this, the State is always seen as a class-State, over which control is exercised by a class that has an independent and prior historical existence. There are of course important questions about what the term 'control' means in this context, and about the degree of 'autonomy' of the State, but these do not negate the basic point that the State is usually seen as an instrument of class rule by a ruling class that has an independent and prior historical existence.

The Magadhan State according to Kosambi was *not* such a State. 'The Arthashastra state', he wrote, 'was not characteristic of a society in which some new class had already come into possession of real power before taking over the state mechanism'.[1] It was of course a class-State, but not of a separately formed and independently existing ruling class; *it was a State in which the king and his subordinate State functionaries themselves could be said to have constituted the ruling class.* It was not a prior class with pretensions to rule that brought about the Magadhan State, but the State itself that *ipso facto* defined the ruling class.

The historical context for the emergence of such a State, the conditions for its dominance, and the methods employed by it to sustain itself in power (even as particular dynasties presiding over this State kept changing), are too well-known to need recounting here. The context was the extension of agriculture through the clearing of forests, and the development of commodity production on the basis of this growing agrarian economy. The conditions for its dominance lay in its control over mineral resources, especially iron, which it employed to clear vast tracts of jungles in the Gangetic plain and elsewhere; the surplus extracted from the producers settled on these 'crown lands' was used to maintain a huge standing army and a flourishing urban life, where the capital city Pataliputra (Patna) became for a considerable length of time the largest city in the world. And the methods used by it to sustain its power, described in Kautilya's *Arthashatra*, included, apart from this standing army, an extraordinarily centralized system of bureaucracy, regulations and espionage.

What is remarkable however was not just the highly centralized polity, but above all the highly centralized pattern of ownership of property in the hands of the State. The *sita* lands, 'settled as well as farmed directly under crown supervision', 'soon formed so great a proportion of the cultivated area that Greek visitors . . . believed all land belonged to the Indian king'.[2] But it was not a matter of land ownership alone. The State had a monopoly of mining and engaged in commodity production on a large scale. There were of course private traders and merchants to whom minerals could be sold by the State, and agricultural produce by both the State and the peasants, but a whole array of restrictions and taxes upon such traders ensured that the overwhelming weight of the State in handling commodities persisted; and likewise the State's domination in mineral processing heavy industry was never threatened.

In Kosambi's words, the

> Kautalyan state appears so fantastic today because it was the main land clearing agency, by far the greatest landowner, the principal owner of heavy industry, and even the greatest producer of commodities. The ruling class was, if not created virtually by and for the State, at least greatly augmented as part of the administration: the higher and lower bureaucracies, the enormous standing army of half a million men (by 300 BC) with its officers of all castes and diverse origins; as important as either, a second but hidden army of spies and secret agents – these were the main supports of the new state.[3]

To be sure, since the State did not have a formal monopoly over either trade or land-clearing, a class of private traders, farmers and *gahapatis* which had come into being earlier, and whose need for security and safe trade routes had been answered by the emergence of the 'unified monarchy', continued to exist. But neither was this class represented in the major echelons of the State (Kosambi contrasts this with the position of merchants vis-à-vis the Chinese empire around this time), nor did the State become an instrument for this class to flourish. Instead, the State itself came largely to occupy the position that this class might have been otherwise expected to occupy; it became virtually the ruling class.

The idea of the State bureaucracy being the ruling class is by no means a new one. It may be invoked, and occasionally has been, to describe certain other instances as well, but the Magadhan State, as Kosambi sees it, was *sui generis*. Let us look at some of these other instances.

From Irfan Habib's (1999) account[4] of the agrarian system of the Mughal empire, where the imperial bureaucracy appears to have appropriated the bulk of the surplus, the conclusion may be drawn that this bureaucracy constituted the ruling class of that period. But there are three obvious differences between the Mughal State and the Magadhan State: first, the imperial bureaucracy under the Mughal empire had to share the surplus with lower echelons (the *zamindars*), and represented in that sense a superimposition upon a pre-existing ruling class with whom it was enmeshed, rather than a separate new arrangement. Secondly, there was no single integral property right on land in the Mughal empire. Indeed Habib (1995) examines the question of property right by looking at the right over the surplus produced on land. By contrast, in the Magadhan empire, according to Kosambi, the resettled peasants on 'crown land' did not necessarily have even hereditary occupancy rights, which suggests something like a single integral property right on such land vested in the State. Thirdly, the Magadhan State, as analysed by Kosambi, was engaged in a whole range of economic activities, including of course mining and forest clearing, which greatly augmented the productive base of the economy, compared to the primarily surplus-appropriating Mughal State whose apparatus of surplus appropriation was so well-developed that it was more or less taken over subsequently by the colonial State and employed with much greater ruthlessness (in so far as the Mughal tax on produce was substituted by a tax on land and enforced through a whole new paraphernalia of juridical property rights backed up by Courts of Law). It follows, for all these reasons, that the class status of the Mughal bureaucracy was vastly different from that of the bureaucracy of the Magadhan State.

The fact that the Magadhan State 'owned' the bulk of the means of production and was engaged in a range of economic activities that augmented the productive base of the economy, may suggest that Magadha was an early instance of a situation that according to ultra-Left writers, characterized the Soviet Union at a later date. Several ultra-Left critics of the Soviet Union, including a section of the Trotskyists (though not Leon Trotsky himself) had persistently characterized the Soviet Union as a class-State where the State bureaucracy constituted a ruling class. They had called it by several names such as State capitalism, Bureaucrat Capitalism, Managerial Capitalism (this last characterization, authored by Burnham and Cartei, being associated with a 'convergence thesis' according to which both advanced capitalist countries like the US and the Soviet Union were 'converging' to 'managerial capitalism'). And the question would naturally arise: to what extent does Kosambi's characterization of the Magadhan State provide theoretical justification to all such characterizations of the Soviet State?

The simple and obvious answer to this question is: none whatsoever. The Soviet Union was formed as a sequel to a revolution in Russia where the working class, in alliance with the peasantry, seized State power and set up a dictatorship of the proletariat. Apart from saving the world from the horrors of fascism, the Soviet Union not only gave succour to anti-imperialist struggles all over the world throughout its existence, but largely contributed to the process of decolonization of the third world. And in addition it set up the most gigantic welfare state system for the workers that the world has ever seen. There were no doubt bureaucratic distortions in the Soviet Union, the prospects of which had been foreseen by Lenin and against which he had warned, but this is not the same as the bureaucracy constituting the ruling class. (Significantly, the protagonists of this view have never tried to explain, though they need to for the sake of completing their argument, why the Soviet bureaucracy was so committed to the anti- fascist struggle, so committed to the anti-imperialist struggle, and so committed to a Welfare State for the workers.) It follows that Kosambi's analysis of the State bureaucracy constituting a ruling class in Magadha cannot be used as an analytical prop for ultra-Left theories about the bureaucracy in the Soviet Union constituting a ruling class. And indeed Kosambi would have been horrified by any such use of his theoretical position. His theory, in short, is completely *sui generis* not just with regard to the historical situation it depicts, but also with regard to its own total structure in depicting that situation.

The question naturally arises: under what circumstances would the State bureaucracy be able to constitute itself as a ruling class? Or putting it differently, if it follows from Kosambi's analysis that in certain historical situations, such as prevailed in the period between the 6th and the 3rd centuries BC in India, a State may come into being which does not reflect the hegemony of a pre-existing class that has been acquiring ascendancy, but whose personnel and bureaucracy itself largely constitute the ruling class, then what is the specificity of this historical situation?

Since the coming into being of such a State is bound to antagonize the pre-existing classes which get hemmed in by it, such a State can survive only if it has certain unique strengths. The access to mineral resources, especially iron, over which the State had a monopoly, and which could be used for cutting forests, and for bringing fresh land under the ownership of the State, provided the Magadhan State with such a unique strength (the post-Kosambi discovery of Megalithic sites where the presence of iron dating back to the second millennium BC has been archaeologically established does not necessarily negate his thesis about the importance of the role of iron for the Magadhan State): the cultivation of such land with the help of a re-settled population provided it with a substantial and growing surplus with which a massive standing army and bureaucracy could be maintained. This was a *sui generis* situation not easily replicable elsewhere (though certain parallel arguments have been made about the 'absolute autonomy' of the Iranian State in certain periods of the twentieth century because of its control over massive oil resources); but Kosambi's boldness in cognizing this phenomenon constitutes a major contribution to the expansion of the frontiers of historical materialism.

II

A class society of the conventional kind began to emerge from the pores of the centralized Magadhan structure as it started to decay (under the initial impact of a fiscal crisis, according to Kosambi). While empires sprouted up periodically, the last in this phase of Indian history being that of Harsha, these were now increasingly based upon a class structure where the oppressed classes, incorporated into the vaishya and the shudra castes, were kept down. But this expanding agrarian class society also absorbed into its fold the tribes and guild castes that were functioning outside of it. It did so through the penetration of brahmanas into their midst in order to assimilate them through a process of 'reciprocal acculturation'.

The tribal deities were accommodated into the brahmanical pantheon, so that the tribes could worship the brahmanical gods together with their own deities, even as the rest of society also worshipped these transformed tribal deities. Matriarchal groups worshipping some mother goddess were assimilated through the 'marriage' of the mother goddess with some male god of the brahmanical pantheon, such as Durga-Parvati (and a number of local variants) being made the wife of Shiva, and Lakshmi that of Vishnu. Together with this there came new myths, new rituals and new places of pilgrimage.

Kosambi expresses the process as follows:

> The mechanism of assimilation is particularly interesting. Not only Krishna, but the Buddha himself and some totemic deities including the primeval Fish, Tortoise and Boar were made into incarnations of Vishnu-Narayana. The monkey-faced Hanuman . . . with an independent cult of his own, becomes the faithful companion-servant of Rama, another incarnation of Vishnu. Vishnu-Narayana uses the great earth-bearing Cobra as his canopied bed to sleep upon the waters; at the same time the same cobra is Siva's garland and a weapon of Ganesha. The elephant-headed Ganesha is son to Siva, or rather of Siva's wife. . . . This conglomeration goes on for ever, while all the tales put together form a senseless, inconsistent, chaotic mass. The importance of the process, however, must not be underestimated. The worship of these newly absorbed primitive deities was part of the mechanism of acculturation, a clear give-and-take.[5]

This acculturation however was a means of assimilation of tribes into the class society. The tribal chief with the backing of a few important tribesmen, would become the ruler of the tribe, acquiring an upper caste, usually kshatriya, status, while the rest of the tribe would get merged into the peasantry with a lower caste status. Sometimes the brahmana would discover an upper caste lineage for the tribal chief in the epics or the *Puranas*, and would occasionally even marry himself into the tribe, creating progeny that would become the new tribal brahmana. 'All this amounted,' says Kosambi, 'to keeping down a newly created set of vaisyas and sudras by Brahmin precept and kshatriya arms'.[6]

What acculturation did was to assimilate tribes into the developing agrarian society *without any explicit use of violence.* Since it simultaneously achieved two distinct outcomes, namely the overcoming of the isolation of the tribe on the one hand, and the splintering of the tribe into two distinct classes in the process of overcoming this isolation on the other, each of which could have been a potentially violent process, the significance of the fact that acculturation obviated the use of violence should not be underestimated.

At the same time however Kosambi looks at the long-term damage it did to India's intellectual and cultural life: despite overcoming the isolation of the tribe, it never fully overcame the isolation of the village society as a whole, and hence inhibited the scope of commodity production, and with it of cultural exchange; it promoted superstition; it led to the proliferation of a mass of senseless ritual; it discouraged codification and recording; it subscribed to the concept of a 'logic' divorced from all reality; it thwarted scientific advance; and it privileged 'hierarchy' over 'equity' which was the original meaning of Ashoka's *dhamma*.

Kosambi's concept of 'acculturation' again is something that falls outside usual Marxist analysis. While acculturation itself consists of the mutual acceptance of each other's deities and rituals, through an act of locating them within a broader, fantastic myth, underlying it is the acceptance of the ideological hegemony of the brahmanas, not only by those being assimilated but also by those with whom assimilation takes place. In fact this assimilation which is the product of this dual hegemony also serves to buttress this hegemony further. Several aspects of it are striking from a Marxist perspective: first, while the acquisition of ideological hegemony following the violent assimilation of a group into society is not uncommon, the use of ideological hegemony *prior to the use of violence and as a substitute for violence* is not. Secondly, the fact of ideological hegemony exercised by an outsider being an instrument for the splintering of the tribe into the ruler and the ruled is itself quite remarkable. Thirdly, the fact of ideological hegemony exercised by the brahmanas over the outside groups serving also to buttress their ideological hegemony over their own society, is also both important and uncommon.

In short, what we have here is not a simple subjugation of tribes by the non-tribal society, but the simultaneous existence of several processes of 'becoming': the 'becoming' of tribal society into class society; the 'becoming' of tribal society into an assimilated segment of a broader agrarian society; the 'becoming' of brahmanical ideology into a dominant force in the tribal society; the 'becoming' of the brahmanical ideology into a dominant force in the broader society by virtue of this fact; and so on. Such a rich and complex process must be historically quite unique; and so is Kosambi's theorizing of it within the literature on historical materialism.

This rich and complex process naturally begs the question: what were the historical specificities underlying it? How is it that acculturation of the sort described by Kosambi could occur in India? What was the basis on which it could occur? Let us construct an answer to this question on the basis of Kosambi's analysis (though Kosambi himself, concerned more with underscoring the phenomenon of acculturation, does not, in my view, discuss it in as much detail as it deserves).

Having tribal deities accepted or 'married' into the pantheon of the brahmanical gods could not in itself have been much of an inducement for tribes to get assimilated into the broader agrarian society. Even though the chiefs would have benefited from such assimilation, in so far as it helped them to get elevated from being mere chiefs to becoming rulers, and thereby presumably control a larger amount of surplus, the ordinary members of the tribes could not possibly have been tempted into such assimilation unless it contributed to an improvement in their economic position. Only such an improvement would have overcome their natural resistance to the introduction of class division within the tribe, to the abandonment of tribal law, and to the acceptance of the status of an inferior caste within an 'alien' universe.

In short, acculturation as a means of assimilation in lieu of violence would succeed only in a situation where such assimilation is beneficial in a more substantive sense, by improving the material position of the assimilated. This could only have occurred in so far as settled agriculture yielded higher incomes than the traditional occupations of the tribes. This, Kosambi's analysis suggests, must have been the case, in which case the brahmana's role in facilitating acculturation was founded upon an even more substantive role which he played, of bringing superior production practices, better technology, better knowledge of markets, and in general, higher income-earning possibilities to the tribal population. The brahmana could play this role because he not only had a pre-eminent position in matters of education, culture and knowledge, but, not having to work for his subsistence and living off the surplus, was also free to move around throughout the country.

Kosambi puts the matter as follows: 'The Brahmins here acted as pioneers in undeveloped localities; they first brought plough agriculture to replace slash and burn cultivation, or food gathering. New crops, knowledge of distant markets, organization of village settlements and trade also came with them. As a result kings or kings-to-be invited brahmins, generally from the distant Gangetic basin, to settle in unopened localities.'[7] It is this knowledge and skill brought to the tribes by the brahmanas that must have prepared the ground for the process of acculturation.

III

Concepts like the 'Magadhan State' and 'acculturation' contain deep insights into the process of Indian history and constitute major building blocks for constructing its totality. In addition however they push the frontiers of historical materialism outward. Kosambi could advance his novel Marxist interpretation of Indian history because he was not bound by a 'closed' reading of Marxism, by a perception of Marxism as a 'closed system'. His Marxism was not a 'formed' theoretical system into which human history had to be fitted, as he felt S.A. Dange to be doing in his book *India from Primitive Communism to Slavery*, but a scientific approach to the concrete study of human history. Marxism necessarily had to be 'open-ended.'

As he put it, 'to remain a living discipline, Marxism must continue to work with newer discoveries in science (including archaeology), and must yield new valid results in history. Its importance lies not only in the interpretation of the past but as guide to future action. By its correct use, men can make their own history consciously, rather than suffer it to be made as helpless spectators, or merely to study it after the event'.[8] The necessity of correct analysis of the past in Kosambi's perception therefore derives from the fact that it aids correct praxis for changing the world. And correct analysis requires not closed minds but those which are open to new discoveries in science and which are alive to new facts: 'The only successful way of dealing with adverse views presented in all good faith is a careful, detailed and factual answer.'[9]

In talking of a 'factual answer' Kosambi is not taking a naïve 'scientist' view of 'facts' and thereby reducing Marxism to a naïve 'scientism'. On the contrary he says:

> Marxism cannot be reduced to a rigid formalism like mathematics. Nor can it be treated as a standard technique such as work on an automatic lathe. The material, when it is present in human society, has endless variations; the observer is himself part of the observed population, with which he interacts strongly and reciprocally. This means that the successful application of the theory needs the development of analytical power, the ability to pick out the essential features in a given situation. This cannot be learned from books alone. The one way to learn it is by constant contact with the major sections of the people.[10]

But then if Marxism is 'open-ended,' if it must continue to work with newer discoveries, then what exactly remains of Marxism? What is the 'theory' whose application Kosambi is talking about? Kosambi's understanding of Marxism is as clear and unambiguous as it is non-heterodox: Marxism accords centrality to social production and its categories. 'The progress of mankind and its history thus depends upon the means of production, i.e. the actual tools and the productive relationships. Society is held together by the bonds of production'.[11] These words of Kosambi could have been almost taken out of *The German Ideology*.

This brings us, finally, to Kosambi's relationship with the Left. Kosambi was associated with the Communist Party during the war years when he wrote occasionally for the Party publications. Even though his association with the Party weakened subsequently, he was extremely active in the Peace movement organized by the Communists. The Sino-Soviet rift weakened the Peace movement, and Kosambi, increasingly disillusioned by the direction it was taking, finally severed his links with it in 1963. But he remained an ardent sympathizer of the Chinese Revolution till the end of his life in 1966, and had agreed to write for an Encyclopaedia that the revolutionary regime in Cuba had planned to bring out. (The project had to be abandoned because of Cuba's economic hardships.) Notwithstanding his differences with the Communists (the Communists themselves it must be remembered had differences among them which eventually led to a split in the Party), the fact that he was considered sufficiently close to them explains perhaps why his proposed Tagore Memorial Lecture at Harvard could not materialize, though the drafts he had prepared for his Encyclopaedia article and for the Tagore Memorial lecture became the basis of his *Culture and Civilisation of Ancient India in Historical Outline*.

Kosambi's political positions were not too distant from those of the dominant section of the Communists. Indeed his political analysis of the Nehruvian era in one of the essays in *Exasperating Essays* is scarcely any different from what the largest Communist party of today would say about that period. And his espousal of Marxism, and commitment to the cause of 'men making their own history consciously', were indubitable.

His main objection to what he called 'Official Marxism,' propounded by his contemporary Communists in India, appears to have been that it treated Marxism as a 'closed' system. This is implicit in his complaint that it considered his writings 'controversial', a criticism which would then exclude according to him 'the main work of Marx, Engels, Lenin, and the best of Stalin and Mao Tsetung'.[12] He decried the fact that Official

Marxism 'too often consisted of theological emphasis on the inviolable sanctity of the current Party Line or irrelevant quotations from the classics'.[13]

None of this makes Kosambi a heterodox Marxist. It is surprising therefore to find no less a person than Romila Thapar writing that Kosambi 'insistently asserted his autonomy from the clutches of contemporary orthodoxies, both of the Left and of the Right.'[14] There are two problems with this remark. First, it puts the Left and the Right, and Kosambi's relationship with the two, on par. But, notwithstanding all his differences from the political Left, Kosambi's relationship with even this political Left can never be considered to be on par with his relationship with the Right. Secondly, it considers 'heterodoxy' and 'openness' as synonymous. One can be a non-heterodox Marxist, *and precisely for that reason,* shun 'closedness' of the mind, which is completely foreign to Marxism.[15] Indeed it is Kosambi's non-heterodox Marxism, which, far from preventing him from pushing the frontiers of historical materialism through novel concepts such as those discussed in the preceding sections, actually motivated him to do so.

NOTES

1 D.D. Kosambi, *The Culture and Civilisation of Ancient India in Historical Outline* (hereafter *Culture*), Routledge and Kegan Paul, London, 1965, pp. 143-44.

2 *Culture,* p.149.

3 Ibid., p. 143.

4 Irfan Habib, *The Agrarian System of Mughal India* (Second Edition), Oxford University Press, New Delhi, 1999.

5 *Culture,* p. 170.

6 Ibid., p. 171.

7 Ibid., p. 172.

8 D.D. Kosambi, *Exasperating Essays,* People's Book House, Poona, 1957, pp. 2-3.

9 Ibid., p. 3.

10 Ibid., pp. 3-4.

11 Ibid., p. 2.

12 Ibid., p. 3.

13 Ibid., p. 3.

14 R. Thapar, 'Early Indian History and the Legacy of D.D. Kosambi', *Economic and Political Weekly,* July 26, 2008.

[15] The proposition that Marxism is necessarily 'open-ended' while various strands of bourgeois thought, including liberalism, are necessarily not 'open-ended' because of their inherent constraint in refusing to recognize the possibility of the transcendence of capitalism, and hence of having to find the resolution of all problems within the bourgeois system itself is developed at length in P. Patnaik, 'The Terrain of Marxist Theory', Safdar Hashmi Memorial Lecture, organized by Jana Natya Manch, November 8, 2008, Delhi. Available online at http://www.pragoti.org/node/2474.

Some Observations on Kosambi's Medieval India

Eugenia Vanina

Luminaries like D.D. Kosambi serve humanity not only by their own contributions into this or that field of knowledge, but by making it possible for the succeeding generations to think over, criticise, visit and revisit, reconstruct and 'deconstruct' their findings. The writings on Kosambi even exceed in number the works by Kosambi himself; a few memorial volumes have been published, and in 2008 *Economic and Political Weekly* brought out a special number on Kosambi with a comprehensive selection of illuminating papers. Among the existing approaches to the legacy of this outstanding historian two seem absolutely fruitless: firstly, overall negation[1] of his contributions to history that even the opponents to Kosambi's methodology and ideology unanimously acknowledge as professionally and intellectually superb,[2] and, secondly, worship-like attitude viewing any criticism of the deified object as a sacrilege. To a person of Kosambi's open-mindedness the former attitude would have been, I dare suggest, even preferable to the latter. For the scholars of my generation Kosambi has been and is doubtlessly a classic of Indian history; however, a classic who lived and worked in a certain epoch, on a certain level of knowledge and methodology. Critical re-assessment of his thoughts and findings deserve a historical approach which, strangely enough, has been more firmly established in science than in humanities: the scientists would never criticise, for example, Newton for not applying in his age Einstein's twentieth century discoveries, while some historians would castigate their predecessors for 'not knowing' or 'not understanding' what the newer generation does (or thinks it does).

My attempt will be to critically assess the relevance of Kosambi's legacy for researching into medieval Indian history – his contributions to ancient Indian studies have been,[3] and will continue to be, more professionally analysed by the concerned scholars. But to properly evaluate Kosambi's views on medieval India it will not be out of place to situate him in the history of medieval Indian studies.

FOLLOWER AND TRAILBLAZER

When in the 1940s the fascinating trajectory of Kosambi's intellectual pursuits brought him to history, medieval Indian studies had already had a record of more than a century and a half. Kosambi was unavoidably influenced by the hitherto existing notions of medieval India and used them as reference point. All in all, there were two major discourses on this subject. The Orientalistic one is to be mentioned first as the most powerful (from administrative, ideological and methodological points of view), long-existing and developed. Some brief observations on what Kosambi had learned from his Western preceptors would be helpful.

Medieval India as a period of history and a subject of study was, so to say, an unloved stepchild of Indology. As is well known, for Orientalists, beginning from Dow, Jones, Wilkins, Halhed, and their successors, only ancient India was worthy of research and of praise as a 'Golden Age' of Indian civilization. These celebrated inheritors of the European Renaissance and Enlightenment for whom ancient Greece and Rome had been the only sources of light, the only law-makers in almost all spheres of life, were happy to find that India had also had its glorious antiquity which could be a certain (although not full, of course) match for the Greco-Roman one. It was ancient India that the 'Indophiles' loved, studied, translated and valiantly protected from the vehement attacks of their 'Indophobic' Utilitarian opponents like James Mill.[4] Criticising the latter, the Orientalists however fully subscribed to his division of pre-colonial history of India into two major periods: 'Hindu' and 'Muslim'. For many of them 'Muslim' period was medieval India as such,[5] everything that preceded it was 'ancient'. This suited well the scheme worked out for West European history: the 'golden epoch' of the highly civilized, enlightened and morally elevated Greco-Roman antiquity was cruelly brought to end by barbarous hordes of Alaric and Attila – in India a worthy parallel to them was seen in the Muslim invaders, likewise projected as destroyers of the shining antiquity of ancient India. To claim such an antiquity, rightfully or not, was a proof of the country's status of civilized: some less fortunate nations even had to 'invent' an antiquity for themselves.[6] At the same time for enlightened Europeans 'medieval' was synonymous to 'barbarian' ('dark Middle Ages' as a standard epithet) and even the poetized glorification of medieval legacy by the Romantics changed the situation but little. The same model was applied to India. For every true Indologist the beginning of the 'Muslim period' was a *Laksmanarekha* to be never trespassed, as had been solemnly declared by William Jones in his famous 1786 discourse.[7] The border between 'ancient' and 'medieval' was established for decades to come as religious (Hindu – Muslim) and, no less significantly, linguistic: the former was to be explored by specialists on Sanskrit (later on with a little addition of Tamil for South India), the latter was, and, unfortunately, to a certain extent still is, studied exclusively on the basis of Persian sources. Translating and analysing Sanskrit texts, European Orientalists viewed almost all of them, including, for instance, those by Bhartrihari, Jayadeva, Somadeva or Kalhana, as 'ancient', not medieval.

The 'Muslim period', treated as almost coterminous with 'medieval',[8] was discussed by Orientalists in an overwhelmingly negative way, as had been most vividly demonstrated by Elliot's vehement preface to his notoriously famous selections from Persian chronicles.[9] It was worth studying, if at all, only to provide colonial administrators with adequate material on their predecessors' experience in agrarian legislation, taxation, etc.,[10] and to demonstrate to the British readers – how fortunate they were not to live under the 'Oriental tyrants';[11] and to the Indian subjects of Empire – how benevolent British Raj was in comparison with the bloodthirsty Padishahs and Nawabs.[12] As for 'ancient' India, it could be studied as a repository of Sanskrit literary classics, philosophical schools, 'pure Aryan spirit', etc. – and also as a record of slowly but surely developing decay and degradation.

Parallel to the European story of how Roman civilization had degraded to become a victim of barbarous hordes, 'ancient' India, as imagined by Orientalists, also decayed, especially with the collapse of the Mauryan and Gupta empires. According to them, the 'true Aryan spirit' of Vedic religion along with philosophically elevated Brahmanism and Buddhism gave way to Hinduism with its chaos of deities, ignorant priesthood and ceremonies, sometimes shocking to a civilized European (of eighteenth or nineteenth century, of course);[13] exquisite Sanskrit classics were pushed back by crude texts in the 'bazaar' vernaculars; enlightened brahmanical asceticism died out to be replaced by moral depravity, hedonism and barbarity.[14] This degradation was, according to Orientalists, inseparable from the collapse of the mighty empires of Mauryas and especially Guptas: what resulted was a chaos of petty states whose 'bewildering annals', according to Vincent A. Smith, could only 'serve to the reader a notion of what India has always been when released from the control of supreme authority, and what she would be again, if the hand of the benevolent power that now safeguards her boundaries should be withdrawn'.[15] The farther Indian society proceeded away from the 'Golden Age' of the Guptas, the more critical and denunciatory was the tone of its Orientalist researchers: the post-Gupta 'Hindu' India, not to mention 'Muslim' period, became, in their view, the realm of all social evils, rectifiable only by the 'hand of the benevolent power', i.e. British Raj.

To Orientalists, the 'Hindu' or 'ancient' Indian society, given its achievements in language, literature and philosophy, was nevertheless stagnant – changes, if any, were only towards 'degradation'. I may suggest that one of major reason why James Tod's concept of Rajput society's feudal character was so passionately opposed and even mocked as 'Romanticist extravaganza' by many Indologists, was that this concept, given its immaturity, factual mistakes and methodological weakness, presupposed by itself a certain changeability of Indian society, its development according to the same historical pattern as European one, the gap between the two being not as wide as previously suggested (Jones found ancient Greece in the late eighteenth century Bengal).[16] India was imagined as a timeless society – in the meaning of both unchangeability and ahistoricity. In the Orientalistic imagination, as summarised by Peter van der Veer, 'India becomes a society without history. It is a frozen society that is only introduced to history by its confrontation with the modern colonial world'.[17] That 'ancient' Indians had neither sense of history nor interest in recording it has become an unchallengeable dogma of Indology. Philosophically substantiated and blessed by Hegel, this misconception has outlived Orientalism[18] despite many painstaking and convincing efforts by a number of modern scholars to disprove it.

The second discourse on medieval history, the nationalist one, owed so much to the findings of Western Orientalists, that some modern researchers have even termed it 'the avatar of Orientalism in the later colonial and postcolonial periods'.[19] Both the reformists and nationalists were students of the British Indologists and read James Mill as a standard textbook. In their condemnation of the dark sides of medieval Indian society (like caste discrimination, impoverishment of the toiling masses, child marriages, widow self-immolation, feudal oppression, religious prejudices, ignorance, etc.) they even outmatched Mill and Utilitarian critics of India, as national humiliation and sincere patriotic desire to serve their country by rectifying social evils added more passion to their argumentation. With a few exceptions[20] they fully subscribed to the dogma of the 'ahistoricity' of Indian civilization before the 'Muslim invasion' and almost overwhelmingly spoke in terms of 'Hindu' and 'Muslim' history of India – it took time for 'secular' or 'inclusivist'[21] wing of Indian nationalist thought to reject this division as uncompromisingly as Nehru did.[22] From the British Orientalists and German philosophers (like Kant, Schlegel, Herder, etc.) they learned about the brave and moral Aryans, the 'Golden Age of the Hindu India' and ancient India as a cradle of world culture, religions, philosophies and 'spirituality',[23] as well as of its subsequent degradation and subjugation by alien aggressors.[24] But, unlike their British mentors, the nationalists did not paint the post-Gupta period in total black; according to them, it could boast of a number of wise and valiant leaders, as well as manifestations of heroic spirit. Medieval rulers, denounced by Orientalists as 'robber chiefs' and 'tyrants', became, like Shivaji, heroes in the nationalist discourse. Opposing inferiority complexes, inculcated by colonial propaganda that portrayed Indians as 'cowardly', 'feminine', 'servile' and 'devoid of patriotism', nationalist leaders, writers and historians actively employed ancient and medieval India to invoke in their audiences the feelings of self-respect, national pride and courage. As nationalist thought developed its own perception of history, according to Partha Chatterjee's paradigm, towards 'past-as-it-will-be',[25] Ashoka, Harsha and Akbar were perceived as precursors of the future national state, while Shivaji and Raj Singh – as inspirers for anti-colonial struggle.[26]

Kosambi doubtlessly inherited from both these discourses, as a researcher into Indian history to which major contributions had been hitherto made by Orientalists, and, in the words of his daughter Meera, as a 'staunch nationalist' himself.[27] He narrated the post-Mauryan and especially post-Gupta history of India primarily as a story of decline: it was, for him, a 'dismal tale of rapid growth and long degradation' which covered 'some fifteen centuries after Asoka'.[28] 'The process of decay', he further wrote, 'was so long and gradual that a book like the present [*The Culture & Civilisation of Ancient India in Historical Outline*] could be terminated at any date after Harsha'.[29] In his uncompromising denunciation of parasitical and obscurantist brahmana priesthood, as well as other exploiter classes of late ancient and early medieval India, he was both the follower of European progressivism, so common for Orientalists, and an Indian patriot who could never stop thinking about the social evils that had been to an extent responsible for colonial subjugation of his country and afterwards blocked its development as an independent state.

Kosambi likewise shared with both Orientalistic and nationalistic historiography the misconception of the 'ahistoricity' of ancient and medieval India: in his opinion, 'India has virtually no historical records worth the name'.[30] Like many of his colleagues, in India and elsewhere, he was convinced that ancient and medieval Indian texts should have been necessarily destined to comply with the historicity criteria as worked out by nineteenth and twentieth century European scholars, and if they failed to do so, they were not 'worth the name' of history. In full compliance with Orientalistic postulates, Kosambi juxtaposed ancient and early medieval Indians with 'historical-minded' nations like Chinese, Greeks, Romans, Assyrians, etc., without taking into consideration that the history of those people would have never been so well researched into if the respective specialists had been judging their ancient texts by modern Western criteria. Recent studies on various ancient and medieval cultures have now convincingly proved that pre-modern societies had peculiar means of recording and understanding their past, and modern criteria of historicity and factual truth are not applicable to them.[31] Kosambi's adherence to the 'ahistoricity concept' is even more regrettable given his own brilliant ability, after the almost ritual lamentations on the absence of Herodotus and Thucydides in India, to successfully use Sanskrit texts of various genres, including literary and mythological ones, as historical sources – this, in Meera's words, 'led the more conservative Sanskritists in India to perceive him as an iconoclast'.[32] Historical consciousness of ancient and early medieval Indians has been by now researched upon with a considerable success by a number of scholars.[33]

However, to reproach Kosambi for sharing the misconceptions of his time would be as meaningless as criticising him for not using a computer or mobile phone. Of much more importance is what he intended to do with this alleged 'ahistoricity'. His suggestion was not to lament the alleged 'abnormality' but to find a constructive way to defy it: 'Certainly, no ancient[34] Indian history is possible with the detailed accuracy of a history of Rome or

Greece. But what is history? If history means only the succession of outstanding megalomaniac names and imposing battles, Indian history would be difficult to write. If, however, it is more important to know whether a given people had the plough or not than to know the name of their king, then India has a history'.[35]

The very idea that historians should concern themselves not with heroes and battles but the life of the people was neither new nor Marxist: even Leo Tolstoy advocated it powerfully in *War and Peace.* Kosambi's trailblazing role was in attempting to find a reliable method of understanding Indian history and a focal criterion of evaluating the historical evolution of its society. The former for him was Marxism; the latter, consequently, was formulated as '*History is the presentation in chronological order of successive changes in the means and relations of production*' (italics in the original).[36]

In the view of some scholars, Kosambi's adoption of Marxism for researching into ancient and early medieval India was a lamentable mistake that dwarfed his otherwise brilliant insight.[37] Rajan Gurukkal was even surprised that Kosambi did not comply with a stereotyped image of a caricatured Marxist: 'Historical materialism was indeed his framework for comprehending the past but his procedure was not exactly as construed in Marxism, the basic presumption of which meant formulation of theoretical truth first and checking it against the theoretically accessible empirical evidence'[38] – here the author, may I suggest, vividly demonstrates the same scholastic approach as attributed by him to Marxism: he first creates a theory of what an imagined Marxist dogmatic should have definitely done and, when 'accessible empirical evidence' of Kosambi's contributions does not match the stereotype, declares it to be 'not exactly' Marxist. It was almost in this vein that Orientalists treated Kalhana for not complying with 'ahistoricity' dogma or Bhartrihari for defying the 'impersonality' one.

Any theory, Marxism being no exception, has blind, dogmatic or just professionally inadequate followers. Kosambi was, as unanimously accepted by even his critics and opponents, nothing like a mechanic chanter of Marxist mantras – in the words of D.N. Jha, he has 'ably demonstrated beyond doubt that dialectical materialism does not make the muse of history lie on the bed of Procrustes'.[39] The task, as seen by him as well as by his co-thinkers and followers, has been and is applying to Indian history the methodology which its founder, Marx, did not use for India himself, the reasons being needful of a separate study. Kosambi deserves credit for doing what some Marxists, in India, USSR and elsewhere, failed to do: demarcating the methodology from Marx's concrete evaluations of the Indian realities. Kosambi's treatment of the latter, as appears from his writings, was a historical approach of a twentieth century Marxist scholar to the mid-nineteenth century research, almost totally substantiated and influenced by Orientalism: 'The adoption of Marx's thesis does not mean blind repetition of all his conclusions (and even less, those of the official, party-line Marxists) at all times. . . . What Marx himself said about India cannot be taken as it stands.'[40]

Indeed, Kosambi, firstly, rejected the applicability to India of the Asiatic mode of production theory, and, secondly and more importantly, refused to view ancient India as a slave-owning society. While the former dogma could be rather easily disproved by the available concrete data on Indian society with its absence of huge state-owned irrigation systems and observably weak state, the latter one was actively debated, for instance, by some Soviet scholars who substantiated their *pro* and *contra* arguments for slavery in ancient India by the available data from Sanskrit and Pali texts of the epoch.[41] A dogmatic of Gurukkal's description would have been fighting tooth and nail for the slave-owning model for ancient India only because the 'five formations' scheme had been established in Marxism (not by Marx himself). Kosambi's analysis of ancient Indian society brought him to the conclusion that slaves were not the major productive force in it. In this aspect India was to a certain extent close to many European and Asian societies where slavery, albeit existing as a social institution, was however not a dominant means of production.

POLEMICIZING FEUDALISM AND ITS CULTURE

Another crucial contribution by Kosambi to Indian history was, doubtlessly, his concept of Indian feudalism. In the view of some colleagues, however, this was one of the major problems with Kosambi's scholarship, since, according to Sheldon Pollock, this concept 'has been singularly sterile. Its dust-dry shastric exercises over tax or rent, peasant or serf, class or caste are often completely *apriori* and devoid of any engagement with real empirical data and actual texts. They have little help to offer to those trying to make any sense of the real nature of polity or the character and grounds of cultural change. After half a century of discourse on feudalism, we still seem to have little idea about the political order in middle-period India'.[42]

A great number of scholars share these negative views on the Indian feudalism concept. An equal number, on the other hand, zealously defend the concept. Contrary to Pollock's accusation, both sides, in their 'dust-dry shastric exercises', do rely upon the analysis of 'real empirical data and actual texts', and, more often than not, one and the same document may be used to substantiate the feudalism concept and to oppose it. The main reason is, no doubt, the very character of medieval texts whose authors would have spent dozens of pages to describe a king's amorous and military feats but never bother to mention who owned land in his kingdom, and how.

Another problem, I may suggest, is that the students of medieval India have been still using a rather limited number of sources. The more than a century long dominance of the 'ahistoricity' dogma became a serious obstacle for the search and analysis of Indian history documents. Indeed, why should one take the labour of searching for something that, as every scholar knows, had never existed? In Western Europe, China or Russia, a discovery of a new medieval text would have caused an international sensation and bring the discoverer state awards, while in India a Ph.D. student may come to an archive, pick up a hitherto unknown document from a dusted heap and use it in his/her thesis without fanfare. No doubt, thanks to the tireless efforts of some scholars, Indian and non-Indian, an impressive number of new sources, including chronicles, family or temple records, apart from oral histories, have been brought to light. But a lot of work is still to be done.

The feudalism idea, for any country, may have lots of applicability problems, first and foremost the evergreen conflict between any concept and any historical or socio-cultural reality which never fully corresponds to the suggested pattern. As Engels once asked in a letter: 'Did feudalism ever correspond to its concept?'[43] The concept is almost inevitably as sterile, dry and 'shastric' as any theory and does not take into consideration the peculiarities of a given society. However, the 'sterility' of the feudalism theory was no obstacle for the scholars from various parts of the globe to assess the history of medieval mentalities and culture in Europe.[44]

Kosambi, to give him full credit, was fully conscious of the fact that not all features of feudalism as established for some European societies had been observable in India.[45] Among such features, as summarized by Romila Thapar, 'was an absence of demesne-farming on a substantial scale on the land of the vassal by those compulsorily made to labour. This involves questions of serfdom, the manorial system and the contractual element in the relations between king, vassal and serf. It was also pointed out that neither trade nor cities had declined in many parts of the subcontinent as was a requirement in some models'.[46] These peculiarities of medieval Indian society, visible to all, made some scholars fully negate the applicability of feudalism to India while others would spare no efforts to find in India demesne-farming, manors, serfdom and urban decay without taking into consideration that the above-mentioned specificities were conspicuous by their absence in some definitely feudal European societies too, like Italy, for example, where peasants were in their majority not serfs, feudal lords preferred manorial castles to urban palazzos, and cities or trade never decayed.

Lots of work is still ahead to redefine the features that undoubtedly make a society feudal. One of Kosambi's major achievements was his research into what Engels had termed as 'the basic relation of the whole feudal system' – the 'granting of land in return for the delivery of certain personal services and dues'.[47] In this peculiar sphere, however, Kosambi was extremely insightful and careful, never treating each and every land grant as a proof of feudalism – this was demonstrated by his criticism of a Soviet scholar, K.A. Antonova, for oversimplification of the emergence of feudalism in India and ignoring crucially important factors like caste.[48] Kosambi and his followers have made a universally acknowledged contribution to describing and analysing many pivotal features of feudalism in India, like specific means of production, methods of accumulating and redistributing wealth, forms of exploitation, relations between and within major social groups, character of state, administration, taxation, development of agriculture and trade.

It is important to point here that these processes have been thereafter studied by various scholars for different stages of Indian history, from early medieval to late medieval. Thanks to Kosambi it became possible to discuss the upper border of medieval epoch in India as different from what Orientalistic imagination had conceived it to be, and, in the words of D.N. Jha, 'to argue that medievalism did not coincide with the advent of Islam but that it was the end of Gupta rule towards the end of the sixth century AD that marks the beginning of some significant developments in India'.[49] However the 'wall', built by Orientalists, still separates in our understanding the 'before' from the 'after' of the 'Muslim invasion', and the lack of coordination between the scholars researching into different periods of medieval history sometimes makes it difficult to even now denote continuity and change between early medieval and late medieval India, as if the studies in, say, Gupta history and Mughal history refer to different countries.

All the above-mentioned aspects of economic, social and politico-administrative development are doubtlessly pivotal for defining a feudal society, in India or elsewhere, but, as mathematicians would say, they are necessary but not sufficient.

When Pollock criticised the 'sterility' of the feudalism concept, he did it as a 'contemporary literary or intellectual historian'. And here, to my mind, he has a point – not because the feudalism concept is irrelevant, but because the scholars who apply it to India have hitherto centred their attention almost exclusively on 'tax or rent, peasant or serf, class or caste', in many cases ignoring a very important aspect of Marxist methodology – the important and in many cases decisive role of superstructure and thus leaving cultural, religious and intellectual history to be analysed by anybody but Marxists. This socio-economic exclusivism was criticised by Engels as

> the fatuous notion of the ideologists that because we deny an independent historical development to the various ideological spheres which play a part in history, we also deny them *any effect upon history.* The basis of this is the common undialectical conception of cause and effect as rigidly opposite poles, the total disregard of interaction. These gentlemen often almost deliberately forget that once a historic element has been brought into the world by other, ultimately economic causes, it reacts, and can react on its environment and even on the causes that have given rise to it.[50] [Emphasis in the original.]

Kosambi, of course, did not insist that history was *only* 'the presentation in chronological order of successive changes in the means and relations of production' and nothing more. He should not be held responsible for the fact that some of his followers understood his statement verbally and followed it dogmatically. His emphasis upon socio-economic aspects of ancient and medieval Indian society was inevitable, in line with Marxist historiography, in an opposition to the previously established approach to history as just a change of dynasties, conquests and royal whims. However, Kosambi never neglected religion and culture as important factors of historical evolution and insisted upon studying the society as a system, not as a set of separated institutions, relations and processes in economy or culture. As noted by Thapar, 'culture for him was not a separate entity, but an intrinsic part of the making of a historical context. This may sound trite today but fifty years ago the inter-weaving of society, economy and culture was a departure from the standard histories of ancient India'.[51] Kosambi laid a special emphasis upon the dialectical interrelation between 'basis' and 'superstructure' and pointed at the latter's relative autonomy, that was at his time indeed an eye-opener for a Marxist discourse on India, and K.N. Panikkar had every reason to attach a special significance to this aspect of Kosambi's methodology.[52] However, Kosambi's application of this dialectic approach to concrete phenomena of Indian culture and literature was not devoid of inconsistencies and contradictions.

For Kosambi, it appears, class interests and conflicts were inevitably and directly influencing culture. 'For what class?' – with this question his analysis of the *Bhagvadgita* began,[53] and this seems to be the first inquiry he made into every text he analysed. Exploiting classes, as appears from Kosambi's analysis, produced culture and literature that had nothing to do with the life of the exploited masses; the sole purpose of any literary or artistic activity by and for the elite was, firstly, to amuse the rulers with endless stories of war and sex and, secondly, to safeguard and sanctify the existing norms and forms of dominance and exploitation. That was how he treated literary texts like Bhartrihari's poetry or the works collected in Vidyakara's anthology *Subhashitaratnakosha.*

This approach by Kosambi was opposed by many scholars from different points of view. As is well known, D.H.H. Ingalls, the author of the English translation of the *Subhashitaratnakosha* and general editor of Harvard Oriental Series where both the Sanskrit original and its English translation had been published, criticised Kosambi for what the American scholar understood as theories of Engels and Plekhanov on class character of literature.[54] Pollock, too, opines that Kosambi's approach to Indian history was 'derived from the darkest and most undialectical period of Marxist intellectual history, Stalin's *Diamat* of the 1940s compounded with Plekhanov's earlier historical materialist vision of literary change'.[55] Such is criticism from those who deny any applicability of social analysis to literature. But there have been polemics from another side, from the scholars who do accept Marxist methods for researching into history, literature and culture. Among them the views of Soviet scholars, whose works have been unfortunately unavailable in English, may be of interest to the readers.

Kosambi was doubtlessly respected in the USSR – as a public figure, as a fighter for world peace, a renowned scientist and, of course, as a Marxist historian. His book *The Culture & Civilisation of Ancient India in Historical Outline* was published in 1968 from Moscow in Russian translation; some of his articles were translated too. His biography was included into various Soviet encyclopaedias. Kosambi visited the Soviet Union and held discussions with scholars working on Indian history; he studied some of their works ('in free translation', as he himself confessed in his critique of Antonova) and objected to some of their misconceptions, to be, in turn, criticised by them for what they termed as 'schematism'[56] and 'certain vulgarization of materialist method [in history]'.[57]

However, Kosambi found in the USSR his most passionate critic and at the same time a most sincere admirer in the person of I.D. Serebryakov (1917 – 1998).[58] A Sanskritologist of classical St Petersburg school, in whose brilliant translations the Russian readers have enjoyed Bhartrihari, *Panchatantra*, *Shukasaptati*, Kshemendra's *Narmamala* and the whole of *Kathasaritsagara*, a Jawaharlal Nehru award winner, he worked at the beginning of his career for some years in India as a correspondent of the leading Soviet newspaper *Pravda*. There he met Kosambi and was fascinated. They met in Moscow too. In his book on Bhartrihari, describing under the rubric 'Genius Meets Genii' those scholars, thinkers and poets who had commented upon, translated and studied this great Sanskrit poet, Serebryakov included a *prashasti*-like essay on Kosambi (I have translated it and added to this paper as an Appendix). However, in his work 'Literary Process in India, Eighth to Thirteenth Centuries' Serebryakov strongly criticised

Kosambi's approach to early medieval literary texts. What in Kosambi's analysis was opposed by a Soviet scholar, a devoted Marxist and Communist to his last breath, even when after the collapse of the USSR?

Giving full credit to Kosambi as 'one of the first Indian scholars who tried to apply Marxist methodology to the study of history and culture of ancient and medieval India', as a 'most experienced textologist whose critical edition of Bhartrihari's three shatakas will remain a standard of textological work for many decades to come',[59] Serebryakov reproduced a lengthy citation from Kosambi's introductory notes to the *Subhashita-ratnakosha* text:

> The analysis must therefore derive from the class division of every society in which literature was cultivated. The professional writer before the machine age was a member of the leisure class, which in turn includes and is appended (as in priesthood) to the ruling class. Hence literature may be viewed in two aspects. The first would be as a closed preserve of a class in power, private literature not accessible to common herd. This is typical for all Sanskrit . . . . At its broadest, this type of literature marks the unity of the upper classes, as the Sanskrit language unmistakably did till AD 1200. There is secondly the broader literature which serves all society; this too becomes saturated with the ideas of ruling class, taking on the appearance of a tool of domination. But the development and technique have to be different here. The theme or approach must be traditionally familiar to the people at large, accepted by society as a whole, thus suitable for embroidery with special class glorification.[60]

To this argument by Kosambi Serebryakov objects in the following way:

> Here we have certain dogmatism, bringing us finally to the well-known concept of Sanskrit literature as aristocratic, as

> separated, like its creators, from the people . . . . According to Kosambi, Sanskrit literature is a literature of social elite. This literature is counterpoised, without any characterization or even linguistic denomination, by some kind of popular literature, determined by the ideas of the ruling class. To note, the unity of this class is significantly over-estimated here. And it was not only the real competition between the ethnically different groups of the feudal lords, but in the concrete dissimilarities in the situation in various feudal states by the end of the first millennium CE.[61]

Further on Serebryakov strongly disagreed with Kosambi's assessment that the *subhashita* literature 'could not reach the people, so its class interests remain unmistakable', that 'poet and priest were brothers in fact and in deed' and, finally, that this literature carried 'with the rank beauty of the orchid the corresponding atmosphere of luxury, parasitism, decay'.[62] He wrote: 'Kosambi's view on the class character of literature is static; it excludes the possibility to discover social protest, albeit expressed individually, in Sanskrit literature. He almost brings literature outside of concrete historical analysis. Therefore, if we put aside "class" terminology and a few interesting guesses, the scheme suggested by Kosambi is hardly different from what S.N. Dasgupta, S.K. De, S.K. Chatterji and C. Kunhan Raja have criticised European colleagues for.'[63] Indian literary historians, mentioned here by Serebryakov, were distinguished critics of the Orientalistic conceptions of Sanskrit literature as 'ornamental', 'aristocratic' and 'fully alien to popular life and culture'. Serebryakov thus denoted Kosambi's approach to Sanskrit literature as having more to do with Orientalism than with Marxism and stated that because of that the above-mentioned criticism by Ingalls of Kosambi's approach as 'Marxist' was 'unsubstantiated'.[64] Significantly, Irfan Habib too viewed Kosambi's earlier work on Sanskrit literature, that on Bhartrihari, as written 'in the best "Orientalist" tradition'.[65]

Serebryakov's book attempted to use Marxism, as well as other methodologies applied by contemporary researchers into literature and culture, to disprove some misconceptions of Sanskrit literature as, firstly, deficient in the realisation of authors' individuality and, secondly, elitist, aristocratic and alien to either social criticism or to patriotic consciousness. He succeeded in denoting strong individual features of style, personality traits and social position, in more than one case very unorthodox one, in Bhartrihari, Bana, Bhavabhuti, Kshemendra, Somadeva, Kalhana, Hemachandra and other Sanskrit authors. Moreover, discussing what he termed as 'pre-national literary communities', i.e. linguistic and literary aspects of ethnic and regional consolidation as manifest in some medieval (by AD 1200) feudal states like Kashmir, Gujarat, Maharashtra, etc., he invoked Kosambi again.

Referring to the great Sanskrit writers from Kashmir, like Kshemendra, Somadeva, Kalhana, he wrote: 'Their works, like the legacy of many other Kashmiri authors, are distinguished by the absence of religious narrow-mindedness, magnitude of thematic range that seemed to embrace almost all significant sides of common people's life, solid interlinks with folklore traditions, vividly expressed patriotic mood, active development of epic genres, in the absence of which Ingalls and Kosambi saw a specific weakness of classical Sanskrit literature'.[66] The fact that most of the authors in question belonged by birth to high and educated strata of society did not prevent them, in Serebryakov's view, from being closely associated in their works with folklore, from reconstructing various aspects of social life and conflicts, as well as in more than one from case criticizing social evils and satirizing those in power.[67] Neither the Soviet scholar's Marxist affiliation nor his adherence to the feudalism concept prevented him from discussing the individuality of a Sanskrit poet's personal experience and literary style.

CONCLUDING SUGGESTIONS

In his comparative analysis of the differences between Indian and European models of feudalism Kosambi included major characteristics of economy, social structure and political system, but did not even mention culture, values, behavioural patterns, worldview and other elements of 'superstructure'. These mental and cultural aspects of medieval society have remained, since Kosambi's time, a weakest side of the Marxist discourse on feudalism in India, and Panikkar has a point when he says that the 'relatively inadequate attention to the study of culture in Marxist historiography has made it easier for communalism to appropriate and imperialism to hegemonise the study of culture'.[68] Despite some valuable contributions on various aspects of medieval religion, political thought, mysticism, and art, a greater number of major studies into medieval mentality, culture, sense of history, social values have been hitherto made by the scholars who work outside the Marxist paradigm or even define themselves not as historians but as cultural anthropologists, specialists on religion, literature, etc.

As D.N. Jha says, 'an in-depth study of the social history of art and religion, the role of language, the social significance of new literary genres and the means and methods of communication and propaganda in the early Indian feudal society [and other stages of medieval epoch too – E.V.] await serious scholarly attention. There is, however, no doubt that in the study of these themes the use of feudal model may be highly rewarding'.[69] Indeed, the concept of feudalism, when limited only to 'exercises over tax or rent, peasant or serf, class or caste' may really be of little help to those researching into literature, arts, mentalities, or culture of a given epoch. But when the concerned scholars realise that feudalism was not only a certain level of production means and relations, surplus distribution and exploitation, etc., but a certain way of thinking and behaving, a certain way of perceiving mundane and divine worlds, a certain set of mental values pertaining to various social groups, the concept in question may indeed be of a considerable help. Peasant or serf, lord or merchant, brahmana, Rajput, Mughal, shudra, etc., were not only statuses of men and women living under such and such economic conditions: they represented, given all the peculiarities of this or that individual character, certain ways of thinking, modes of assessing the surrounding world and themselves. Their worldview as gleaned from the available sources and studied in historical development may be situated in time as pertaining to feudalism, to medieval epoch, and as such distinct from the epochs before and afterwards. And if we discuss a poet or artist, his/her language, technique, genre, style, aesthetic principles, personal experience and psychological profile, were undeniably, albeit not mechanically, linked to a given epoch and its social milieu – *Chanson de Roland* or *Prithvirajrasau* could by no means be authored by Balzac or Tagore.

Whatever the deficiencies of the feudalism concept may be, nothing valuable has been hitherto counterpoised by its opponents to situate in world history a given epoch with all implications of its societal, political, cultural and mental development in this or that country in question. Simply 'medieval' or, as suggested by Pollock, 'middle-period', is not helpful, for it inevitably provokes the query 'middle between what and what?' Nor do terms like 'pre-modern' or 'pre-colonial' help, as they presuppose the view of the whole of the Indian history, from Indus Civilization and Vedic times to the coming of the British Raj as an indivisible and unchangeable entity. One of the major contributions by Kosambi and other Marxist scholars has been that the concept of feudalism, given its shortcomings, pre-supposed and proved a certain changeability of Indian society before the colonial era. Modern scholarship has gone far enough from Sir William Jones to view *Gitagovinda* as an 'ancient' text and ignore the numerous facts that make it possible to place the Valmiki *Ramayana* in ancient India and *Ramcaritmanas* by Tulsidas or *Ramacandrika* by Keshavdas in medieval, i.e. feudal.

In his analysis of ancient and medieval India Kosambi never treated the history of India as isolated from the outside world. To him, it was an integral part of humanity's general history and hence his never-ending comparisons of Indian developments, personalities, events and texts with their counterparts from other parts of the world – Egypt, Greece, Rome, China, medieval West Europe. Some modern critics see this as one more fallacy – Pollock, for instance, could not agree with the very idea 'the world works in uniform, lawlike ways, and these laws have been discovered by western science'.[70] For Kosambi, a patriotic Indian as he was, the fact that the laws of historical development had been discovered by Western scholars, was no obstacle for studying these laws and their applicability to India – just in the same way he used other Western discoveries in his research and everyday life. His attempt was to situate ancient and early medieval India in world history presupposing that different societies developed not in uniform, as interpreted by Pollock, but according to some general laws and patterns. To quote a convincing argument by Hermann Kulke: 'Once we agree to the existence of continuously interrelated Eurasian historical process in which India and Europe participated, just as other regions of the Eurasian continent did, the question of Eurocentric periodisation does not arise. The mere fact that this periodisation was developed just in early modern European historiography should not be sufficient reason for its not being allowed to be used in its broader Eurasian context'.[71]

Kosambi's numerous references to historical events, texts and personages from various countries and comparing them with India doubtlessly testify to his fascinating knowledge and erudition, enviable for many modern scholars. The problem however is of the purpose of those comparisons. It appears from Kosambi's writings that in many cases he followed the Orientalistic path in presenting other societies, especially ancient and medieval European and sometimes Chinese, as models of 'correct' historical and cultural development in contrast with the 'incorrect' and 'deviated' Indian one. Thus, in the above-mentioned elaborations on the 'Indian ahistoricity' Herodotus, Thucydides, Polybius, Livy, Tacitus were invoked; early medieval Indian kings like Harsha were reproached for not writing *Commentaries* like Caesar.[72] In another work, Karna, Bhishma and Abhimanyu were compared with a host of Western warriors among whom only Achilles and 'Horatius at the bridge' could be viewed as belonging to approximately the same epoch with that of the *Mahabharata* or, more precisely, its literary recording. The others he mentions were

Roland (eighth century), Hereward the Wake (eleventh century), Grettir the Strong (thirteenth-fourteenth century), and even Bussy d'Amboise (sixteenth century); all these were summoned by Kosambi to lament 'how great the difference!' (between the West and India) and to point how considerably India had lagged behind the 'correct' model.[73] Similarly, in *An Introduction to the Study of Indian History*, West European and Indian models of feudalism were juxtaposed, by the very tone of the narrative, as 'standard' and 'deviant' paths of historical evolution. The book ends with a brief review of late medieval India, based mainly upon Western travelogues (especially Bernier) and some later observations by colonial administrators, to demonstrate, how backward and incapable for indigenous development towards capitalism medieval India was in comparison with the 'progressive' proto-bourgeois West.[74]

This aspect of Kosambi's legacy, inherited by him from Orientalist and from him by many subsequent scholars, especially working on late medieval India, needs, I suggest, a critical revision. India's model and tempo of historical evolution may be definitely juxtaposed with those of other countries, West or East, but only on condition that both sides, similarly well known to the concerned researcher, be compared as equal participants in world history, not as a 'right' and 'wrong', 'progressive' and 'backward' model of development and social organisation, feudalism or whatever. There has never been and is no 'standard' in history, and if on one stage a certain society makes a breakthrough, it does not necessarily mean that such a forward position had been guaranteed for it in the past and will be likewise booked for the future. Comparison of different societies as equally valid human experiences may help us denote the general laws of historical evolution as well as the specificities of every given country and epoch.

It has to be noted here that the development of any theory, in sciences or in humanities, is a historical process and, like any other in the sphere of ideas and culture, it has its stages, not to be covered in 'big leaps', as well as breakthroughs and setbacks. Without medieval alchemists and eighteenth-nineteenth century chemists, Boyle, Cavendish, Faraday, there would have been neither Mendeleyev nor modern chemistry. And the misconceptions of an earlier stage, to be rectified by the succeeding one, were inevitable as they corresponded to the level of knowledge and, implicitly, socio-historical development of a society. The same happened with Marxism: in its initial stage, the major emphasis, by Marx, Engels, and their followers, was unavoidably on means of production, feudal rents, exploitation techniques, surplus value and its redistribution, class interests, and so on, at the expense of other aspects, especially of superstructure. In Indian historiography too, Marxism, trail-blazed by Kosambi, Muhammad Habib and others, had to pass through this initial stage. The interest in and emphasis on technologies, agrarian relations, rent, distribution, village community, etc., was enforced by the specific circumstances of colonial and early independent India where many feudal institutions had been still alive. Unlike their Western counterparts, Indian Marxists studied *zamindar*s, *jagir*s, rents and bondage so passionately because for them all these were not of a remote past, but of the contemporary present. Hence, too, the condemnatory tone of their narrative on medieval society, inherited from the preceding generation of nationalists – in India feudalism was too near and its effect too painful to be idealised.[75]

It is now time to carry forward the theory that has tarried too long on its initial stage of development. The creative and innovative potential of Marxist methodology, as discovered by Kosambi, needs to be reconsidered and developed to cover hitherto neglected areas like culture, literature, mentalities, ethical values, religions, scientific views, etc., and thus to bring our researches on Indian history and its medieval period closer to historical truth. This will be the most effective contribution to Kosambi's memory by his numerous followers and admirers all over the world.

APPENDIX

A Talk with a Friend[76]

I.D. Serebryakov

On the staircase of the 'Ukraina' hotel, under the bright Moscow sun stands Damodar Dharmanand Kosambi – mathematician, historian, philologist, textologist, Vice-President of Indian Peace Council, member of the World Peace Council . . . His eyes are ablaze with never-ending fire of knowledge thrust that no life shocks had been able to extinguish. Encyclopaedic vastness and thoroughness of his erudition as well as his multi-dimensional activities in research and knowledge make him akin to the Renaissance titans.

He is in Moscow to attend the World Peace Council session, and his thoughts are concentrated upon how to achieve peace for all mankind, how to safeguard his country from the spider web of military blocks, spread by imperialism. But his academic interests never abandon him, curiously but naturally interweaving with his political activities. He is extremely precise in his estimations of the overall capacity of the US nuclear arsenals that threaten not only to turn our planet into a lifeless radioactive desert but to destroy it as a cosmic body. The scholar scrupulously calculates how many schools, hospitals, houses, libraries and centres of science and culture could be built if swords be beaten into ploughshares. Nevertheless he believes in humanity freed from hunger, diseases, poverty and ignorance, sufferings and cruelty, from the enslavement of man by man; he believes in the bright world of future.

Kosambi has deeply researched into the history of his country, widely and expertly applying methods borrowed from natural sciences – but should we talk of borrowing in this case? Kosambi is a mathematician himself. Historical studies brought him to historical materialism, to realising the fundamental laws which govern human society.

Our talk, however, refers mainly to Bhartrihari – for Kosambi this poet is like first love that never gets old. For me Bhartrihari is a poet who had fully and vividly disclosed his individuality in the hour of deep personal crisis. I felt it necessary to understand him and familiarise my people with him. Who could help me better than Kosambi? Now the readers may judge my attempt to answer some questions associated with Bhartrihari,[77] to a considerable extent inspired by the advice from my late friend.

One question was consciously reserved by me for the end of our talk. One of Kosambi's works, perhaps his magnum opus, the critical text of the *Shatakatrayam* was dedicated 'To the sacred memory of the great and glorious pioneers of today's society, Marx, Engels, Lenin'. This dedication was sincere and emotional. And I asked the scholar, what kind of link did he perceive between the poet of early medieval India and the creators of the world-changing theory?

He answered: 'First and foremost, the poetry of Bhartrihari resonates with the groans of an oppressed man whose dignity had been tramped under the feet by the exploiters. That's what makes him a great poet. Marx had said that Balzac's novels enriched his knowledge of capitalism more than bulky treatises on economy. Likewise, Bhartrihari's lines and the tradition initiated by him contribute to the understanding of early medieval India much more than *dharmashastra*s.

Quickly and energetically did Kosambi give me an illuminating lecture on his understanding of class character of literature. Maybe he was too straightforward sometimes, but his sincerity and dedication were unquestionable. He proceeded:

– Take Bhartrihari. I used to write that he might have been a brahmana, but a brahmana of a considerably later epoch, when this *varna* had no reliable economic position...

– But why should he necessarily be a brahmana?

– Well, because his views . . .

He stopped here. And recalled that every new idea comes to

life within the dominant ideology and inevitably becomes opposed to it. Indeed, the whole burden of this struggle had to be carried by the bearer of the new idea, and woe betide him if he was alone, if his idea had not yet been supported by masses – he had to put his head upon the scaffold, to be crucified, taken to stakes or gallows. And there always existed a method of killing him 'without shedding blood' – by the bony hand of poverty, hunger, humiliation . . .

– No, even this was not the case. I dedicated my work to Marx, Engels and Lenin because Bhartrihari, whatever class he might belong to, crossed the borders of this class as well as the limits of the whole society in his epoch. By his genius, by the whole treasure of his poetic talent, by the whole of his literary activity he pointed at the necessity to reject the oppression of man by man.

In Kosambi himself there was something from Bhartrihari – passionate fidelity to science, his friends, his country and the whole of Humanity! Unlimited devotion to the Truth, tireless and uncompromising quest for it in whatever field – be it in mathematics, history of India or struggle for peace, against nuclear and other bombs, against imperialism. He was himself a rare blend of best human qualities which his beloved poet Bhartrihari could dream of.

NOTES

1 For instance, in his scathing review in the *Hindu* (April 22, 2003) of the *Combined Methods in Indology and Other Writings*, a collection of Kosambi's papers edited by Brajadulal Chattopadhyaya (Oxford University Press, Delhi: 2002), Sudhanshu Ranade opines that 'Kosambi was *incapable* of making any contribution to the *history* of ancient India' (italics in the original).

2 To quote from A.L. Basham, who disagreed with Kosambi on many methodological and ideological points: 'His *An Introduction to the Study of Indian History* is in many respects an epoch making work, containing brilliantly original ideas on almost every page; if it contains errors and misrepresentations, if now and then its author attempts to force his data into a rather doctrinaire pattern, this does not appreciably lessen the significance of this very exciting book, which has stimulated the thought of thousands of students throughout the world'. *'Baba'. A Personal Tribute*, available at http://www.webcitation.org/query?url=http://www.geocities.com/dialecticalmethod/basham.html&date=2009-10-25+19:29:26.

3 One of the earliest analysis of his contribution to the history of early India was

convincingly made by D.N. Jha just two years after Kosambi's death in his paper presented to the Sixth Annual Conference of the Institute of Historical Studies (Srinagar, 1968) and published as D.N. Jha, 'D.D. Kosambi', in *Historians and Historiography in Modern India*, ed. S.P. Sen, Institute of Historical Studies, Calcutta, 1973, pp. 121-32.

4 See in more detail on British Indophilia and Indophobia: Thomas R. Trautmann, *Aryans and British India*, University of California Press, Berkeley-Los Angeles-London, 1997, pp. 62-130.

5 For a convincing analysis of how 'medieval' became synonymous for 'Muslim' in Orientalist and Nationalist historiography, see Harbans Mukhia, '"Medieval India": An Alien Conceptual Hegemony?', in *Exploring India's Medieval Centuries: Essays in History, Society, Culture and Technology*, Aakar Boors, Delhi, 2010, pp. 38-42.

6 A good example is Russia where the initial periods of its recorded history, from ninth-tenth century CE up to the Mongol invasion in the twelfth-thirteenth century, and textual sources pertaining to this epoch, have been since nineteenth century being denoted as 'ancient Rus'.

7 William Jones, The Third Anniversary Discourse (delivered 2 February, 1786, by the President, at the Asiatick Society of Bengal), in *The Works of Sir William Jones. With a Life of the Author, by Lord Teignmouth* [John Shore], John Stockdale and John Walker, London, 1807) Vol. III, p. 37. It is worth reminding here that the first Asian language mastered by Jones, before coming to India, was Persian; his translations from this language won Sir William the nickname of 'Oriental Jones'. But the Indian Persian, spoken by many Hindu and Muslim contemporaries of Jones, along with literary texts in it, never attracted the great Indologist.

8 This Orientalistic paradigm has not gone to the oblivion, as we might suppose. In a recently published and otherwise very illuminating paper, Max Harcourt states: '. . . my use of the term "medieval" is not to imply any close European parallels but to indicate the period between the Islamic invasions of the 11th century CE that ended the relative isolation of the classical Hindu/Buddhist ecumene, and the imposition of British colonial rule'. Max Harcourt. 'Devi's lion herders: bards and bardic goddesses and the moral regulation of power in late-medieval Rajasthan', in *The Iconic Female: Goddesses of India, Nepal and Tibet*, eds. Jayant Balchandra Bapat and Ian Mabbett, Monash Asia Institute, Melbourne, 2008, p. 149.

9 *The History of India as Told by Its Own Historians. The Muhammadan Period.* Edited from the posthumous papers of the late Sir H.M. Elliot, K.C.B., East India Company's Bengal Civil Service, by Professor John Dowson, M.R.A.S., Staff College, Sandhurst. Vol. I. (Trübner, London, 1867), pp. xv – xxvii.

10 This attitude was observable even in the British classics on 'Muslim' India. Interestingly, K.A. Antonova, a Soviet specialist in Mughal history, criticised W.H. Moreland's treatment of Mughal agrarian economy 'from the view point of a colonial administrator'. K.A. Antonova, *Ocherki obschestvennykh otnosheniy*

i politicheskogo stroya Mogolskoi Indii vermyon Akbara (1556 – 1605) (Essays on Social Relations and Political Establishment of Mughal India in the Time of Akbar (1556 – 1605), Academy Publishers, Moscow: 1952, pp. 26-27.

11 This was clearly expressed as early as in 1767 by Alexander Dow in the Dedication to the King of his History of Hindostan: *The history of Hindostan; from the earliest account of time, to the death of Akbar; tr. from the Persian of Mahummud Casim Ferishta of Delhi; together with a dissertation concerning the religion and philosophy of the Brahmins; with an appendix, containing the history of the Mogul empire, from its decline in the reign of Mahummud Shaw, to the present times by Alexander Dow* (London: Printed for T. Becket, and P.A. De Hondt, 1768). Even much before Dow, this motif was very strong in Bernier too.

12 *The History of India as Told by Its Own Historians*, Vol. I, pp. Xxii-xxiii.

13 A representative of the 'civilized' Greco-Roman antiquity with animals and human beings slaughtered on the altars and animal innards inspected by priests to foretell the future would have hardly been shocked by Aryan sacrifices, not to mention later Hindu offerings of fruit and flowers to the deities.

14 See in more detail, D. Kopf, *British Orientalism and the Bengal Renaissance. The Dynamics of Indian Modernization, 1773 – 1835*, University of California Press, Berkeley and Los Angeles, 1969, pp. 22-42; Ronald Inden, *Imagining India*, Basil Blackwell, Cambridge MA-Oxford UK, 1992, pp. 8-9; Peter van der Veer, 'The Foreign Hand: Orientalist Discourse in Sociology and Communalism', in *Orientalism and the Poscolonial Predicament: Perspectives on South Asia*, eds. C.A. Breckenridge and P. van der Veer, University of Pennsylvania Press, Philadelphia, 1993, pp. 25-26; Thomas R. Metkalf, *Ideologies of the Raj: The New Cambridge History of India*, Cambridge: Cambridge University Press, 1995, pp. 68-92; Richard King, *Orientalism and Religion: Postcolonial Theory, India and 'The Mystic East'*, Oxford University Press, Delhi, 1999, pp. 101-05; D.N. Jha, *Ancient India in Historical Outline*, Manohar, Delhi, 2000, pp. 17-26, 172 - 73; Vasudha Dalmia, *Orienting India: European Knowledge Formation in the Eighteenth and Nineteenth Centuries*, Three Essays, Delhi, 2003, pp. 3-15.

15 Vincent A. Smith. *The Early History of India from 600 BC to the Muhammaddan Conquest*, Clarendon Press, Oxford, 1924, p. 372.

16 On Tod's concept of feudalism, see Jason Freitag, *Serving Empire, Serving Nation: James Tod and the Rajputs of Rajasthan*, Brill, Leiden-Boston, 2009, pp. 103-29. To colonial administrators and ideologues this idea was dangerous, being able, in their opinion, to facilitate unnecessary and dangerous 'expectations', lest one day the Indian 'knights' considered themselves equal to the British ones and question the latter's superiority. See Thomas R. Metkalf, *Ideologies of the Raj*, p. 74-80.

17 Peter van der Veer, *The Foreign Hand*, p. 31.

18 See, for instance: Louis Dumont, *Homo Hierarchicus: The Caste System and Its Implications*, tr. Mark Sainsbury, Vikas Publications, Delhi, 1970, p. 195; Jan E.M Houben, 'The Brahmin Intellectual: History, Ritual and "Time Out of Time"', *Journal of Indian Philosophy*, Vol. 30, No. 5, 2002, p. 473 (Sanskrit

Knowledge Systems on the Eve of Colonialism. Columbia University Research Project, 2002, available at http://www.columbia.edu/itc/mealac/pollock/sks/papers/Houben-Brahmin_Intellectual.pdf); Vinay Lal, *The History of History: Politics and Scholarship in Modern India*, Oxford University Press, Delhi, 2003, p. 14.

[19] Breckenridge and van der Veer, *Orientalism and the Poscolonial Predicament*, Editorial Preface, p. 12.

[20] As early as 1839, Peary Chand Mittra, a founding member of the Bengali reformist Society for the Acquisition of General Knowledge, opposed the dogma of the 'ahistoricity of Hindus' and noted that the early history of every nation inevitably contained a mixture of myth and reality, so the accounts on Aeneas, Achilles, Romulus and Remus were 'as mythological as that of Rama and Yudhishthira' – an argument that even some modern scholars fail to consider. See Peary Chand Mittra, 'State of Hindoostan Under the Hindoos, No. 1, Read on the 14th September 1839', in *Awakening in Bengal in Early Nineteenth Century*, ed, Gautam Chattopadhyay, Vol. I, Progressive Publishers, Calcutta, 1965, pp. 130-81.

[21] For 'inclusivist' and 'exclusivist' trends in Indian nationalism, see Romila Thapar, 'The Future of the Indian Past', *Outlook*, April 1, 2004.

[22] Jawaharlal Nehru, *The Discovery of India*, Meridian Books Limited, London, 1947, p. 233.

[23] See Romila Thapar, 'Ideology and Interpretation of Early Indian History', in *Cultural Pasts*, Oxford University Press, Delhi, 2000, p. 8; Partha Chatterjee, *The Nation and Its Fragments: Colonial and Postcolonial Histories*, Oxford University Press, Delhi, 2001, pp. 73-94; Chetan Bhatt, *Hindu Nationalism: Origins, Ideologies and Modern Myths*, Berg, Oxford-New York, 2001, p. 111.

[24] For a poetic summarization of this concept in the nationalist discourse, see Maithilisharan Gupta, *Bharat bharati*, Chirganv, Jhansi, 1954.

[25] Partha Chatterjee, *The Nation and Its Fragments*, pp. 55.

[26] See, among others, M.G. Ranade, *Rise of the Maratha Power and Other Essays*, University of Bombay, Bombay: 1961, pp. 3-4; Jawaharlal Nehru, *The Discovery of India*, pp. 123-26, 257-58; James Laine, *Shivaji: Hindu King in Islamic India*, Oxford University Press, Delhi, 2000, pp. 71-77, 81-82; Chetan Bhatt, *Hindu Nationalism*, p. 34; Naheem Jabbar, *Historiography and Writing Postcolonial India*, Routledge, London-New York, 2009, pp. 91-92.

[27] Meera Kosambi, 'D. D. Kosambi, the Scholar and the Man', *Economic and Political Weekly*, July 26, 2008, p. 40 (hereafter *EPW*).

[28] D.D. Kosambi, *The Culture & Civilisation of Ancient India in Historical Outline* (hereafter *Culture*), Vikas Publishing House, Delhi, 1976, p. 175.

[29] Ibid., p. 193.

[30] Ibid., p. 9-10.

[31] See, for instance, Thomas Luckmann, 'The Constitution of Human Life in Time', in *Chronotypes: The Construction of Time*, eds. John Bender and David E. Wellbery, Stanford University Press, Stanford, 1991; Gabrielle M. Spiegel, *The*

Past as Text: The Theory and Practice of Medieval Historiography, The John Hopkins University Press, Baltimore and London, 1997.

32 Meera Kosambi, 'D. D. Kosambi, the Scholar and the Man', p. 37.

33 Romila Thapar, 'Society and Historical Consciousness: The *Itihasa-Puraoa* Tradition', in *Situating Indian History: for Sarvepalli Gopal*, eds. S. Bhattacharya and Romila Thapar, Oxford University Press, Delhi, 1986; Romila Thapar, *Time as a Metaphor of History: Early India*, Oxford University Press, Delhi, 1996; Brajadulal Chattopadhyaya, 'Confronting Fundamentalisms: The Possibilities of Early Indian History', *Studies in History*, Vol. XVIII, 1, January-June, 2002; Arvind Sharma, *Hinduism & Its Sense of History*, Oxford University Press, Delhi, 2003. Also in my forthcoming book *Medieval Indian Mindscapes: Space, Time, Society, Man*, Primus Books.

34 Kosambi's reference to ancient India here was fully applicable to early medieval period too, since, according to the ahistoricity concept, historical consciousness and the tradition to record the events of the past came to India only with 'Muslim invaders'.

35 *Culture*, p. 10.

36 Ibid., p. 10.

37 See, for example, Sheldon Pollock, 'Towards a Political Philology: D. D. Kosambi and Sanskrit,' *EPW*, July 26, 2008, pp. 52-59.

38 Rajan Gurukkal, 'The Kosambi Effect: A Hermeneutic Turn That Shook Indian Historiography', *EPW*, July 26, 2008, p. 90.

39 D.N. Jha, *D. D. Kosambi*, p. 123.

40 D.D. Kosambi, *An Introduction to the Study of Indian History* (hereafter *Introduction*), Popular Book Depot, Bombay, 1956, p. 10.

41 About this discussion, see Eugenia Vanina, 'Russian Studies in Medieval History of India: An Insider's View', *Medieval History Journal*, October, 1999, Vol. 2, No. 2, p. 371-72.

42 Sheldon Pollock, 'Towards a Political Philology', p. 56.

43 Karl Marx and Friedrich Engels, *Selected Correspondence*, tr. I. Lasker, Moscow: Progress Publishers, 1975, p. 458.

44 To mention a few: George Duby, *The Three Orders*, tr. Arthur Goldhammer, University of Chicago Press, London-Chicago,1980; A.A. Gurevich, *Categories of Medieval Culture*, tr. G.L. Campbell, Routledge & Kegan Paul, London-Boston, 1985; *Fifteenth-Century Attitudes: Perceptions of Society in Late Medieval England*, ed. Rosemary Horrox, Cambridge University Press, Cambridge,1994.

45 *Introduction*, pp. 326-28.

46 Romila Thapar, 'Early Indian History and the Legacy of D.D. Kosambi', *EPW*, July 26, 2008, p. 50; for similar views, see D.N. Jha, 'Early Indian Feudalism: A Historigraphical Critique', Presidential Address, Ancient India Section, Indian History Congress, Waltair, 1979; D.N. Jha (ed.), *The Feudal Order: State, Society and Ideology in Early Medieval India* , Manohar, Delhi, 2000, Editor's Introduction.

47 Friedrich Engels, 'On the Decline of Feudalism and the Emergence of national

States' in Aijaz Ahmad (ed.) Karl Marx and Friedrich Engels, *On the National and Colonial Questions*, Delhi: LeftWord, 2001, p. 27.

48 D.D. Kosambi, 'On the Development of Feudalism in India', *Annals of the Bhandarkar Oriental Research Institute*, Vol. XXXVI, Pt. III-IV, pp. 258-69.

49 D.N. Jha, *Ancient India in Historical Outline*, revised and enlarged edition, Delhi, Manohar 2000, p. 25.

50 Marx and Engels, *Selected Correspondence*, p. 435.

51 Romila Thapar, 'Early Indian History and the Legacy of D.D. Kosambi', p. 44.

52 K.N. Panikkar, 'Culture as a Site of Struggle', *EPW*, February 14, Vol. XLIV, No. 7, pp. 40-41.

53 D.D. Kosambi, 'Social and Economic aspects of the Bhagavad-gita', *Myth and Reality: Studies in the Formation of Indian Culture*, Bombay: Popular Prakashan, 2005, p. 12.

54 *An Anthology of Sanskrit Court Poetry: Vidyakara's Subhashitaratnakosha*, tr. Daniel H.H. Ingalls, Harvard University Press, Cambridge, Mass., 1965, (Harvard Oriental Series, No. 44), p. 50.

55 Sheldon Pollock, 'Towards a Political Philology', p. 57.

56 For example, G.M. Bongard-Levin and G.F. Ilyin, leading Soviet specialists on ancient India, wrote that 'D. D. Kosambi's generalizing works contain many illuminating thoughts on social history of ancient India; however, they are not free from certain schematism'. G.M. Bongard Levin and G.F. Ilyin, *Indiya v drevnosti* (*Ancient India*), Moscow: Vostochnaya literatura, 1985, p. 24.

57 This was the opinion of C.Z. Ashrafyan, a Soviet specialist on late medieval India, who criticised Kosambi for 'establishing an unreasonably direct dependence between, on one side, the development of means and relations of production and, on the other, phenomena of cultural life, ideology and religion'. C. Z. Ashrafyan, *Feodalism v Indii. Osobennosti i etapi razvitiya* (*Feudalism in India: Specificities and stages of development*), Vostochnaya literatura, Moscow: 1977, pp. 11 – 12.

58 He also worked on Punjabi literature. Most of his works were in Russian. Among his English publications are *Sketches of Ancient Indian Literature*, tr. H.C. Gupta, Indian Studies, Calcutta, 1972; 'In Quest of Methodology: With Special Reference to Indian kavya', in *History and Society: Essays in Honour of Professor Niharranjan Ray*, ed. Debiprasad Chattopadhyaya, K.P. Bagchi, Calcutta, 1978, pp. 55-66; 'A note on the *Ramayana* in Somadeva's *Kathasaritsgara*', in *Indian Epic Values: Ramayana and its Impact*, ed. G. Pollet, Peeters Press, Leuven, 1995, pp. 43-46.

59 I.D. Serebryakov, *Literaturny process v Indii VII – XIII veka* (*Literary process in India. Seventh to Thirteenth century*), Moscow, Vostochnaya literatura, 1979, p. 21.

60 D.D. Kosambi, 'The Social Functions of Literature', *The Subhashitaratnakosha*, compiled by Vidyakara, ed. D.D. Kosambi and V.V. Gokhale, with an Introduction by D.D. Kosambi, Harvard University Press, Cambridge, Mass., 1957, p. lvii.

61 I.D. Serebryakov, *Literaturny process v Indii*, pp. 21-22.

62 D.D. Kosambi, 'The Social Functions of Literature', pp. lviii-lxi.

[63] I.D. Serebryakov, *Literaturny process v Indii*, pp. 22-23.

[64] Ibid., p. 23.

[65] Irfan Habib, 'Kosambi, Marxism and Indian History', *EPW*, July 26, 2008, p. 85.

[66] I.D. Serebryakov, *Literaturny process v Indii*, p. 107.

[67] To add, the class theory of Marx never presupposed that an author's aristocratic origin should undeniably determine his views as elitist and alien to common people. Gorky, for instance, had recorded Lenin's witty saying on Tolstoy: 'Before this count there was no peasant in Russian literature'. See also Lenin's article 'Tolstoy as Mirror of Russian Revolution', *V.I. Lenin on Literature and Arts*, Moscow, Progress Publishers, 1967, p. 28-31.

[68] K.N. Panikkar, 'Culture as a Site of Struggle', p. 41.

[69] D.N. Jha, ed., *The Feudal Order*, Editorial Introduction, p. 29.

[70] Sheldon Pollock, 'Towards a Political Philology', p. 56.

[71] Hermann Kulke, 'Periodization of Pre-Modern Historical Processes in India and Europe: Some Reflections', *Indian Historical Review*, Vol. XIX, 1-2 (July 1992-January 1993), p. 36.

[72] *Introduction*, pp. 1-2.

[73] D.D. Kosambi, *Myth and Reality*, pp. 7-8.

[74] *Introduction*, pp. 326-72.

[75] I am obliged for this argument to Prof. D.N. Jha who has considerably increased my knowledge on the development of historical studies in India.

[76] I.D. Serebryakov, *Bhartrihari*, Moscow: Vostochnaya literatura, 1983, pp. 141-43.

[77] Serebryakov means his book on Bhartrihari (see previous note).

Kosambi and the Religious Histories of India

Krishna Mohan Shrimali

The year 2007 marked the centenary of the birth of Damodar Dharmanand Kosambi, who had heralded a significant paradigm shift in the writing of Indian history in general and that of early Indian history in particular. Barring a very late realisation on the part of the Indian History Congress, the oldest organization of professional historians in India, which organized a small symposium (at its 68th session held at Delhi in December, 2007) to mark the occasion, the contributions of this significant mover did not inspire much celebrations.[1]

It is somewhat intriguing that in October 2007, the Jawaharlal Nehru University (New Delhi) in collaboration with the Embassy of Romania in India and the Nehru Memorial Museum and Library preferred to hold an international symposium to reflect on the life and works of Mircea Eliade, whose birth centenary year coincided with that of Kosambi. Eliade is known for being a prime mover in the domain of history of religions – an area that interested Kosambi as well. Both published a monograph with the same title, namely, *Myth and Reality*. There was nothing else that was common between the two. It was only in mid-2008 that Kosambi Birth Centenary witnessed some feverish activity.[2]

As India attained freedom in August, 1947, cries of building the 'nation' afresh reverberated all over. Of course, it was clear even then, that there were differing visions of that 'nation'. In the domain of history writing, one vision materialized in the shape of *The History and Culture of the Indian People*, popularly known as the Bharatiya Vidya Bhavan Series. It was conceived and planned by the noted Hindu chauvinist K.M. Munshi, who was the founder of that educational society and had spearheaded the reconstruction of the Somanatha temple (destroyed by Mahmud Ghazni in the 10th-11th centuries) immediately after India's independence. The General Editor, too, was a known Hindu chauvinist. Of the planned ten volumes, as many as five (I: *The Vedic Age*; II: *The Age of Imperial Unity*; III: *The Classical Age*; IV: *The Age of Imperial Kanauj*; and V: *The Struggle for Empire*) were devoted to the 'ancient' period (up to *c.*1300 CE) and only two (VI & VII) covered more than four centuries of the 'Delhi Sultanate' and the 'Mughal Empire'. One century of the 'Hindu *padpadshahi*' of the 'Maratha Supremacy' (1707-1818) constituted volume VIII and the rest were concerned with the 'British Paramountcy and Indian Renaissance' (1818-1905, in two parts) and 'Struggle for Freedom' (1905-1947). The first five volumes were published within the first decade of independent India and it took nearly two decades to complete the remaining volumes (for Kosambi's critique of the first three volumes of the series, see Kosambi 1955(a): 790-96). The series clearly buttressed the colonialist vision of the Indian 'nation' fragmented by religious divides. The overall 'communal' bias of the entire series is well established. No wonder, the present day 'Cultural Nationalists' who swear by 'fragmented nationalism', accept this series as their role model.

The Bharatiya Vidya Bhavan Series had also rooted itself within the framework of political power and, therefore, titles of its several volumes included words such as 'Empire', 'Imperial', 'Supremacy', 'Paramountcy' and so on. While this series was underway, studies on early Indian history had also initiated a move away from the humdrum political/dynastic histories within the first decade of India's Independence. Interest in routine mélange of dates and events, wars and conquests, 'achievements/ failures' of individual potentates started dwindling when two very significant works came out in the 1950s. A.L. Basham's *The Wonder That Was India* (1954; hereafter *Wonder*) and D.D. Kosambi's *An Introduction to the Study of Indian History* (1956; hereafter *Introduction*) epitomized this new shift. A doyen amongst Indologists, Basham romanticized the vast sweep of India's history.

He pleaded for a new emphasis on cultural and religious history of India in university curricula. *Wonder* was written to interpret ancient Indian civilization to ordinary western readers who had little knowledge of the subject but some interest in it. But this masterly kaleidoscope of early India's social structure, cults and doctrines, and arts, languages and culture has been such an engrossing venture that it won for Basham the love and appreciation of scholars and laypeople alike, both in India and outside. It is regrettable, however, that his fascination for the inclusive aspect of Hinduism has been completely distorted, put upside down, and turned into a straitjacket of glorious Hindu India by some self-appointed guardians of Indian cultural traditions.

Kosambi's *Introduction* is an iconoclastic critique of the undulating path of historical changes. For him 'the subtle mystic philosophies, tortuous religions, ornate literature, monuments teeming with intricate sculpture, and delicate music of India all derive from the same historical process that produced the famished apathy of the villager, senseless opportunism and termite greed of the "cultured" strata, sullen un-coordinated discontent among the workers, the general demoralization, misery, squalor, and degrading superstition. The one is the result of the other, the one is the expression of the other' (*Introduction*: xi-xii). Such an understanding not only enabled Kosambi to question the stereotypes of the colonialist-imperialist and the so-called 'nationalist' historiography but also to bring into focus a more positive and constructive approach to comprehend prime movers of history.

Since in his vision society is held together by bonds of production, answers to the following questions become crucial: who gathers or produces things and with what implements? Who lives off the production of others, and by what right, divine or legal? Who owns the tools, the land, and sometimes the body and soul of the producer? Who controls the disposal of the surplus, and regulates quantity and form of the supply? Why did India never have large-scale chattel slavery as in classical Greece and Rome? When did regular coinage appear? Why do Buddhism, Jainism, the Ajivikas, and so many other contemporary religious sects of the type arise in Magadha, and all becoming prominent at about the same time? Why did the Gupta empire and not the Mauryan empire produce great Sanskrit literature? Such searching questions had set the agenda for a new kind of history writing.

Answers provided by Kosambi to such questions have been the subject of animated discussions amongst historians in the last fifty-odd years. Understandably, some have been accepted, others completely rejected, and a few others modified/redefined. Today, of course, it has almost become fashionable to be dismissive about his numerous forays into India's social, economic, political, literary and cultural histories. However, even a modicum of objectivity demands that a proper assessment of his contributions to the writing of Indian history must take cognizance of the times when he produced his essays and monographs. Further, a quantified analysis also needs to be factored in to suitably assign his place in the annals of Indian historiography. The focus of this presentation would be on Kosambi's disparate contributions on India's religious history. The foci of writings in this domain would have to be situated within the ambit of specificities of Kosambi's method, which was indeed, keeping the times in mind, extremely forward looking and scientific. Though characterized as 'Combined Methods in Indology' by the author, it would perhaps be fair to rechristen it as 'The Kosambian Method'.

Today, inter-disciplinary studies have become a buzzword. But nearly half a century ago, Kosambi applied the methodologies of statistics, mathematics, numismatics, linguistics, anthropology, genetics, archaeology, etc., to the study of history. Ironically, when his method should be celebrated, Kosambi is being shunned like an *antyaja*. It would be hard to find amongst researchers and historians of the age group of 40s, who would show any familiarity even with the two basic monographs of Kosambi, namely, *Introduction* and *The Culture and Civilisation of Ancient India in Historical Outline* (1965; hereafter *Culture*).

The marginalization of Kosambi is not unrelated to the present-day historian's intellectual context which is dominated by the marginalization of all varieties of Marxism and an academic shift to the so-called 'cultural studies'. Much of this has to do with mis-reading of Marx as well as over-simplification and mis-reading of Kosambi, and reminds us of what Hobsbawm called 'vulgar-Marxism' (Hobsbawm 1968 [1997]: 141-156).

THE KOSAMBIAN METHOD

In referring to Kosambi's historical approach, and in comfortably and securely keeping him ensconced in a Marxist basket, the following statement made by him in *Introduction* as well as in *Culture* is underlined: '*History is the presentation in chronological order of successive changes in the means and relations of production*'. The belief that 'the economic factor is the fundamental factor on which the others are dependent' is listed at the top of the criteria of elements of 'vulgar-Marxism'. Even when loudly proclaiming himself to be a Marxist, Kosambi does not leave anyone in doubt about the paramount need of working out an India-specific method for understanding its history and culture. As early as 1956 he had made this absolutely clear: 'Marxism is far from the economic determinism which its opponents so often take it to be. For that matter, any intelligent determinism must discuss "conditions" rather than "causes"' (*Introduction*: 10).

Reiterating a similar notion almost a decade later in 1965, Kosambi went a step further and clarified: 'Our position has also to be very far from a mechanical determinism, particularly in dealing with India, where form is given the utmost importance while content is ignored. *Economic determinism will not do.* It is not inevitable, nor even true, that a given amount of wealth will lead to a given type of development. The *complete historical process* through which the social form has been reached is also of prime importance'(emphases added). For Kosambi, 'the complete historical process' was the uniquely Indian process, to be explained by the logic of India's societal developments and in terms of Indian cultural elements, *culture* being understood 'in the sense of the ethnographer, to describe the essential way of life of the whole people' (*Culture*: 10-12).

Getting away from the rigid and unilinear 'historical laws and historical inevitability', Kosambi had, in his critique of D.A. Suleikin's note on periodization of Indian history, written in 1951: 'India is not a mathematical point but a very large country, with the utmost diversity of natural environment, language, historical course of development. Neither in the means of production nor in the stages of social development was there overall homogeneity in the oldest times. Centuries must be allowed to pass before comparable stages of productive and social relationships may be established between the Indus Valley, Bengal and Malabar. Even then, important differences remain which makes periodization for India as a whole almost impossible except with the broadest margins.' (Kosambi 1951: 49-50). Almost at the same tangent was his refusal to accept mechanically the model of 'base/basis and superstructure' (in spite of Marx and Engels' own warnings, used most widely to explain the history of ideas) allegedly representing relation of dominance and dependence.

> I have adopted a certain method of historical analysis *only because it works.* We have not the dates and episodes which fill out European history. No chronicles, family records, church annals are to be found – a symptom of local rustic production, the idiocy of village life as lived from year to year, absence of the trader's influence. We have therefore to abandon the scissors-and-paste method. Our history has to be written without solid documentation of episodes, in large outline. At the same time treating history as a science, regarding it not as successive waves of emergency or acts of god but the combined effect of human effort enables one to realize that the future is not a blank, that a correct analysis of present factors tells us what is to come, and may enable us to *make* history. (Kosambi 1954: 71; emphases in the original.)

MIRCEA ELIADE'S HISTORY OF RELIGIONS

While this essay focuses on Kosambi's writings on Indian religions, it would be appropriate to reflect on the method and writings of Eliade as well, because he has been a strong influence in developing the discipline of history of religions across the world.

Eliade in his long academic career produced a phenomenal number of monographs, including the last major undertaking in his life, namely, the planning and completion of the first edition of the sixteen volume *The Encyclopedia of Religion* (1986). The range of his writings included novels such as *Maitreyi* (1933), based on his amorous relationship with the daughter of his renowned Indian host and *guru* Professor Surendranath Dasgupta. Eliade was, in fact, expelled from the Dasgupta household after this liaison became know. In dramatic fashion, the University of Chicago Press in 1994 coupled the publication of Eliade's *Bengal Nights* (from the title of the French translation of *Maitreyi*) and Maitreyi Devi's response *It Does Not Die: A Romance* (originally published in Calcutta by P. Lal and in Connecticut by some obscure publisher named Inter-Culture Associates). Surprisingly these publications did not appear while Eliade was still alive. *The Forbidden Forest* (1978) is a sort of historical novel dealing with the events and activities of the protagonist and his lovers, friends, and foes during the turbulent years from 1936 to 1948, in Romania, London, Lisbon, Russia and Paris. Eliade skillfully creates characters all of whom are caught by 'destiny', as people often are in his other stories. He also published his *Autobiography* (in the 1980s), *A History of Religious Ideas* (1978-86; in four volumes, though his health prevented his work on the fourth volume himself).

The themes and religions covered by him were no less expansive as is reflected in such titles as *The Yoga: Immortality and Freedom* (1936; wherein he attempted a new interpretation of the myths and symbolism of archaic and oriental religions – it attracted the attention of such eminent European scholars as Jean Przyluski, Louis de La Poussin, Heinrich Zimmer, and Giuseppe Tucci), *Birth and Rebirth* (1958; representing the Haskell Lectures delivered by Eliade when he was invited by the University of

Chicago in 1956), *The Sacred and Profane* (1959), *Shamanism: Archaic Techniques of Ecstasy* (1964), *From Primitive to Zen* (1968; thematic work dealing with religious data from non-literate, ancient, medieval, and modern religions), *Images and Symbols* (1969), *Australian Religions* (1973), etc. This is by no means an exhaustive list of his publications.[3]

An idea of Eliade's concept of history of religions and methods of studying them may be worked out with the help of his *Myth and Reality* (1963). This is particularly desirable because Kosambi, too, had brought out an anthology of his essays on Indian religions with an identical title: *Myth and Reality* in the previous year (1962).

Early in his career, Eliade had ventured to look for 'universal man' – a quest that had brought him to India and, more importantly, to the Himalayas. Eliade always had a strong case of destiny, from his youth until his last day in Chicago. 'Perhaps, without knowing it, I was in search of a new humanism, bolder than the humanism of Renaissance, which was too dependent on the models of Mediterranean classicism . . . Ultimately, I dreamed of rediscovering the model of a "universal man"' (*No Souvenirs: Journal, 1957-69*, London, 1978, 17). He explored several avenues and thought of combining history of religions, Orientalism, and ethnology. At the height of McArthyism in the USA, he was invited to don the prestigious Chair at the Department of the History of Religions at the University of Chicago in 1956.[4] There he founded, in the summer of 1961, a new international journal for comparative historical studies called *History of Religions.* Providing an answer to the question 'Is there a history of religion?' in the inaugural issue of this journal, Eliade wrote the famous article entitled 'History of Religions and a New Humanism'. While he did exhort readers to engage in twin tasks of the history of religions (namely systematic and historical), to him, ultimately the history of religions was more than merely an academic pursuit. Seeking a justification for and reflecting upon the prospects of the distinctive discipline of the history of religions, he wrote:

The History of Religions is destined to play an important

> role in contemporary cultural life. This is not only because an understanding of exotic and archaic religions will significantly assist in a cultural dialogue with the representatives of such religions. It is more especially because . . . the history of religions will inevitably attain to a deeper knowledge of man. It is on the basis of such knowledge that a new humanism, on a world-wide scale, could develop. (*History of Religions*, I: 2-3)

The first chapter of *Myth and Reality* entitled 'The Structure of Myths' outlines essentials of Eliade's approach to study of religions, myths and symbols. A few extracts from this chapter would be quite illustrative:

> Myths describe the various and sometimes dramatic breakthroughs of the sacred (or the 'supernatural') into the World. It is this sudden breakthrough of the sacred that really *establishes* the World and makes it what it is today. Furthermore, it is as a result of the intervention of the Supernatural Beings that man himself is what he is today, as a mortal, sexed, and cultural being . . . It is necessary to emphasise a fact that we consider essential: the myth is regarded as a sacred story, and hence a 'true history', because it always deals with *realities*. The cosmogonic myth is 'true' because the existence of the World is there to prove it; the myth of the origin of death is equally true because man's mortality proves it, and so on . . . Because myth relates the *gesta* of Supernatural Beings and the manifestations of their sacred powers, it becomes the exemplary model for all significant human activities . . . The same justification is alleged by the Hindu theologians and ritualists. 'We must do what the gods did in the beginning' (*Shatapatha Brahmana*, VII.2.1.4). 'Thus the gods did; thus men do' (*Taittiriya Brahmana*, I.5.9.4) . . . As we showed in *Cosmos and History: The Myth of the Eternal Return*, . . . the foremost function of myth is to reveal the exemplary models for all

> human rites and all significant human activities – diet or marriage, work or education, art or wisdom.

Further, enumerating characteristic qualities of structure and function of myths, as experienced by archaic societies, Eliade underlines that:

> (1) it constitutes the History of the acts of the Supernaturals; (2) this History is considered to be absolutely *true* (because it is concerned with realities) and *sacred* (because it is the work of the Supernaturals); (3) that myth is always related to a 'creation', it tells how something came into existence, or how a pattern of behavior, an institution, a manner of working were established; this is why myths constitute the paradigms for all significant human acts; (4) that by knowing the myth one knows the 'origin' of things and hence can control and manipulate them at will; this is not 'external', 'abstract' knowledge but a knowledge that one 'experiences' ritually, either by ceremonially recounting the myth or by performing the ritual for which it is the justification; (5) that in one way or another one 'lives' the myth, in the sense that one is seized by the sacred, exalting power of the events recollected or re-enacted . . . 'Living' a myth, then, implies a genuinely 'religious' experience, since it differs from the ordinary experience of everyday life. (Emphases in the original.)

Eliade concludes his own understanding of the nature and function of myths in 'primitive societies' by citing, what he calls 'classic passages' from Bronislav Malinowski's *Myth in Primitive Psychology* (1926; reprinted in *Magic, Science and Religion*, New York, 1955: 101, 108):

> Studied alive, myth . . . is not an explanation in satisfaction of a scientific interest, but a narrative resurrection of a primeval reality, told in satisfaction of deep religious wants,

> moral cravings, social submissions, assertions, even practical requirements. Myth fulfills in primitive culture an indispensable function: it expresses, enhances, and codifies belief; it safeguards and enforces morality; it vouches for the efficiency of ritual and contains practical rules for the guidance of man. Myth is thus a vital ingredient of human civilization; it is not an idle tale, but a hard-worked active force; it is not an intellectual explanation or an artistic imagery, but a pragmatic charter of primitive faith and moral wisdom . . . These stories . . . are to the natives a statement of a primeval, greater, and more relevant reality, by which the present life, fates and activities of mankind are determined, the knowledge of which supplies man with the motive for ritual and moral actions, as well as with indications as to how to perform them.

This concluding observation based on Malinowski needs to be questioned. What about other 'Functionalists' such as Alfred Raginal Radcliffe-Brown in his famous monographs *Andaman Islanders* (1922) and *Taboo* (1938)? He was less bothered about 'origins' of rites. Instead, his focus tended to be on the functions *after* they got established – they arouse as well as allay anxiety. Even Malinowski has been cited very partially. In *Myth in Primitive Psychology* Malinowski had not only argued that myths are validation of the social order, but also more importantly, he had gone far ahead of the 19th century ethnologists such as Levy Bruhl (author of *Primitive Mentality* in six volumes) who were loath to attribute power of 'reason' to the so-called archaic societies and 'primitives'. Malinowski made a clear distinction between magic and religion in his two famous monographs, namely, *Argonauts of the Western Pacific* (1922) on the Trobriand Islanders (fishermen) and subsequently *Coral Gardens and Their Magic* (1935) on Trobriand agriculture. Substantially, then, the two outstanding 'Functionalists' were keen to locate human religious behavior in society as well as to argue that myths were products of discerning intellectual capacities of the so-called 'primitives'.

The core of Eliade's approach to the study of religions is the plea for an autonomous history of religions. It comprised of recognizing the danger of 'reductionism' in the history of religions as much as in the interpretation of art and literary works. He insisted that a work of art, for example, reveals its meaning only when it is seen as an autonomous artistic creation and nothing else. In the case of the history of religions he realised that the situation is complex because there is no such thing as a 'pure' religious datum and that a human datum is also a historical datum. But this does not imply that, for historians of religions, a historical datum is in any way reducible to a nonreligious, economic, social, cultural, psychological, or political meaning. No wonder, he could unhesitatingly pronounce: 'every rite, every myth, every belief or divine figure reflects the experience of the sacred and hence implies the notions of being, of meaning, and of truth' (*A History of Religious Ideas*, I, Chicago, 1978: xiii). Eliade, like his great phenomenologist predecessor Gerardus Van der Leeuw, did not think that such an approach to religion could be empirical.

Even if the case for the discipline of 'history of religions' is conceded, it need not rest on such premises as were espoused by Eliade. First, a distinction needs to be made between 'history of religions' and 'religious histories'. Second, even if the former formulation is accepted, we would still like to underline pluralities thereof, resist the temptation of homogenizing such ventures, and make a plea for '*histories* of religions'. Third, the discipline deserves utmost attention because such histories give us important entry-points to understand 'the other' not necessarily in the quest of 'universal man' but because these help us understand ourselves better. And finally, the discipline needs to be worked out not through Eliade's phenomenological approach with its trademark anti-reductionism and no space for the empirical. A more analytical approach is needed, especially if we do not wish to fall prey to the fast rising 'fundamentalism/s' all over the world. This analytical approach must rest on the spirit of questioning – questioning even the so-called 'sacred', and ought to situate religions *in* society. And that, indeed, is what Kosambi attempted to do.

KOSAMBI'S APPROACH TO RELIGIOUS HISTORIES

In his two landmark histories of India, i.e., *Introduction* and *Culture* Kosambi had expressed himself freely and fearlessly on functional aspects of early India's numerous religions. Thus, his views on the role of religion in the Harappan society, specially the ritualistic significance of the Great Bath at Mohenjo-daro (as a centre of performance of fertility rites); his hypotheses about the simultaneous emergence of Buddhism, Jainism and Ajivikas in the middle Ganga valley being the result of growing nexus of trade, monetization and mineral wealth of the emerging empire of Magadha; his ideas about the ideological role played by Buddhism in providing spurt to urbanization and trade through the centuries; and so on, have been analysed by several historians (see, e.g., Shrimali 2003: 1-59, Chakrabarti 2008: 60-70, Ratnagar 2008: 71-77). We intend focusing on Kosambi's approach to writing religious histories of India through a detailed exposition of the anthology of five seminal essays, namely, *Myth and Reality* (Kosambi 1962; hereafter *MR*). His other major essays, i.e., 'The Avatara Syncretism and Possible Sources of the *Bhagavad-Gita*' (1948-49, reprinted in *CMI*) and 'The Historical Krishna' (1965, reprinted in *CMI*), though very provocative, need not be dwelt upon extensively as their essentials have been incorporated in the essay on the *Bhagavad Gita* in *MR*.

The following extracts from the Introduction of *Myth and Reality* give us a fair idea of Kosambi's objectives and overall approach of addressing problems of religious histories:

> These essays have one feature in common, namely that they are based upon the collation of field-work with literary evidence. Indian critics whose patriotism outstrips their grasp of reality are sure to express annoyance or derision at the misplaced emphasis. Why should anyone ignore the beautiful lily of Indian philosophy in order to concentrate upon the dismal swamp of popular superstition? That is precisely the point. Anyone with aesthetic sense can enjoy the beauty of the lily; it takes a considerable scientific effort to discover the

psychological process whereby the lily grew out of the mud and filth.[5]

Our present task is to trace the primitive roots of some Indian myths and ritual that survived the beginning of civilisation and indeed survive to this day. This is not too difficult in a country where contemporary society is composed of elements that preserve the indelible marks of almost every historical stage. The neglect of such analysis leads to a ridiculous distortion of Indian history and to a misunderstanding of Indian culture, not compensated by subtle theology or the boasts of having risen above crass materialism.

The religious observances of the various human groups in India, particularly those that are lowest in the social, cultural and economic scale, show roughly the order in which the particular groups were enrolled into a greater, productive society. In a general way, this is true of many higher strata as well . . . . Change of economic status is reflected in, and acted till recently through some corresponding transformation in caste; sometimes by change in cult as well. One of the main problems for consideration is: Why is a fusion of cults sometimes possible and why do cults stubbornly refuse to merge on other occasions? Naturally, this question cannot be answered on the 'highest plane' of Shankara and Ramanuja, for it simply does not exist on that level. Cults do not clash by themselves. It is the people who observe the cults that find it impossible to come to terms . . . . Upanishadic riddles which display so much mysticism and philosophy are only a step above the deadly riddles asked by *yakshas* of strangers at sacred springs . . . . Surely, primitive superstition was not so very much worse than the economic philosophy of a modern affluent society which destroys surplus grain and potatoes in a hungry world, or the political philosophy which glorifies the ultimate thermonuclear deterrent.

Parallels between European Ice-Age drawings and

> modern Indian representations of certain deities need not imply a direct line of descent. Without discussing any of the numerous diffusionist theses, I merely say that people who live by similar methods and techniques often produce similar cults, just as they produce similar artifacts of stone.

Kosambi's *MR* comprises of five essays, four of which were originally published between 1947 and 1960. Most of these were subsequently revised for various publications and then included in this anthology. The essay entitled 'Pilgrim's Progress: A Contribution to the Prehistory of the Western Deccan Plateau' was first published in this collection, which came out in 1962 – a year before Eliade's work of the same title. However, the sub-title of Kosambi's anthology, namely, *Studies in the Formation of Indian Culture* is indicative of the substantive difference in the overall approaches and methods of the two savants of religious studies. Evidently, Kosambi is convinced that religion is not *sui generis*, it is rooted in society and must be studied in totality of the culture of the concerned societies. Kosambi's defining parameters of 'culture' have been mentioned above. His sensitivity towards the temporal and spatial concerns and his eagerness (sometimes bordering on over-enthusiasm) to locate historical processes within the larger social formations make his forays into religious histories truly historical. This is not the place to discuss the veracity of various chronologies constructed or accepted by Kosambi in *MR* – be it the date of the *Bhagavad Gita* (considered as a 'remarkable interpolation' datable between '150-350 AD, nearer the later than the earlier date', p. 16) or the first time announcement of the radio-carbon dates of the Buddhist caves at Karle (3rd century BCE – 'the caves in the portion now collapsed may even have been a century earlier').[6] The totality of his approach and method leave us in no doubt that he cannot be accused of being 'ahistorical' or 'ahistoricist', which is one of the most repeated criticisms of Mircea Eliade (Jones 2005: 2761).

Of the four hitherto published essays included in *MR*, the first two, namely, 'Social and Economic Aspects of the Bhagavad-

Gita' and 'Urvashi and Pururavas' stand out for their iconoclastic deconstruction of texts that have been used by generations of students and scholars alike for over two hundred years. Like Kosambi, many pre-Kosambi scholars, too, have seen the *Bhagavad Gita* as a work of a remarkable synthesis of several rel-igions and philosophies. However, when Kosambi asked questions such as 'When does a synthesis work?' and 'Why Krishna?', those who thrive on weaving mysteries around Indian religions and philosophies started getting nervy. If this wasn't sufficient blasphemy, Kosambi, by asking yet another question, 'For what class?' further demystified the *Bhagavad Gita*. '*The Gita furnished the one scriptural source which could be used without violence to accepted Brahmin methodology, to draw inspiration and justification for social actions in some way disagreeable to a branch of the ruling class* upon whose mercy the Brahmins depended at the moment' (*MR*: 15; emphases in the original).

'Urvashi and Pururavas' starts with *Vikramorvashiyam*, the famous play of Kalidasa, but sees it as the culmination of a process that actually began with the *Rigveda* and passed through the later Vedic text, namely, the *Shatapatha Brahmana*. Different layers of the same myth have been peeled off very delicately, not just to trace the gradual development of the narrative itself – the transition from ritual to drama, but more importantly, to correlate these layers of the various stages of the Pururavas-Urvashi legend with differences in social structure. In the process, we stand enlightened about the notions of 'apsarasas as water goddesses', 'traces of different types of "hetaerism" in the *Rigveda*' with an accent on the 'hetaera-hierodule-bayadere' character of Urvashi and postulation of the cult of pre-Aryan mother goddess (even mentioning in passing: 'Indian mother-goddess temples are a direct growth from primitive tribal cults, each of local origin, later brahmanised'),[7] 'ritual sacrifice of the male hero' (with hints of the denial of cannibalism as a motive for killing the hero), 'primitive sacred marriage', and 'group marriages'/ 'fraternal polyandry'. However, a major hypothesis of Kosambi, namely, the myth represents the transition from 'matriarchy to patriarchy' has been questioned not just on the bases of semantic formulations (modern-day historians and anthropologists prefer the use of 'matriliny' and 'matrilocality'. Incidentally, Kosambi was not unaware of these, as shown by his reference to Malinowski's *Dynamics of Cultural Change* and Oedipus complex in *Introduction*: 51, n. 10) but also because it is contended that such a proposition made in the 19th century by the Swiss jurist and historian of Roman law J.J. Bachofen and followed by Friedrich Engels, that seems to have provided inspiration to Kosambi, is vulnerable on count of absence of empirical evidence from long human history.[8]

Just as 'Urvashi and Pururavas' takes off from a classic Sanskrit work of Kalidasa, similarly *Mrichchhakatika*, the popular Sanskrit-Prakrit drama of Shudraka provides Kosambi an entry point to investigate the location of the mother-goddess cult sites at the crossroads (*tvamapi chatushpathe matribhyo balim upahara* – 'go thou, offer (this) *bali* to the Mothers at the crossroads'). It resulted in 'At the Crossroads: A Study of Mother-Goddess Cult Sites'. This essay, and the subsequent one entitled 'Pilgrim's Progress: A Contribution to the Prehistory of the Western Deccan Plateau', may be seen as complementary pieces in terms of their methodology and overall hypotheses. Both are concerned with the survival of autochthonous religious rites in varied forms with indicators of their brahmanization over the years. The former concludes thus: 'The crossways were, from the stone age, places where the Mothers were normally worshipped by savages whose nomad tracks met at the junction. . . . However, nothing prevented any brahmin's adopting it in the manner of the Puranas, which have been specially written to justify and even to glorify so many primitive autochthonous rites. *This was a regular mechanism for assimilation, and acculturation*' (emphases added). Elsewhere, too, Kosambi had asserted: 'what most observers miss is the reciprocal influence of tribesmen on the Indian peasant and even on the upper classes' (*Culture*: 44; emphasis in the original).[9] And the latter, 'Pilgrim's Progress', begins thus:

> Field work based upon Poona leads to the conclusion that

> certain rustic traditions and observances in Maharashtra have their roots in the late stone age. Many nameless village gods have risen from gruesome origins to identification with some respectable Brahmin deity. A transformation of the cult seems clearly to reflect a change in its human worshippers, from the food-gathering savage, through pastoralist, to agrarian food-producer. The development was not continuous, nor always in direct line. Conflict between the gods generally reflects human group-conflict. Divine marriages, acquisition of a family or entourage, and successive incarnations are theological manifestations of social fusion. Such parallel changes in society and religion were repeated in different localities. The apparently senseless myths so illogically put together in our Puranas have a peculiar basis in reality.[10]

Much of the ingenuity of both these essays lies in Kosambi's field work in Poona (now Pune) and its environs, specially the distribution patterns of microliths and megaliths as well as identification of what he called the 'highland' culture and 'lowland' track. The earliest food-gathering cultures had goddess worship involving blood sacrifice, whereas male divinities came with pastoralist intruders. 'The fixed cult-spots for pre-agricultural people would necessarily be those where their regular paths crossed, places where they met for their pre-barter exchange with the ceremonial and communal ritual that always accompanied it, or where several groups celebrated their periodic fertility cults in common. *Thus, the crossways are logically the original sites for the mother-goddess cults*' (emphases in the original). Embedded in this construct is an answer to the question as to why numerous Buddhist monasteries are located in the western ghats. The prehistory of the trade routes of the early first-millennium BCE influencing the location of these establishments could perhaps be related to the prehistoric tracks. Kosambi extended the course of such developments down to more recent times – analysing the routes of the great annual pilgrimages of the Varkari believers of the western Deccan to Pandharpur (centre of the Vitthala cult). 'Pilgrimages were originally the seasonal movement of prehistoric lowlanders' (*MR*: 130). Apart from 'transformation' of cults, the 'migration' of cults in relation to changes in subsistence pattern and mutations in social formation also constitutes an incisive line of enquiry, which had a direct and an indelible impact on the path-breaking studies of Gunther-Dietz Sontheimer.[11]

The theme of transformation of divinities on account of migration of varied social groups and communities recurs in the last essay of *MR*, 'The Village Community in the "Old Conquests" of Goa'. Though this essay deals with a relatively later period, i.e., the 16th-18th centuries, the aforesaid theme provides the historical background of the analyses of the formation of 'village community'. Kosambi's quest starts with an observation that in the village communities of Old Conquests (term for the areas including districts of Ilhas, Bardez, Salcete, etc., that came under the Portuguese dominion soon after Albuquerque's final victory in 1511 – the remaining eight districts were annexed after 1763) '*the best rice producing land is still common property*' (emphases in the original). In order to assess the actual bearing of this feature, he enters into a 'fairly complicated historical analysis'. 'All extant evidence seems to me to point to an ancient migration of Brahmins from the Gangetic plain of India over a thousand miles away, and the settlement in communities with a profit-sharing must have come with them'(*MR*: 166). This migration of Brahmins, which continued for almost a millennium from *circa* 4th to the 12th centuries CE, also unleashed forces that transformed local cults. An example of this phenomenon is outlined thus: 'the god *Mangesha*, one of the five principal deities of southern Sarasvat Brahmins (of Goa), has been forcibly converted into an image, though originally (and still under the golden mask) a stone phallic symbol of Shiva. What influence this change of cult had upon private land ownership we cannot say, but it did not change either the god's name or the community system' (ibid.: 167).

ELIADE AND KOSAMBI CONTRASTED

Having seen the objectives, methods and important works of both Mircea Eliade and Kosambi, a brief comment on the essential differences between them may not be out of place before we look into the issues involved in critique of the Kosambian method.

Eliade had a phenomenal legacy to fall back upon – a long tradition of historians of religions in the western world, both in Europe and the Americas. Kosambi was a loner in the field. No doubt, there are endless monographs on different religions of India but they lack critical historical focus. If we exclude the writings of social historians of art such as Niharranjan Ray, Amita Ray and Devangana Desai, who inevitably had to take cognizance of religious developments, none can be truly identified as harbinger of religious histories of India through millennia. Even the post-Kosambi writings have not seen much spurt in the field.

Eliade wrote a phenomenal number of works on different aspects of religions, both from their morphological and historical standpoints. Kosambi, on the other, produced only a few, though very provocative and incisive essays. While Eliade's active academic career spanned over more than fifty years, Kosambi died when he was only 59.

The works of Mircea Eliade on religions of the world have come under careful scrutiny and the impact of his writings, including the dwindling of his influence since the 1980s, have been widely debated.[12] However, an assessment of Kosambi as a harbinger of a new kind of religious history of India is yet to be attempted. Even B.D. Chattopadhyaya's Introduction to his anthology of 52 contributions of Kosambi (*CMI*) is reticent about it. It is no surprise, therefore, that his landmark contributions have gone completely unnoticed in the concerned historiographic surveys undertaken in the West. Thus, for example, Wilhelm Halbfass' and Arjun Appadurai's 'Indian Religions: History of Study', originally written for the first edition of *The Encyclopedia of Religion* (1987, edited by Mircea Eliade) and now included with a revised bibliography in the 2nd edition (Jones 2005: 4445-4451), does not even mention Kosambi.

Kunal Chakrabarti's reasonably balanced review of Kosambi's contributions on religion (2008) is a recent exception. However, following Romila Thapar's lead (Thapar 1993: 93, 111), Chakrabarti has also contended, though mildly, that Kosambi took no notice of the French anthropologist Levi-Strauss' structuralism. This needs some probing. After all, Eliade's numerous works show little application of Levi-Strauss' method of studying myths. Surely, this is more surprising than the absence of Levi-Strauss in Kosambi's writings. Eliade lived in Paris for a decade between 1945 and 1955 when Levi-Strauss emerged on the French intellectual scene. During his stay in Paris, Eliade had solidified most of his important concepts and categories, including those of *homo religious*, *homo symbolicus*, *axis mundi*, hierophany, etc., to give shape to what he later called a total hermeneutics.

More than this, it would be pertinent to ask how many studies on Indian religions since the publication of Levi-Srauss' *Structural Anthropology* in 1958 have invoked that method. One can perhaps recall only *Shiva, the Erotic Ascetic* (1973, reprinted in India in 1975 under the title *Asceticism and Eroticism in the Mythology of Shiva*, OUP) by Wendy Doniger. While it was then rightly hailed as a landmark work, Doniger's interest in the Straussian method waned immediately and her subsequent works tended to be more psychoanalytical than anthropological. And her latest work *The Hindus: An Alternative History* (2009; for its critique, see Shrimali 2010: 66-81) shows still greater departures. Howsoever sophisticated, challenging and provocative the methodologies are, their utility for a historian rooted in temporal and spatial concerns becomes suspect. Wendy Doniger in all her prolific writings has always been 'ahistorical'. That Eliade too has always been criticized for being 'ahistorical' or perhaps 'ahistoricist' should add sharpness to our contention.

Further, we need to recall the strong warning expressed by R.S. Sharma in the context of invoking new conceptual terminologies and methods: 'what is needed is not only an awareness of the various models that are being peddled in the field but also their careful examination, otherwise we would just become middlemen and paraphrasers. I would prefer to be damned as old-fashioned than go in for the latest without assessing its analytical validity and social relevance. New terms are needed to express new ideas, but phrase-mongering should not be confused with advance in historical knowledge' (Sharma 2007: 13-14).

CRITIQUE OF KOSAMBI'S ARCHAEOLOGY FOR RELIGIOUS HISTORIES

Making a special reference to essays ('At the Crossroads' and 'Pilgrim's Progress') included in *MR*, Shereen Ratnagar has dubbed Kosambi's archaeology 'amateurish' (Ratnagar 2008: 71-77). In this extremely strong critique, and that too in an almost vituperative language, she argues: 'Kosambi's archaeology, as far as I can tell, left no lasting legacy. His site locations were not precise; . . . he was neither trained in nor interested in the typology of stone tools; and his correlations of tool occurrences with sacred sites, of the tribe with an absence of plough agriculture and of iron technology with agricultural surpluses, were flawed. . . . Typology and classification are indispensable: as indispensable as is the knowledge of an ancient language for the historian. Failure to engage in the grammar of these entities and an ignorance of site formation processes give rise to faulty generalization.' Additional arguments include faulty drawings of stone tools making her doubt even their 'actual tool' status and considering them only as 'waste flakes'; Kosambi's findings of microliths and identification of megaliths not finding place in the official publications of the Archaeological Survey of India (hereafter ASI) such as its annual reports *Indian Archaeology – A Review* and *Ancient India – Bulletin of the Archaeological Survey of India*; and archaeologists such as H.D. Sankalia and F.R. Allchin disagreeing with him.[13] Concluding her assessment, Ratnagar contends, in a pontificatory tone: 'Given the current disposition in which academic status often rests on ideological positions, one does not expect much self-correction. Yet in the long term it is not enough to be proclaimed as a leftist/ secularist/Marxist – the gloss of identification with a charmed circle will inevitably wear off over time, and then the scrutiny of a person's scholarship will be of a different order altogether. An object lesson, perhaps, for young and not-so-young scholars with professional ambitions.' This critique requires probing on almost all counts.

One does not have to labour hard to underline that Kosambi was not a professional archaeologist trained in its so-called 'indispensable' grammar. For that matter, he was neither a professional numismatist, nor a professional historian, nor a professional religionist, etc., etc. Indeed, towards the end of his career as Professor of Mathematics at the Tata Institute of Fundamental Research (Mumbai), he was accused of being an 'amateur Indologist' (Banerjee 1974: 316). Like a true academician, Kosambi had himself confessed: 'I fell into Indology, as it were, through the roof' (Kosambi 1972: 158-59). Equally importantly, he was humble enough to conclude his Introduction to *MR* thus: 'It is not the purpose of these essays to judge but to analyse in so far as the essayist's knowledge suffices for the purpose. It seems to me that a great deal more in the way of field work is needed in every part of the country before we can begin to theorize. However imperfect, the beginning is made here' (*MR*: 11).

Reading Ratnagar's critique, I was reminded of the distinctions between 'archaeology from above' and 'archaeology from below', and between 'official archaeologist' and 'independent archaeologist' made by Faulkner in 2000. He castigated the 'bureaucratic professional tendency' within the British archaeological establishments and made a strong case for 'democratic archaeology'. 'Professional associations sometimes develop the approach of the old medieval craft guilds, where mystification and artificial barriers are used to create an exclusive elite, and group interests are advanced in opposition to other would-be practitioners deemed "unskilled" and "amateur". This attitude is sometimes represented in official archaeology . . .' (Faulkner 2000: 21-33). If 'technical training' and understanding is 'as indispensable' for an archaeologist as is the 'knowledge of an ancient language for the historian', it needs to be stressed that 'intuitive understanding' is no less indispensable for being a thinking and creative archaeologist.

Ratnagar has strong reservations about stone-age tools and even goes to the extent of calling them 'waste flakes' largely on the basis of the technically imperfect drawings. Should the professional archaeologist have passed such a judgment without physically examining the antiquities herself? Further, in the process, she also misquotes or only partially quotes both Kosambi and the Allchins. Referring to *Introduction* (51, n. 5) she contends: 'Kosambi says his collections were verified by F.R. and B. Allchin, although it is not specified which particular collections were shown to them. Actually, in a volume dedicated to his memory [this is with reference to Allchins 1974, and the cited page should be 49, not 45], the Allchins' remark that Kosambi's archaeology was less successful than his other works.' To put the record straight, Kosambi's aforesaid note is in the context of the 'general tool sequence' and the absence of uniformity in their classificatory modes. 'The total material is scanty, particularly when infinite local variation over the vast size of the country is considered' (*Introduction*: 19). And referring to F.R. Allchin's work summarizing most of the then available evidence, Kosambi says: 'My gratitude is expressed here for stimulating discussions with Dr. and Mrs. Allchin, who also verified my finds of stone-age tools *and corrected the old-fashioned terminology*' (emphases added). Since the tool typology is quite central to Ratnagar's critique, the Allchins need to be cited *in extenso*:

> It is to the lasting credit of the late D.D. Kosambi that he recognized, *perhaps more clearly than any of his countrymen had done before*, the extent to which such depressed or peripheral social groups (tribal people) constituted 'priceless evidence for the interpretation of some ancient record or archaeological find; their survival as backward groups also furnishes the real problem for explanation in the light of historical development' [*Introduction*: 7-8]. It is also to his

> credit that he recognised in the people on his own backdoor-step in Poona the presence of this evidence, and that from his observations he formulated one of the fundamental propositions of Indian social history: '*The entire course of Indian history shows tribal elements being fused into general society.* This phenomenon, which lies at the very foundation of the most striking Indian social feature, namely caste, is also the great basic fact of ancient Indian history. The different methods whereby the different elements were formed into a society or absorbed into existing society are prime ethnic material for any real historian [emphases in the original but missed by the Allchins]. . . . It is unfortunate . . . that his archaeological thinking appears as the weakest part of his arguments. *Had he lived longer, advances in archaeological methods and interpretation, in the world in general and in India in particular, might have supplied him with the material to substantiate his hypothesis even more fully than he hoped . . .* (emphases added).

Notwithstanding their relative assessment of Kosambi's 'archaeological thinking', the Allchins concluded their own essay on the Neolithic-Chalcolithic period and its relationship with the Late Stone Age hunters and gatherers with full-throated compliment for Kosambi thus: 'All these arguments lead us to the conclusion that certain elements of the Neolithic-Chalcolithic cultures of central and peninsular India may reasonably be regarded as intrusive, but other no less important aspects of technology, and no doubt more general cultural elements were already indigenous to these regions. Therefore the Neolithic-Chalcolithic cultures themselves are likely to represent an early synthesis or partial synthesis of groups at different technological levels, and perhaps of occupational specialization on a group basis, as was noticed by D.D. Kosambi around his home in Poona and seen by him as so fundamental a part of the Indian life and culture (Allchins 1974: 65-66).

Much is made of Sankalia's reservations about Kosambi's

claims about megaliths in the Poona district and allusion to his 1979 writing (Sankalia 1979: 117) has been invoked in this context. First, in an earlier publication of 1974, Sankalia had categorically stated 'Here I must say that I had myself decided not to contradict him [Kosambi] on the spot because this would have lead [sic.] to a very furious argument' (Sankalia 1974: 337). Isn't it unethical from a professional point of view to maintain silence in the presence of the concerned scholar and then criticize him posthumously? Second, the citation invoked by Ratnagar to underline Sankalia's disagreement also mentions R.C. Gaur's view on the same megaliths which upholds Kosambi's position. How ethical is to accept professional opinion of one and conceal that of another? Recollecting vicissitudes in his relations with Kosambi, Sankalia observed: 'Whether one agrees with his conclusions or not, one must admire the great tenacity of purposes and interest with which Prof. Kosambi had moved about in these parts [Poona District] of the Deccan and observed things for himself'(ibid.).

An important element of Ratnagar's critique of Kosambi's archaeology concerns the notion of 'tribe' / 'tribal people'. She writes: '[Kosambi] tends to mistake Stone-Age hunter-gatherers for tribes, when in fact hunting-gathering-fishing constitutes the pre-tribe stage of cultural development. *The tribe as a social formation came into existence only with the coming of agriculture*' (emphases added). This assessment seems to be only partially true. It is not as if Kosambi was not aware of such 'pre-tribe' groupings as clan, band, etc. While he was certainly conscious about subsistence patterns of early social groups and does mention hunting-gathering-fishing, and processes involving both splitting and coalescence amongst tribes and clans – 'presumably on the basis of exchange of food products', it is indeed the factor of social formation that turns out to be the central hallmark in his definitional parameters of 'tribe'. Let us remind ourselves that the second chapter of *Introduction* is titled 'The Heritage of *Pre-Class* Society' (emphases added) and not 'Tribal Society'. Sure, archaeologists not trained in Marxian methodology or familiar only with vulgar Marxism (scholars of such breed have flooded the stream of Indian official archaeologists) are not expected to appreciate such nuances. No wonder, while Ratnagar's explanation of the use of the expression 'scheduled tribes' for hunter-gatherer groups (that runs counter to her own understanding of tribe) in independent India's Constitution is that it 'does not set out to define the tribe or the caste, its purpose being to select groups for positive discrimination' (Ratnagar 2008: 77, n. 12), Kosambi sees no problem in describing the modern day remnants of tribal society thus: 'Some practice head-hunting, others combine the pastoral life with small agriculture, a goodly number have drifted into the casual-labour market' (*Introduction*: 26).

Commenting upon Kosambi's proposition that the prehistoric tracks seem to have developed into trade routes of the historic period, Ratnagar indirectly indicts Kosambi's field work: 'Students may also beware the notion that intensive fieldwork and on-the-ground observation will reveal the exact placing of millennia-old roads or tracks. It is one thing to do basic map work and realize that, at the regional level, Ujjain rather than Chhota Udepur, or Nasik rather than Dahanu, lie on major routes. But on the ground, routes are hard to pinpoint . . .'. The underlying assumption of this seems to be implying that Kosambi's conception of fieldwork was somewhat mechanical and pre-determined. This is very far from being the case. In the Preface to *Introduction*, Kosambi wrote: 'Going over to the common people is not easy work . . . Such field-work has to be performed with critical insight, taking nothing for granted, or on faith, but without the attitude of superiority, sentimental reformism, or spurious leadership which prevents most of us from learning anything except from bad textbooks'. In the revised edition, he says:

> In the revision, I had expected to learn a great deal more than has actually been possible from reviews by professional historians. The paramount importance of field work in the study of Indian history seems altogether to have escaped their attention. Such work in the field falls into three inter-related classes: archaeology, anthropology, and philology.

> All three need some preliminary knowledge of local conditions, the ability to master local dialects, and to gain the confidence of tribesmen as well as peasants. In all field work, it is necessary to develop a technique and critical method during the course of investigation itself. Fitting observation into rigid, preconceived mould is ruinous. The technique of asking the right questions in the proper way cannot be taught nor mastered except in the field.

Further, distinguishing between the 'field archaeology' and 'site archaeology', he says: 'The actual technique developed by O.G.S. Crawford for England in his fine book *Archaeology in the Field* cannot be transferred to Indian territory'. And by this logic certainly, what is feasible and desirable in Ujjain may not work in Chhota Udepur and what may be good for Nashik may not yield any fruitful result in Dahanu.

By field work Kosambi was not referring to archaeological investigations alone. One suspects that this is where he was somewhat skeptical of the work being done in his time, by professional, institution-based archaeologists. Though his vision of archaeology essentially involved study of the total contemporary context, yet Kosambi was not oblivious of the limits of field-based ethno-archaeology. He clearly wanted the practitioners to know not only the difference between old functions of artifacts and their current uses but also cautioned them against mechanical application of technical training. In a letter to V.N. Sisodia, one of the young fieldworkers associated with him and later a student at the Institute of Archaeology, London, Kosambi wrote on October 16, 1963: 'By all means concentrate upon new techniques like soil analysis. Pollen does very well in Denmark, with peat bogs for example; but what will work in India I don't know. The best indicator in this area is the impregnation of the soil with lime absorbed from below (Deulgao Gada, Coraci Alandi); also some peculiar whitening of microliths, perhaps also due to such absorption. If these could be used in some way for dating, all the better' (*CMI*: xxxiv, n. 28). As an illustration of Kosambi's passion for underlining the indispensability of field work even for comprehending literary texts, his review of John Brough's translation of *Gotra-pravara-manjari* of Purushottama Pandit (under the title *The Early Brahmanical System of Gotra and Pravara*, Cambridge University Press, Cambridge, 1953) of medieval times (not later than *c.* 1450 CE) may be cited (Kosambi 1953: 178-88). The late G.D. Sontheimer, who had done some field work with Kosambi in the Pune area and whose subsequent researches on the folk deities of the Deccan came to be based on regular field work, recording of oral traditions and written texts, received this communication (dated May 24, 1962) from his mentor: 'The old methods for Indology will simply not do; without fieldwork the literary sources will not convey any real meaning. You must have realized by now, but have the senior scholars?'(*CMI*: xxxv, n. 29).

Finally, a word about the 'legacy' of Kosambi's archaeology. This has little to do with the quality and quantity of Kosambi's writings in the field. On the contrary, it is a reflection on the training received by archaeologists. As far back as 1950 Wheeler wrote: 'Archaeologists should bear in mind that their aim is not to dig up mere things but dig up people' (Wheeler 1950: 126). Unfortunately most of the post-independence archaeologists have largely been only digging, and have, in the process, created phenomenal mass of antiquities and their typologies and perhaps also mastered their grammar. The type of archaeology in which Kosambi was interested, was concerned with digging up people, and for that one needed to be adept in classical languages and literary texts created over several millennia, epigraphic and numismatic resources, and exposure to other allied disciplines such as anthropology, sociology, and so on. In India, 'official archaeology' is being done by people whose grounding in classical languages is almost non-existent. Similarly, the breed of well-trained epigraphists and numismatists is also dying out fast and one would find it almost impossible to identify archaeologists grounded in such and other allied disciplines. To illustrate, H.D. Sankalia, the doyen of Indian archaeologists had this to say about Kosambi and his own training in handling coins: 'By a careful examination of the coins, he [Kosambi] found out how the statistical approach could be made use of to find out their age. So when I happened to acquire a similar hoard of punch-marked coins from Nagari in Rajasthan in 1955 and published the results in 1956, I sent him a copy of the article. He said that the hoard was welcome because it gave us a large number of punch-marked coins in the graded series, though they were not useful from the statistical point of view. *And then I realized how very ignorant I was of the statistical method*, because I thought that this hoard would be as precious as the one studied by Prof. Kosambi, namely, of Gupta coins' (emphases added).[14] How many archaeologists today would be courageous enough to own their limitations?

Ratnagar has rightly spoken very highly of B. Subbarao, the author of *The Personality of India* (M.S. University, Baroda, 1958), a classic work. If one tries to identify the 'legacy' of such a genius professional archaeologist, it would be found that Indian archaeologists have largely remained unaffected by him. Why should we then expect an 'independent' archaeologist such as Kosambi to leave much impact in the field that is so overwhelmingly dominated by what Faulkner had called the 'bureaucratic professional tendency'?

RELIGION, IDEOLOGY AND POWER

We have, in one of our earlier contributions, discussed the role of religion as an ideological force (Shrimali 1988 (1989): 83-88, 101-02). Kosambi, it seems, has been overawed by the absence of violence in the Indian psyche. Prima facie such an understanding, like the alleged tolerance of Indians in general and of Hinduism in particular is a stereotype and has been rightly contested (Jha 2009: 27-47, Shrimali 2003: section IV, Ratnagar 2008: 72). Looking for the modus operandi of the formation of the social consciousness amongst peace loving Indians, Kosambi wrote: 'what it was about India that was characteristic, to ask ourselves wherein the history of India *differs* from that of other countries? . . . How is it to be characterised? Certainly by strong grip of religion – without an organised church as in Medieval Europe . . . India has the unique social division, the (endogamous) caste system. *Caste is class at a primitive level of production, a religious method of forming social consciousness in such a manner that the primary producer is deprived of his surplus with minimum coercion.* This is done with the adoption of local usages into religion and ritual, being thus the *negation* of history by giving fictitious sanction from 'times immemorial' to any new development, the actual change being denied altogether. To this extent and at a low level of commodity production, it is clear that *an Asiatic mode did exist*, reaching over several stages; at least, the term is applicable to India, whatever the case elsewhere' (Kosambi 1954: 59; emphasis in the original). This endorsement of the Asiatic Mode of Production was vehemently denied by Kosambi later in *Introduction*. Notwithstanding this denial, the matter is debatable. For the present, however, let us accept Chattopadhyaya's observation: 'This is not the same as understanding, as many do, the much published religiosity of the Indians or producing specialized tomes on Indian religions and philosophies. On the other hand, it meant understanding how ideology bore upon relations between disparate groups in society, how it acted as an integrative mechanism, strengthening at the same time the basis of inequality' (*CMI*: xxviii). Elsewhere Kosambi wrote: 'tribal society could not have been converted peacefully to new forms nor free savages changed into helpless serfs – though peace between tribes (whose normal intercourse means war) and change from hunting or pastoralism to agriculture guarantee a decidedly more secure livelihood for the tribesmen. Only an imposing ritual, or overpowering force, or modern socialism could have won the savage over. The Indian method reduced the need for violence to a minimum by substitution of religion; caste and the *smritis* adopted or replaced totem or taboo with more power than the sword or bow' (Kosambi 1955: 309-10).

POSTCOLONIALISM AND OTHER 'TURNS'

In recent years we have been hearing about various kinds of 'turns' – the 'cultural turn', the 'linguistic turn', the 'performative turn', the 'pictorial turn', and so forth. On the question of religion-ideology-power nexus, a different twist of 'power' is seen in a recent work that seeks to locate the real meaning of the construct of 'The Mystic East' in the modern Western consciousness. Richard King's *Orientalism and Religion* (1999) pleads that religious studies as a discipline might better conceive of itself as a form of 'cultural studies' rather than as an offshoot of theology. It argues for an awareness of 'mutual imbrication of religion, culture and power as categories' by denying the exclusivity of both materialist and culturalist reductionism assuming that they deny 'culture' and 'power' respectively. The approach here is 'to look at the categories of mysticism and religion, some of the presuppositions involved in the disciplines of religious studies and Indology, and the ways in which Indian religion became located within contemporary notions of "the mystical".' Its aim is 'to *change the subject* (that is, mysticism and the comparative study of Indian religion), not by changing what we talk about (that is, by looking at something else) but rather by suggesting ways in which one might redirect the intellectual trajectory of comparative study in the light of postcolonial and post-structuralist theories' (King 1999: 1-6; emphasis in the original). King seeks to demonstrate that there are in fact a number of heterogeneous facets to Indian religions (he uses 'religion' in singular almost throughout the monograph) and that not all of these are what might be called 'mystical', for, he believes that it does not involve questioning the basic assumptions underlying the description of these movements. His interests lie in demonstrating that 'both philosophy and history of ideas should take more seriously not only the social location of the concepts under examination but also their involvement in a wider cultural field of power relations, or what has become known as "the politics of knowledge".'

There are several problems with this construct – both methodological and ideological. To begin with, the methodology deployed here consists of an inherent contradiction. Though critiquing the alleged 'textualist bias' within Western approaches to religion, and Indian religion in particular, King himself relies exclusively on 'texts'. He considers them to be of 'special reverence' for the history of religious ideas and undertaking field work for such a venture an impossibility. This sounds almost ridiculous, especially because King is aware that 'of the thousands of languages that have been spoken by humans throughout history only some 106 have ever produced anything that might be described as literature' (ibid.: 62). Also, to read such a pronouncement almost half a century after Kosambi's demonstrations of the indispensability of combining textual studies and field work, is extremely disheartening.

Further, King admits that his interest is in 'those traditions, doctrines and classical texts of Indian religion that are most liable to be described as "mystical" – that is, Advaita Vedanta, the Yoga traditions, the Madhyamaka and Yogachara schools of Mahayana Buddhism'. It is obvious that these textual traditions belong exclusively to the Sanskritik tradition (though not necessarily brahmanical), and, therefore, cannot be taken as representative of 'Indian' traditions. King is aware that scholars in the early 19th century had already spoken about discrepancy between 'textual Buddhism' and 'actual Buddhism' (ibid.: 70). To this may be added the phenomenal work of Gregory Schopen who has illustrated similar discrepancies between the Buddhism of scriptures and Buddhism in epigraphic texts in more recent years. Mahayana Buddhism has received his special attention.

These numerous contributions since the 1990s (now available in useful anthologies: Schopen 1997 and 2004) make an incessant plea for inscription-aided study of Buddhism, for, such an approach goes beyond the world-view of the small literate, almost exclusively male, and certainly atypical professionalized subgroups. Instead, it provides evidence of what religious people of all segments of a given community actually did – how monks and nuns owned property, supported transfer of merit and how the Buddhist community disposed its dead. Such analyses would go a long way in questioning the stereotype of treating Buddhism in general and Mahayana Buddhism in particular as 'mystical'. Nothing would have excited Kosambi more than questioning such stereotypes.

Ideology plays an integral part in the very act of understanding, interpreting or studying anything. King is conscious of this. His overall construct is self-confessedly rooted in 'postcolonial' theories. Essentially, this notion comes to us from literary critics based in the Western world. Michel Focault's project of unraveling multiple relations of knowledge and power, Edward Said's 'Orientalism', etc.,[15] have been its guiding spirits. The 'postcolonial' brings to our attention the relations between colonialism and nationalism in the 'politics of culture' and 'politics of representation'.

Apparently, concerned with the 'exploding the myth of objectivity', as is the wont of the postcolonialist, Richard King (King 1999: Chapters 3 and 5) draws his hermeneutical inspiration from Hans-Georg Gadamer's 1960 work *Wahrheit und Methode* (translated as *Truth and Method* by Joel Weinsheimer and Donald G. Marshall in 1975; 2nd revised edition, New York, 1989). He underlines: 'The nature of Indian post-colonial identity provides support for Gadamer's suggestion that one cannot easily escape the normative authority of tradition, for, in opposing British colonial rule, Hindu nationalists did not fully transcend the suppositions of the West, but rather legitimated Western Orientalist discourse by responding in a manner that did not fundamentally question the Orientalists' paradigm.' Further, commenting on the more recent indigenous discourses by the 'new' Indian intelligentsia, educated in colonially established institutions, influenced by European cultural standards and moulded in the postcolonialist frame, King finds them to be deeply indebted to Orientalist pre-suppositions and failing to criticize the essentialist stereotypes embodied in such narratives.

This rejection of British political hegemony but from a standpoint that still accepts many of the European presuppositions about Indian culture is a sign of neo-colonialism (ibid.: 116).[16] Significantly, King's own deconstruction of 'the Mystic East' also does not question the construct of 'the Mystic East' *per se* and its underlying assumptions of 'the Other'. He notes, without irony: 'The rise of Hindu- and Buddhist-inspired groups throughout the West, much of contemporary New Age mythology as well as media advertising and popular culture in general, demonstrates the ongoing cultural significance of the idea of the "Mystic East", and the continued involvement of the West in a romantic and exotic fantasy of Indian religions as deeply mystical, introspective and other worldly in nature' (King 1999: 142). In King's hands it is simply projected onto Indian religious culture as a way of manipulating, controlling and managing the Orient. After all, his larger project is to pay greater attention to power relations in the history of ideas. How is it different from the 'Orientalist' discourse? Isn't it an apology for the second colonization, not through gunboats, but through an influx of the so-called 'cultural studies'?

Some of the contributions in a recently published volume entitled *Text and Context in the History of Literature and Religion of Orissa* (Malinar, Beltz, et al. 2004: 1-42, 203-38, 457-81) also deal with some theoretical issues related with the 'turns' currently in vogue. The thesis of the 'readability of cultures' is taken up by Dietrich Harth, who highlights the difficulties involved in the task of translation. Recognizing the boundaries of language as the boundaries of culture, translation and its synonym, i.e., 'interpretation', are seen as crossing borders. A lot of translation has to be enacted. Neither text (something mute and absent) nor context are 'given' phenomena, they are selected and validated by the interpreter. 'The interpretation changes the text, the changed text calls forth a new interpretation, and so on and so forth.' Cultures perceived as readable become portable cultures and this mirrors the fact that cultures in our times are losing their centers and show more and more the features of migrant and interlacing performative patterns (for similar assertions and convictions, see also King 1999: ch. 3). Axel Michaels argues: 'when reading the text one must also consider those who are not within the text'. There is plea for special collaboration of anthropologists and philologists and Michaels calls it 'Ethno-Indology'. Michaels argues that Indology needs to become more bare-footed, both orally and socially.

Broadening the notions of 'text' is welcome but haven't some of these theoretical interventions been in practice for decades, though without semantic jargon? What is this great fuss about reading/translating/interpreting cultures and 'interplay of texts and contexts'? Haven't generations of undergraduate students in history been told that 'facts' do not speak for themselves and it's the historian who makes them speak? Haven't historians of the last numerous generations endeavoured to make them speak by looking beyond and reading between the lines of their sources (or 'text', as the current fashion goes), and by analysing the background and milieu (including class biases, which post-modernist and post-colonialist practitioners are often shy of exploring) of 'authors' and their 'agencies'?[17]

Kosambi, a polyglot who knew more than a dozen languages, Indian and foreign, modern and classical, spent his whole academic life in developing a method of reading 'texts' of different *genres*, studying their transmission and stratifications, and in editing and translating them.[18] His seminal writings on the *Mahabharata*, Kautilya's *Arthashastra*, *Bhartrihari's* trilogy, Vatsyayana's *Kama-sutra*, and Kamandaka's *Nitisara*, and comments on Geldner's translation of the *Rigveda* and John Brough's editing of the *Gotra-pravaramanjari*, etc., remain unparalleled. Again, we need to ask how the parameters of Michaels' 'cultural turn' and 'Ethno-Indology' differ from those of Kosambi's 'Combined Methods in Indology' (with its special accent on combination of textual studies and fieldwork) and 'Living Prehistory', which the latter had worked out in the 1960s? Kosambi is not even acknowledged by Michael. Ironically, his essay is 'In Memory of G.D. Sontheimer', who himself never tired of admitting that Kosambi was his mentor and a major inspirational figure.

Another recent contribution within the larger project of 'cultural studies' is Sheldon Pollock's 'Towards a Political Philology' which analyses Kosambi's work as a Sanskritist and is emphatic about the need for a cultural difference for advancing frontiers of the history of textuality. This is, however, underlined in the backdrop of his lopsided understanding of the notion of modes of production and what he has called skewed interpretation of scientific Marxism. The debate on feudalism in early India, Pollock says, 'has been singularly sterile. Its dust-dry shastric exercises over tax or rent, peasant and serf, class or caste are often completely a priori and devoid of any engagement with real empirical data and actual text . . . . The participants in the debate often interpreted a cultural production mechanically according to an inflexible economism and equally dismal functionalism'. In fact, Kosambi, who initiated this allegedly 'sterile debate', categorically refused to accept 'economic determinism' as the sole factor in historical and social (including religious) change.

CONCLUSION

Given Kosambi's iconoclasm and his reluctance to be overawed by the orthodox base-superstructure and a unilinear development of historical processes proposed by the 'Official Marxists'; his unequivocal view of locating the 'power of ideology' in the specificities of the Indian caste system; and his boldness in overcoming the traditional Marxist distrust of psychoanalysis, as Kunal Chakrabarti shows (2008: 68-69), make the task of categorizing him within the straight-jacketed 'Marxist' fold all the more difficult. Kosambi believed that 'Marxism is not a substitute for thinking, but a tool of analysis' (Kosambi 1949: 789). It is often argued that the materialist reductionism of Marxism denies religion and culture. It is not just that this is one of the elements of 'vulgar Marxism' but the problem lies precisely in taking religion outside the domain of culture. Numerous contributions of Kosambi take the bull by its horns, demolish the myths surrounding the nature of materialist reductionism and define contours of religious histories afresh. Significantly, he did not study religions as part of the so-called superstructure or accord it any particular hallowed and autonomous status. Instead, for him, it was an integral part of the larger and dynamic cultural process involving an interaction between historical contexts and the development and influence of ideas. A proper assessment of his specific contributions to religious histories of India must recognize that in many ways he boldly ventured to extend the frontiers of what, in Friedrich Max Müller's words, we can call the 'science of religions'.

NOTES

1 One of the earliest initiatives, that unfortunately went without much notice outside West Bengal, was taken by the Centre for Archaeological Studies & Training, Eastern India (located in Kolkata) with the support of Kolkata Museum Society in November 2007. The theme of this twelfth Annual Seminar of the Centre was 'Remembering Kosambi: A Centenary Tribute'. It attracted nearly twenty speakers.

2 The Indian Council of Historical Research held a symposium 'Looking Back in 2008: The Life and Work of D.D. Kosambi' in July 2008. The three speakers revisiting the work of an extraordinary scholar included Irfan Habib, D.N. Jha and the author of this paper. Around the same time, *Economic & Political Weekly* put together a collection of ten papers on the theme: 'D.D. Kosambi: The Man and His Work' (Vol. XLIII, No. 30, July 26-August 01, 2008). The contributors included Meera Kosambi, Romila Thapar, Sheldon Pollock, Kunal Chakrabarti, Irfan Habib, Rajan Gurukkal, B.D. Chattopadhyaya, Shereen Ratnagar, Kumkum Roy and Vivek Monteiro. Thereafter, *The Marxist*, Theoretical Quarterly of the Communist Party of India (Marxist) also brought out Kosambi Centenary Issue (Vol.XXIV.4, October-December, 2008) with contributions from D.N. Jha, Irfan Habib and Prabhat Patnaik.

3 Some other notable publications of Eliade include *The Hooligans* (1935), *Cosmos and History: The Myth of the Eternal Return* (1954), *Yoga* (1958), *Patterns in Comparative Religion* (1958), *Myth, Dreams and Mysteries* (1960), *The Forge and the Crucible* (1962) and *The Quest* (1969).

4 This may not have been unrelated to Eliade's strong anti-Left and pro-Fascist political position. He joined that University in 1957 and remained there till his death. At the time of his death in 1986, he was the Sewell L. Avery Distinguished Service Professor Emeritus. For a recent assessment of the notorious politics of Eliade, see Horst Junginger (ed.), *The Study of Religion under the Impact of Fascism*, Brill, Leiden-Boston, 2008, specially the editor's Introduction, and the articles of Eugen Ciurtin, 'Raffaelle Pettazzoni and Mircea Eliade: Generalist Historians of Religions and the Fascisms (1933-1945)' and Istvan Keul, 'Political Myopia, Mystical Revolution, 'Felix Culpa'? Mircea Eliade and the Legionary Movement: Recent Romanian Perspectives'. Abstracts of these two articles are also available in English. See also Mac Linscott Ricketts, 'Eliade on diplomatic service in London', *Religion: An International Journal*, Vol. 38 (4), December 2008, pp. 346-254, sketching the history of Great Britain's early involvement in World War II, the dramatic political events in Romania during Eliade's diplomatic service in London, and the British government's intrigues that held him a virtual 'captive' from September 1940 to February 1941.

5 This reminds us of the Periyar E.V. Ramasamy Naicker, the founder of the

Dravida Movement (Dravidar Kazhagam) in Tamil Nadu in the early 20th century, who often said that it was easy to be a theist but one requires a lot of courage to be an atheist.

6 See especially Kosambi's comment (n. 5 on p. 149) on the British Museum laboratory, where the sample of the wood from the ceiling beams of the great Chaitya was dated.

7 An important post-Kosambi study, also based entirely on literary data, argues that the *Devi Mahatmya* of the *Markandeya Purana* (*c.* sixth century CE) is the first comprehensive account of the Goddess to appear in Sanskrit – the explanation is sought in terms of Sanskritization. It is clearly underlined that the basic impulse behind the worship of goddess is of non-Aryan and non-Sanskritik origin (Coburn 1984: specially Prolegomenon).

8 See Chakrabarti 2008: 69. For Kosambi's own reservations on the subject, though feeble, see his comments on why he could not use *The Mothers* (1927), the 'powerfully documented and inspiring three-volume work of R. Briffault' (*MR*: 76, n. 17). However, for a competent survey of the current position of historians, sociologists, anthropologists, archaeologists, religion specialists in these and other allied fields such as folklore, psychology and comparative mythology, including the contributions of the so-called 'feminist scholars' on the question of 'matriarchy to patriarchy' transition, see Preston 2005: 3611-3616.

9 This approach stands in marked contrast to what the American anthropologist Robert Redfield identified as 'the great' and 'the little' traditions in peasant civilizations in his monograph entitled *Peasant Society and Culture* (1956). A collection of essays edited by McKim Marriott titled *Village India* (1955) also showed the continuity of this idea. Milton Singer's *When a Great Tradition Modernizes: An Anthropological Approach to Indian Civilization* (1972: with a foreword by M.N. Srinivas) marks its zenith. Indeed, the prehistory of this idea may be seen in the concept of *Sanskritization* expounded in *Religion and Society Among the Coorgs of South India* (1952), the seminal work of Indian sociologist M.N. Srinivas. Both these concepts of 'Sanskritization' and 'the great tradition' rested on the assumption of a critical historical, linguistic, and conceptual gap between local religious beliefs and customs and those of the so-called 'Sanskritik Hinduism', i.e., the 'Hinduism' of esoteric Sanskrit texts, literate priests, and cosmopolitan centres. In contrast, 'the little tradition' is typically illiterate, customary, and embodied in the common beliefs and practices of the mass of ordinary folk. The exclusivity of 'Sanskrit texts' and its assumed 'higher' status remains debatable and certainly stands exposed by Kosambi's accent on the concept of 'acculturation' that was marked by coalescence of different traditions and had no place for regarding popular (and vulgar for some) religions as a 'lower' form of expression. An important contribution based on the application of this concept of 'acculturation' is Sharma, 'Material Milieu of Tantricism', in R.S. Sharma (ed.; in collaboration with Vivekanand Jha), *Historical Probings – In Memory of D.D. Kosambi*, People's Publishing House, New Delhi, 1974. Another more recent work influenced by Kosambi's approach is Nath: 2001.

[10] For the skeptics of Kosambi's methods and analyses, it should be incisive to learn that if zealously pursued, such processes could be shown to be valid for other regions as well, depending of course on the efficacy with which such field work is carried on. An encouraging example of this comes from south India in the form of David D. Schulman's *Tamil Temple Myths: Sacrifice and Marriage in the South Indian Shaiva Tradition*, Princeton University Press, Princeton, 1980, especially ch. 4. Incidentally, Kosambi did not take all accounts of the Puranas in an uncritical manner. Apart from critically analysing Pargiter's use of the Puranic texts vis-à-vis Vedic textual allusions and also making a case for relating information available in these texts with the evidence of settlement patterns unearthed in archaeological excavations (Kosambi 1953 (a): 410-15), he had left no one in doubt about his contempt for 'ludicrous "Indian history" that is still being written, with the *puranas* as gospel, dating the Vedas back several million years, crediting our mythical sages with every modern scientific discovery down to the electron and the bacteriophage' (Kosambi 1955 (a): 793).

[11] Some of Sontheimer's prominent works include *Pastoral Deities in Western India* (translated by Anne Feldhaus, Oxford University Press, New York, 1989) and *King of Hunters, Warriors, and Shepherds: Essays on Khandoba,* edited by Anne Feldhaus, Aditya Malik and Heidrun Bruckner, Indira Gandhi National Centre for the Arts/Manohar, Delhi, 1997. For a more detailed list of Sontheimer's writings inspired by Kosambi, see Heidrun Bruckner, Anne Feldhaus and Aditya Malik (eds.), *Essays on Religion, Literature and Law,* Indira Gandhi National Centre for the Arts/Manohar, Delhi, 2004. The closest parallel to Kosambi/Sontheimer type of construct that one can locate in Eliade's writings lies in his belief that a substratum of peasant cultures of southeastern Europe was preserved to this day, underneath the cultural influences of the Greeks, the Romans, the Byzantines, and Christianity. He went to the extent of suggesting that the peasant roots of Romanian culture could become the basis of genuine universalism, transcending nationalism and cultural provincialism.

[12] As recently as 2008, *Religion: An International Journal,* devoted an entire issue (38 (4), December 2008, jointly edited by Douglas Allen and Michel Gardaz) to mark the centennial of Eliade's birth and to discuss various dimensions of his legacy. It described him as 'the most influential theorist of religion and the foremost scholar of religious myth and symbolism', though controversial, too. Another useful contribution that assesses the status of the phenomenological approach to study religions and Eliade's position is Michael Stausberg, 'The Study of Religion(s) in Western Europe III: Further Developments after World War II', *Religion: An International Journal,* 39(3), September 2009, pp. 261-282. The concept of 'Implicit Religion' and the launching of *Implicit Religion: The Journal of the Centre for the Study of Implicit Religion and Contemporary Spirituality* in 1998 also owe considerable debt to Eliade's phenomenological approach to religion. See in this context, Edward Bailey, 'Implicit Religion', *Religion: An International Journal,* 40 (4), October 2010, pp. 271-78.

[13] Curiously, Ratnagar has maintained mysterious silence on the thoroughly

unprofessional conduct of the ASI when it comes to the publication of such reports – the publication of *Ancient India* ceased with Number 22 for the year 1966 (actually published in 1973) and the latest issue of the *Indian Archaeology – A Review* is for the year 2003-04 but published in 2011. Official reports of excavations at important Harappan sites such as Ropar and Kalibangan have either not been published at all or published only partially, though these sites were excavated almost half a century ago. The list of such unpublished sites is huge.

14 Sankalia 1974: 335. There seems to be some confusion in his mind though, for Kosambi is not known to have undertaken any statistical analysis of 'Gupta coins'.

15 Ronald Inden's use of Edward Said's 'Orientalism' in his *Imagining India*, Basil Blackwell, Oxford, 1990 provides illustrations of Indian specificities. For a critique of his work, see Shrimali 1993: 25-39.

16 The issue of an interplay between indigenous and orientalist discourses of power, specially the resemblances between pre-colonial brahmanical discourse and oriental scholarship has also been underlined by Pollock 1994: 76-133.

17 In his critique of the first three volumes (1951-54) of the *The History and Culture of the Indian People* Kosambi did not mince words: 'The specific feature of Indian history, progressive exploitation of the worker under a dual burden of caste and class, cannot long remain buried under such vainglorious praise of Indian "culture" and philosophy. The effort to prove equality of the present ruling class (and of the supposed ancestors it has found for itself) with the ruling class in some western countries may help secure foreign intervention in time of need; it will not prevent the internal struggle from maturing all the more rapidly.'(Kosambi 1955(a): 796). I regret that no historian of my generation (including me) or later, has ventured to critique several volumes (brought out since the late 1990s) on early Indian history published under the Project of History of Indian Science, Philosophy and Culture with D.P. Chattopadhyaya as its General Editor. The Series is entitled *History of Science, Philosophy and Culture in Indian Civilization*, and its class bias is not very different from that of the Bharatiya Vidya Bhavan Series. It calls for serious introspection on the part of the present-day historians.

18 In a posthumously published contribution (Kosambi 1979: 271) Kosambi prioritises: 'The order proposed here, *Arthashastra, Mahabharata, Kamasutra*, Kamandaka, Somadeva, is bound to be contested by those who retain their faith in the antiquity of the epic, unshaken by common sense or modern scholarship.' Recently, Upinder Singh (Singh 2010: 29-62) has situated Kamandaka's *Nitisara* 'at the threshold or the advent of the early medieval' (*c.* 500-700 CE) without assigning any particular reason. She does not even mention Kosambi's ordering of this text mentioned above, which would not have militated against her ascription. Second, Kosambi had underlined: 'There must have been the heavy emphasis upon ethics that Kamandaka and the still later *Nitivakyamrita* of

Somadeva Suri thrust into their treatises.' Though conceding an important place to ethics in the *Nitisara*, Singh conspicuously ignores Kosambi.

BIBLIOGRAPHY

Allchin, Raymond and Bridget Allchin 1974. 'The Relationship of Neolithic and Later Settled Communities with those of Late Stone Age Hunters and Gatherers in Peninsular India', in R.S.Sharma (in collaboration with Vivekanand Jha), ed., *Indian Society: Historical Probings – In Memory of D.D.Kosambi*, People's Publishing House, New Delhi, pp. 45-66.

Banerjee, A.K., 1974. 'D.D.K.—A Rough Diamond', in *Science and Human Progress: Essays in Honour of Late Prof. D.D. Kosambi, Scientist, Indologist and Humanist*, Prof. D.D. Kosambi Commemoration Committee, Popular Prakashan, Bombay, pp. 311-17.

Breckenridge, Carol A. and Peter van der Veer (eds.), 1994. *Orientalism and the Postcolonial Predicament: Perspectives on South Asia*, Oxford University Press, Delhi.

Chakrabarti, Kunal, 2008. 'The Lily and the Mud: D.D. Kosambi on Religion', *Economic Political Weekly* (*EPW*), XLIII, 30, July 26-August 1, pp. 60-70.

Coburn, Thomas B., 1984. *Devi Mahatmya: The Crystallization of the Goddess Tradition*, Motilal Banarsidass, Delhi.

Eliade, Mircea, 1963. *Myth and Reality* (being volume Thirty-one under the Series 'World Perspectives', planned and edited by Ruth Nanda Ashen), translated from the French by Willard R.Trask, Harper & Row, New York and Evanston.

Faulkner, Neil, 2000. 'Archaeology from below', *Public Archaeology*, 1, 1, pp. 21-33.

Hobsbawm, Eric, 1997. 'What Do Historians Owe to Karl Marx?' (first written in 1968), reprinted in *On History*, Weidenfeld & Nicolson, London.

Jha, D.N., 2009. *Rethinking Hindu Identity*, Equinox, London Oakville.

Jones, Lindsay (Editor-in-Chief), 2005. *Encyclopedia of Religion*, 2nd edition, Thomson Gale, Detroit/New York.

King, Richard, 1999. *Orientalism and Religion: Postcolonial Theory, India and 'The Mystic East'*, Oxford University Press, Delhi.

Kosambi, D.D., 1949. 'Marxism and Ancient Indian Culture', *Annals of the Bhandarkar Oriental Research Institute (ABORI)*, Vol.29 (1948), pp. 271-77; reprinted in *CMI*, pp. 784-89.

———, 1951. 'On a Marxist Approach to Indian Chronology', *ABORI*, 31, pp.

258-66; reprinted in *CMI*, pp. 49-56.

———, 1953. 'Brahmin Clans', *Journal of the American Oriental Society*, 73, pp. 202-08; reprinted in *CMI*, pp. 178-88.

———, 1953(a). 'The Study of Ancient Indian Tradition', *Indica*: The Indian Historical Research Institute Silver Jubilee Commemorative Volume, St Xaviers College, Bombay, edited by Radhakumud Mukherji, Mohammad Habib, Ramachandra Dikshitar, H.D. Sankalia, Bhaskar Saletore, J.M. Unvala; reprinted in *CMI*, pp. 407-429.

———, 1954. 'Stages of Indian History', *ISCUS: Journal of the Indo-Soviet Cultural Society*, 1, 1, January; reprinted in *CMI*, pp. 57-72.

———, 1955. 'The Basis of Ancient Indian History (I)', *Journal of American Oriental Society*, 75, pp. 35-45; reprinted in *CMI*, 309-326.

———, 1955(a): 'What Constitutes Indian History, *ABORI*, 35, pp. 194-201; reprinted in *CMI*, pp. 790-96.

———, 1956/1975. *An Introduction to the Study of Indian History*, Popular Prakashan, Mumbai, first published in 1956; Revised Second Edition, 1975.

———, 1962. *Myth and Reality: Studies in the Formation of Indian Culture*, Popular Prakashan, Mumbai.

———, 1965. *The Culture & Civilisation of Ancient India in Historical Outline*, Routledge and Kegan Paul, London.

———, 1972. 'Adventure into the Unknown', in K. Satchidananda Murty and Ramakrishna Rao (eds.), *Current Trends in Indian Philosophy*, Andhra University Press/Asia Publishing House, Waltair, pp. 152-167.

———, 1979. 'The Line of *Arthashastra* Teachers', *The Indian Historical Review*, V, 1-2, July 1978-January 1979, pp. 1-15; reprinted in *CMI*, pp. 260-278.

Malinar, Angelika, Johannes Beltz and Heiko Frese (eds.), 2004. *Text and Context in the History, Literature and Religion of Orissa*, Manohar, New Delhi.

Marty, Martin E. and R. Scott Appleby, (eds.), 1991-1993. *Fundamentalisms Observed* (1991), *Fundamentalisms and the State: Remaking Polities, Economics, and Militance* (1993) and *Fundamentalisms and Society: Reclaiming the Sciences, the Family, and Education* (1993), University of Chicago Press, Chicago & London.

Nath, Vijay, 2001. *Puranas and Acculturation: A Historico-Anthropological Perspective*, Munshiram Manoharlal, New Delhi.

Pollock, Sheldon, 1994. 'Deep Orientalism? Notes on Sanskrit and Power Beyond the Raj' in Breckenridge and van der Veer 1994, pp. 76-133.

———, 2008: 'Towards a Political Philology: D.D. Kosambi and Sanskrit', *EPW*, XLIII, 30, July-August, 2008.

Preston, James J., 2005. 'Goddess Worship: Theoretical perspectives' in Jones 2005: 3611-3616.

Ratnagar, Shereen, 2008. 'Kosambi's Archaeology', *EPW*, XLIII, 30, July 26-August 1, pp. 71-77.

Sankalia, H.D., 1974. 'The Late Prof. D.D. Kosambi', in *Science and Human Progress: Essays in Honour of Late Prof. D.D.Kosambi, Scientist, Indologist and Humanist*, Prof. D.D. Kosambi Commemoration Committee, Popular Prakashan, Bombay, pp. 335-337.

———, 1979. *Indian Archaeology Today*, Ajanta Publications, Delhi.

Schopen, Gregory, 1997. *Bones, Stones and Buddhist Monks: Collected Papers on the Archaeology, Epigraphy and Texts of Monastic Buddhism in India*, University of Hawai'i Press, Honolulu.

———, 2004. *Buddhist Monks and Business Matters: Still More Papers on Monastic Buddhism in India*, University of Hawai'i Press, Honolulu.

Sharma, R.S., 2007. *Material Culture and Social Formations in Ancient India*, 2nd edition, Macmillan, Delhi-Bangalore.

Shrimali, Krishna Mohan, 1988 (1989). 'Religion, Ideology and Society', Presidential Address, Section I (Ancient India), 49th Session of the Indian History Congress held at Karntaka University, Dharwad in 1988, *Proceedings of the Indian History Congress*, Delhi, pp. 59-102.

———, 1993. 'Reflections on Recent Perceptions of Early Medieval India, *Social Scientist*, 21, 12 (247), pp. 25-39.

———, 2003. 'Constructing an Identity: Forging Hinduism into Harappan Religions', *Social Science Probings*, 15, 1-2, Summer, pp. 1-59.

———, 2010. Review article on Wendy Doniger: *The Hindus: An Alternative History*, Penguin/Viking, New Delhi/New York/Toronto 2009, *Social Scientist*, 38, 7-8 (446-47), July-August, pp. 66-81.

Singh, Upinder, 2010. 'Politics, violence and War in Kamandaka's *Nitisara*', *The Indian Economic and Social History Review*, XLVII, 1, January-March, pp. 29-62.

Thapar, Romila, 1993. 'The Contribution of D.D. Kosambi to Indology', in *Interpreting Early India*, Oxford University Press, Delhi, pp. 89-113.

Wheeler, Mortimer, 1950: 'What Matters in Archaeology', *Antiquity*, 24, 95, pp. 122-130.

Kosambi on Caste

Suvira Jaiswal

A brilliant and innovative mathematician, D.D. Kosambi was impelled to take up the study of Indian history owing to his deep concern with the problems of hunger, poverty and backwardness of the Indian masses. In the preface of his trail-blazing book, *An Introduction to the Study of Indian History*, he quotes official statistics indicating miserably deficient food consumption per adult. 'The grim tale', he points out, 'is made still more tragic by the fact that it is a rare Indian who can afford to buy even the food assigned to him by statistical averages.' (The situation remains grim for the vast majority of Indian people even today!) To change this situation of 'passive suffering that has perpetuated Indian life from generation to generation', we have to reshape and take control of our history, for which the first step is to acquire a scientific understanding of our past with a firm grasp of its material realities. For Kosambi, the study of history was quite indispensable for 'correct thinking' but by history he meant not the 'drums and trumpets' history obsessed with historical episodes, lists of kings and their conquests, but the 'presentation in chronological order of successive changes in the means and relations of production'.[1]

With this perspective it was logical that Kosambi should devote a good deal of attention to the history of the caste system, since 'caste is an important reflection of the actual relations of production, particularly at the time of its formation',[2] and belief in its 'inevitability',[3] an important factor in the maintenance of class structure in India. A proper assessment and analysis of its role was important, for, as he puts it, the relations of production 'are not determined simply by the economic level, nor immediately by the tools, but depend also upon the previous social history of the particular group of men'.[4] The remark is particularly significant in the context of caste. Kosambi was an outstanding Marxist who made a creative use of the tools provided by historical materialism; but it is fallacious to accuse him of economic determinism or of sticking to a mechanical unilinear scheme of periodization and theorizing that 'every society was destined to experience all those forms in a sequence'.[5] His devastating criticism[6] of S.A. Dange's *India from Primitive Communism to Slavery* is well known, and his analytical rigour, intellectual honesty and 'reverence'[7] for facts won admiration from his critics as well. It was his scrupulous regard for the data culled from a variety of primary sources, over which he had a profound mastery, that led him to reject the stage of slavery in Indian history and underline the specific features of Indian feudalism, which, he pointed out, was greatly different from the European type. It also made him probe deeply into the textual and ethnological evidence relating to caste, a neglect of which meant throwing away of 'what little remains to us of source material in Indian History'[8] particularly as the system 'represents nothing more or less than the attempt to fix a class structure at a primitive level of production'.[9]

Why and how did India develop caste, a unique system of social divisions which spread over the entire subcontinent despite the existence of tremendous geographical and racial diversity? Among the current explanations Sir Herbert Risley's theory of the racial origin of castes was perhaps the most influential one. It traced the origin of castes to hypergamous unions between the fair-complexioned Aryan invaders and dark aborigines. The descendants of such mixed groups were ranked hierarchically in proportion to the presence of aboriginal blood in them, which factor ultimately resulted in the formation of endogamous groups or multitudinous *jatis*. Alternative explanations, while rejecting the theory of racial origin, put forward the 'voluntarist' or 'artificialist' view laying emphasis on the role of brahmanas. S.V. Ketkar[10] spoke of the 'spiritual authority' of the brahmanas who organized the entire system on the basis of the religious principle of purity and pollution. Hocart[11] traced its origin in the hierarchy of ritual functions performed by separate groups of people, which groups later crystallized into closed castes. B.R. Ambedkar[12] regarded the system as a 'diabolical contrivance' of the brahmanas to maintain their superior position and suppress and enslave the lower castes. Kosambi, on the other hand, taking a dispassionate view, presented a hypothesis on its origins, which was reconstructed imaginatively through careful collation and analysis of the textual, archaeological and ethnological data available to him.

Kosambi repeatedly emphasizes[13] that the Aryan tribes, which entered India from the north-west, were genetically or physically not homogeneous and did not constitute a 'race' in the biological sense. He points out that the purity of blood does not mean much in the life of tribes.[14] Nevertheless, these nomadic pastoral tribes were conscious of being Aryans in an ethnic sense.[15] The Aryan intrusion does not seem to have been very large in terms of numbers, but they had superior weapons and fast moving horse-driven chariots. They defeated the pre-Aryans of the Indus Valley and destroyed the dams which sustained their agricultural economy. The conquered pre-Aryans, the *dasas* and *dasyus* of the *Rigveda* were reduced to helot-like servitude and not chattel slavery, for the Aryan tribes had not yet developed individual property norms. They herded their cattle as common tribal property and even tilled their land in common. So the conquered population was transformed into a menial labour class serving the conquerors as a whole.

This was the first stage in the emergence of the caste system with the two *varnas*, the Arya and the *dasa*, constituting a 'class division without intermarriage'.[16] However, the gift of a few *dasas* to specific lineage groups by the tribal chieftains – as reflected in the *danastutis* – is indicative of a process of socio-economic differentiation, which is further accentuated as the Aryan tribes move eastward into the doab region using servile labour and improved techniques of food production to found new sedentary settlements. The earlier tribal organization is subverted and relations of production crystallise in the form of four *varna*-castes, namely, the brahmana (priest), kshatriya (warrior and ruler), vaishya (settler/husband man) and shudra (non-Aryan helot);

the last was initially the name of a defeated tribe, but soon acquired a generic significance. However, Kosambi is categorical that *varnas* are not just classes but castes practicing endogamy; and he is critical of those who deny that the four caste system ever existed[17] ignoring the plentiful evidence of Indian sources. Kosambi argues that the original Aryan priesthood was expanded and transformed by the adoption of a number of 'ritually superior' priesthood of the conquered Harappans. The new priesthood with significant non-Aryan elements took over Vedic rituals and sacred lore refashioning them in many cases. Thus a new caste of brahmanas was born, which caste was able to free itself from Aryan tribal bonds and serve chieftains of different tribes transcending tribal boundaries. This also led to the separation of the brahmanas from the kshatriyas – the latter constituting the Aryan tribal chieftains and warriors – and to the practice of endogamy. He writes:

> It seems clear to me that the formation of an internal, Aryan caste system, essentially the separation of the Brahmin in function and discipline from the kshatriya and the setting of both above the householder vaishya, after the *dasas* had been conquered, must have been accelerated by the assimilation of a subjugated priesthood, for otherwise there is no reason for demarcation into endogamous castes.[18]

Kosambi accepted the theory of Aryan invasion current at the time among Indologists and supported it by interpreting Rigvedic myths of Indra's conflict with Vrta in a strikingly original fashion. However, archaeology does not provide any evidence of direct confrontation and destruction of the Indus civilization by the Aryan pastoral tribes. So the invasion theory has been generally abandoned. At the same time, leaving aside the political and 'religious nationalist' contentions, serious scholarship does not subscribe to the view that the Rigvedic Indo-Aryans were of indigenous origin.[19] The balance of evidence is in favour of the view that the Aryans entered India from the north-west perhaps several centuries after the decline of the Harappan culture.

Nonetheless, it is important to note that Kosambi's thesis on the origin of the *varna*-caste organization does not depend on the invasion theory. He concedes the possibility of the pre-Aryan Indus valley civilization having died out because of the shift of the Indus river[20] and talks of the probability of 'centuries of a fearfully hungry existence in the forests'[21] of the pre-Aryan priestly clans.

Nevertheless, he was quite convinced that a section of Indus priests went over to Aryans, who adopted them owing to their superior knowledge of ritual and a religious ideology which had earlier helped the Indus cities to maintain their class structure with the use of minimum violence. This is suggested, according to Kosambi, by the poor weaponry and apparent lack of a strong military or police force in Indus cities. He goes on to argue that initially only a few brahmana priests and a great many shudras were 'extraneous tribal recruits' into Aryan tribes[22] giving rise to the Rigvedic two-*varna* divisions. But the assimilation of indigenous pre-Aryan priests with the Aryan priesthood had far reaching consequences bringing about 'Brahmanaism itself into being'.[23] It facilitated the disintegration of Aryan tribes into a four-*varna*-caste structure defined by the rules of endogamy, as is stated in the citation given above.

Although a few scholarly studies had appeared in the early decades of the twentieth century showing the absorption of foreign, particularly Scythian, priestly lineages in the brahmana *varna* as Karhada[24] or Maga brahmanas,[25] Kosambi's attribution of the very genesis of the brahmana caste to non-Aryan roots was a radical statement quite at variance with the politically loaded popular version of the invasion theory, which interpreted it in terms of the domination of the Aryan invaders over the subjugated autochthonous population, the former constituting the upper castes and the latter condemned and exploited as shudras. Kosambi, on the other hand, convincingly argued that there was assimilation of the Aryan and non-Aryan tribal population at every level and the process has continued throughout the course of Indian history. However, his attempt to trace the very concept of 'brahmana'[26] and religious basis of stratification to Indus culture, and thereby explain the separation of the brahmana and the kshatriya and emergence of an endogamous caste structure, rests on dubious grounds.

It has been contended[27] that the defence system of the Indus cities and their weapons were not so inadequate as Kosambi imagined. Although one need not discount the possibility of religion playing a role in the legitimization of class structure, one cannot ignore the role of force in the maintenance of a class society, and it seems that the institution of slavery did exist in the Indus Valley civilization, which fact implies the use of force. Mesopotamian texts of the period 2350-2000 BC mention slaves being exported from Meluhha,[28] identified generally with the Indus Valley. Hence, it is reasonable to infer that the small two-room quarters excavated at Harappa and Mohenjodaro resembling modern 'coolie lines' were dwellings for slaves engaged in pounding grain and not isolated quarters of menial castes as assumed by Iravati Karve and some other scholars.[29]

However, it is not implausible that some elements of Harappa culture survived its decline, although their precise nature will remain in the realm of speculation until we come across more reliable evidence. But Kosambi's emphasis on the recombination of the Aryans with pre-Aryans and non-Aryans and his assertion that it was a gradual process of acculturation after the initial phase of conflict between the Aryan tribes and non-Aryan local population remains valid. Appearance of chiefs with non-Indo-Aryan names such as Balbutha and Turuska as patrons of Rigvedic seers is an indication of this process,[30] and it is not without significance that these appear in the Eighth Book of the *Rigveda*, which is generally regarded as a later composition.

Moreover, if we leave aside Kosambi's assumption that the infiltration of Indus priesthood played a catalytic role in the formation of an endogamous four-*varna* structure, his basic thesis that there was a recombination of the Aryan and non-Aryan priesthood is supported by later linguistic researches which find substratum influence of Dravidian and Munda languages in Rigvedic Sanskrit. Was it merely due to co-existence and incidental encounters of the speakers of Indo-Aryan with those of non-Indo-Aryan languages? Considering that the hymns manifesting such influences had a religious and ritual significance, it is not unreasonable to assume that there were some non-Aryan or rather Aryanized non-Aryan priest-composers among them. Kosambi cites several examples of the induction of non-Aryan/tribal priests in the brahmana caste, the brahmanas of Nisada-gotra mentioned by Panini is one such example.[31] However, there is no unanimity of linguistic opinion on the subtratum theory, and Madhav M. Deshpande[32] has argued that the non Indo-Aryan traits in the *Rigveda*, particularly the occurrence of retroflexion, were not a part of the language of the original composers, these crept in due to increasingly Dravidianized oral transmission of the text as the Aryans progressed towards the east. Massive retroflexion is seen in the languages of central and eastern parts of the north India; and it is important to note that the only recension of the *Rigveda* available to us is Shakalya, which is based on the Mandukeya version that was prevalent in the north-eastern region of Magadha and had a long history of oral transmission.

Whatever the case may be, Kosambi clearly brings out the mixed character of the brahmana *varna* in one of his early articles written in 1947. He quotes[33] Patanjali's comment on Panini II 2.6, which informs that 'fair skin, cleanliness of habit, brown (eyes), tawny hair – these are the intrinsic qualities that make brahmanahood . . . . When one has seen a certain black (person), the colour of a heap of black beans seated in the market place, one definitely concludes that that is not a brahmana'. This is compared with the information culled from the *Brihadaranyaka Upanisad*,[34] which recommends the brahmana parents to have a certain type of diet if they want to have black complexioned (*shyama*) son with the ability to recite the three Vedas, and to have a different type of diet if one wishes to have a tawny (*kapilah*) son with reddish brown eyes (*pingalah*). Kosambi comes to the conclusion that divergent perception of the physical attributes of a brahmana in the two accounts is indicative not only of regional difference but also of the fact that the brahmanas of eastern U.P., the cradle of

Upanishadic discourse, were a mixed lot. He is quite emphatic that soon after initial confrontations the new Aryan colonies, which came up with increased food production as a result of transition from pastoral-raider to settled agrarian economy, had a mixed population, and these later developed into exclusive 'Aryan' tribes. For, now 'Aryan' came to mean a way of living based on plough cultivation.

This was a new mode of production, as in his view, the pre-Aryans of the Indus valley used harrow and did not know plough-cultivation, which was introduced by the Aryans. Kosambi was not aware of the existence of a pre-Harappan ploughed field excavated at Kalibangan in Rajasthan in the nineteen-sixties, and he strongly discounted the possibility of the Munda speaking Austro-Asiatics having any knowledge of plough agriculture.[35] However, it is now generally conceded that the term *langala* meaning plough occurring in the *Rigveda* (IV 57.4) is a proto-Munda loan word, the hymn itself is perhaps a late interpolation.[36] The Rigvedic Aryans relied mainly on pastoralism, which had high prestige value, but Kosambi's basic argument that the Aryan way of life was produced by a mixing of the Aryan and the non-Aryan and the four-*varna* structure was rooted in the transition from a pastoral to plough-based agricultural economy remains valid.

The separation of the brahmana and the kshatriya, fragmentation of social structure through the practice of endogamy by each individual unit and other behavioral restrictions have given a unique character to brahmananical society, roots of which are often seen as embedded in the religious ideology of purity and pollution. Louis Dumont built the entire edifice of his *Homo Hierarchicus*[37] on this presumption, contrasting the Hindu world view with the western, described as Homo-equalius.[38]

Kosambi, on the other hand, looked for an explanation in the specific historical circumstances suggested by the available evidence. He presented a hypothesis that the adoption of the Indus priesthood by the Aryan warrior-chiefs gave rise to a separate brahmana *varna* with the recognition of the latter as rulers-kshatriyas; and this distinction was solidified through the practice of endogamy. However, in my view the separation of the *brahma* and *ksatra* categories can be explained more convincingly without attributing it to the pecularities of a 'hierarchical mind' as is done by Dumont or presuming a hypothetical crossing over of Harappan priests to Aryan invaders. It has been noted[39] in several cases that among pastoral tribes two elite categories emerge: the warriors, who specialize in cattle-raids while protecting their own and thus increase the cattle wealth of their tribe, and priests, who specialize in ritual-sacrifice of cattle, offering to gods the most valued items of their society and thus help in increase of cattle-wealth through divine favour.

The Rigvedic evidence shows that initially these two categories were functional and not hereditary or kin-based. But later with the greater availability of surplus through sedentary agriculture-cum-pastoral economy and its unequal distribution, the rights and privileges of the priest and warrior groups were appropriated on a hereditary basis; and there was interdependence and cooperation between the two groups. Vedic sacrificial ritual became a very elaborate affair and its specialized knowledge was confined to priestly lineages.

Kosambi seems to be right in interpreting the term '*varna*' in its early Rigvedic uses as a mark of ethnic distinction but later acquiring a sense of class-cum-caste marked by genealogical and kin boundaries at the disintegration of tribal ethos. As long as the brahmana and kshatriya were open, functional categories, the term '*varna*' is not applied to them, and even the order of precedence of those who engage in priestly activities over those who function as *ksatra* is not observed at least in one hymn (*Rigveda* I 113.6),[40] which invokes the goddess Ushas to wake up people engaged in different activities. This is indicative of the solidification of the *varna* categories from functional divisions.

Textual evidence clearly suggests the separation of *varnas* on the basis of function, rank and the practice of hypergamy/endogamy, the last feature being essential instrumentalization of the female sex for the maintenance of a hierarchical patriarchal order. The so-called 'confusion' among the brahmanical law-givers in their indiscriminate use of the terms '*varna*' and '*jati*' is rooted in the fact that *jatis* emerge as separate sub-groups within the *varnas* through various historical processes; but the assimilation of the marginal communities into the *varna* system was possible only by observing its value system and maintaining their boundaries. It is for this reason that the law-giver Manu[41] emphatically asserts at one place (X 4) that the brahmana, kshatriya and vaishya *varnas* are *dvijatis* and shudra is *ekajati* and there is no fifth (*varna*) but a little later enumerates fifteen *hina varnas* (*varnanpanchadashaiva tu*, X 31), when he really means fifteen low *jatis* or castes.

Kosambi has been roundly criticized for his alleged 'unscientific' use of the category of tribe, mistaking hunter-gatherers as tribes, whereas analytically 'tribe as a social formation came into existence only with the coming of agriculture'.[42] Shireen Ratnagar quotes the work of Marshall D. Sahlins[43] to buttress this point. It is curious that in the very monograph she cites for reference, Sahlins devotes a section discussing 'Hunting, Fishing and Gathering Tribes' and remarks that the western fringe of North America 'was occupied in aboriginal times by *tribes without agriculture or husbandry*'![44]

No doubt anthropologists distinguish analytically between band, tribe as a segmentary system, and chiefdoms. But, as Andre Beteille wrote in 1980,[45] by and large anthropologists have continued to apply the term tribe 'to all three modes of tribal organization'. He goes on to add, 'the several hundred units that comprise the Scheduled Tribes of India cover all the modes of tribal organization from the band to chiefdom'. Kosambi's main concern was to investigate the dynamics of caste society which gradually engulfed the entire subcontinent absorbing tribal societies at various stages of development and not with the details of the internal structure of individual tribes. He wrote:

> *The entire course of Indian history shows tribal elements being fused into a general society.* This phenomenon, which lies at the very foundation of the most striking Indian social feature,

namely caste, is also the great basic fact of ancient Indian history.[46]

The absorption of tribes into the mainstream caste society has been a topic of engrossing interest among the sociologists, most of whom have analysed it as a cultural phenomenon facilitated through a process of sanskritization.[47] Kosambi showed that in pre-British times the crucial factor was integration with the dominant mode of production, 'The advance of plough-using agrarian village economy over tribal India', he writes, 'is a great historical achievement by itself'.[48]

Kosambi ascribed a pioneering role to the brahmana caste in this transition. Initially it helped in the internal disintegration of Aryan tribes and consolidation of the four *varna* structure. Ritually restricted from making a living out of the 'plough or bow', those who could not find adequate employment in the existing settlements penetrated the forested regions interacting with the food-gatherers in the manner of Baka Dalbhya, taking note of non-Aryan tribal rituals, and the Kosalan brahmana Bavari, a contemporary of the Buddha, who established his hermitage on the river Godavari in the Assaka country. The process received a major fillip in Gupta and post-Gupta times when brahmanas were given tax-free land in tribal areas to cultivate it themselves or have it cultivated. Acting as pioneers and educators the brahmanas employed aboriginal tribes to do the actual work of cultivation, providing them a more secure means of livelihood but assimilating them as a cultivating caste of low status in the manner of Gavadas of the Western Ghats.

Kosambi was of the view that the Indian method of organizing production deprived the primary producer of his surplus with the minimum use of violence. 'Caste and smrtis adopted or replaced totem and taboo with more power than the sword or bow' and obviated the need for chattel slavery.[49] Writing about the same time, B.R. Ambedkar forcefully argued[50] that the *de facto* condition of untouchables in India under the caste system was far worse than that of the slaves in the Roman Empire. Unlike a Roman slave, an untouchable was never allowed to take up clean and intellectual professions like that of a doctor, teacher, artist, etc., nor could he hope for emancipation from the 'unfree social order' in which he was born. A sharp divide separated the *savarnas*, which included the shudras, from the untouchables, the *avarnas*, whose labour was freely exploited but who could never be allowed to cross the line. And unlike the Roman slaves the untouchables did not have any security of job or minimum earning. In our view, the concept of untouchability is a logical extension of the social hierarchy envisaged in terms of 'pure' and 'impure' functions. The depressed groups were condemned to carry out filthy and menial work on a hereditary basis. But its main function has been to ensure the availability of a large labour force for hard agricultural labour with no right to ownership of land or even recognition as regular peasants.

Scholars have noted the close connection between the spread of agrarian villages, intensive cultivation, and increase in untouchable groups dependent on agriculture.[51] It has been argued[52] that the availability of untouchable labour helped in diffusing the tension of the direct producers, the vaishyas and the shudras, and thus contributed to the stability of the social order. In fact, in south India, there are some 'untouchable' castes such as the Pallars, who have no other occupation except agricultural labour. Kosambi had concentrated mainly on early north Indian sources in the formulation of his thesis. But the emergence of a large number of *ati-shudra* castes or castes considered outside the *varna* system as *avarnas* living on the margins of peasant settlements and providing the essential drudge labour is an early medieval phenomenon.[53]

That brahmannical ideology did succeed to a certain extent in securing its acceptance among the depressed castes and mitigating violent class confrontations need not be gainsaid.[54] But Kosambi is very explicit about the class role of the brahmana caste. 'This class was perhaps the most convenient tool of the ruling power, whether indigenous or foreign, in the enslavement of the Indian people'.[55] He quotes[56] Manu's dictum (VIII 148) that the king should use force and compel the primary producers, the vaishyas and the shudras, to perform their prescribed duties. The brahmanical code of conduct had to be buttressed by the temporal power of the kshatriya; and the worker, the lowly shudra, was deprived of access to knowledge and learning with much of his superstitious beliefs, practices and rituals left intact in the process of acculturation. Caste ideology limited the options available to brahmana intelligentsia too for earning a living. It had to be forever in search of a generous patron or could be reduced to dire poverty and hunger. Nevertheless, as an auxilliary class appended to the ruling class its literary creations reflect a preoccupation with the interests and inclinations of the upper classes and not of the masses. Sanskrit was the language of the ritual and of upper classes and it was kept alive by the brahmana priests and poets, who wrote voluminous books on ritual, theology and philosophy and developed intricate literary forms for the amusement of the leisured classes. But, 'there is no Sanskrit work of any use to the blacksmith, potter, carpenter, weaver, ploughman'.[57]

Kosambi's characterization of classical Sanskrit poetry as class literature produced and preserved by the brahmanas has been criticized by Sheldon Pollock[58] on the ground that Buddhists and Jainas too wrote it. Moreover, a 13th century anthology mentions eulogistically a poet of the potter caste named Ghrona and another of the chandala caste named Divakara, the latter adorning the court of king Harsha and considered equal to Bana and Mayura. So Pollock argues that Sanskrit was accessible to a much wider range of people than Kosambi supposed, and his assertion that Sanskrit literary culture is upper class culture is seriously flawed.

Nevertheless, it is undeniable that the adoption of Sanskrit language by Mahayana Buddhism[59] and Jainism is symptomatic of the growing penetration of brahmanas and elitism in these religions. The Jainas developed a caste system similar to that of brahmanism. In the *Adipurana* of Jinasena and *Adishvaracharita* of Hemachandra, Adinatha Rishabha creates kshatriya, vaishya and shudra *varnas* from his arms, thighs and feet respectively, but brahmanas are created by his son and successor Bharata for practicising religious duties according to Jaina precepts.[60] The Jainas were as vehement as the brahmanical law givers in denouncing the miscegenation of castes and prescribing the pursuit of occupation on a hereditary basis[61] and show similar prejudice against shudras and artisans by excluding them from religious initiation[62] and regarding the Chandalas as impure.[63] No doubt the Jaina emphasis on the importance of scriptural knowledge in attaining liberation encouraged literacy and education among the higher castes, but the Sanskrit compositions of Jaina and Buddhist monks show the same upper class influence[64] upon erudition as remarked by Kosambi.

The question of the identity of the poet Divakara is much more complex. Pollock takes him to be a Chandala, but the verse in the *Suktimuktavali* speaks of him as a Matanga. Matangas were an aboriginal tribe often bracketed with Medas, Kiratas, Savaras, Pulindas, Chandalas and Nisadas in the brahmanical sources.[65] The 'untouchable' caste of Mangs of Maharashtra has very likely originated from them. The brahmanical ideologues looked down upon the aboriginal tribes as *mlecchas* outside the *varna* system, but their reduction to *Ati-shudra* status was a gradual affair consequent to their assimilation in the expanding agrarian society of the Middle Ages. It has been pointed out that even in late medieval period only a section of the tribe had become *Ati-shudra*, a majority of the tribesmen were still hillmen with some of them holding the office of naiks and guards.[66] In the *Mahabharata* such jungle tribes are described as degraded kshatriyas,[67] and king Prasenjit of Kosala, a contemporary of the Buddha and a great patron of the brahmanas, is said to have been born in a Matanga family (*Matanga-kula*).[68] Social attitudes towards tribesmen were much more liberal than towards the *Ati-shudras*; and if the identification of Matanga Divakara with the Jaina author Manatunga, the writer of the *Bhaktimara-stotra* is accepted,[69] apparently this solitary exception was made possible through a more liberal attitude of earlier Jainism.

However, Kosambi's staggering command over textual

material notwithstanding, he was no arm-chair academic developing his theories in ivory tower isolation. Through his field work and keen observation he was able to demonstrate how and why Brahmanism could modify and absorb primitive symbols and rites giving a sense of continuity but transforming their inner essence; whereby the tools and taboos devised by primitive peoples to control nature or increase production become instruments for maintaining the status quo in favour of a definite class, smothering opposition and absorbing 'any destructive excess of social energy',[70] thus reinforcing the ideal of an unchanging caste structure. The ideological superstructure which evolved in this manner integrated the local with pan-Indian cultural traditions accommodating social change within the *varna* hierarchy. Thus the reality of social change was cloaked in the fictitious legends of continuity, resulting in an apparent negation of history and producing a mentality which attached utmost importance to form while ignoring the content.

Kosambi ascribes crucial role to religious beliefs in the sustenance of caste. He argues[71] that in India, because of the comparative ease with which primitive communities could survive on food-gathering, they co-existed side by side the food producing communities, and their productive relationships were regulated through religion and superstition, i.e., through caste, rather than violence as compared to the history of Europe or America. Initially it helped in agrarian expansion, but later in the stagnant village economy it imposed the dual burden of caste and class upon the worker, becoming a major hindrance to progress.

Kosambi does not have the naïve faith that a change in the mode of production will automatically change ideas in people's heads. He writes, 'it is not necessarily true that caste will disappear with modern means of production any more than the feudal ideology disappeared from Japanese society with modern machinery'.[72] Indeed, 'no Materialist can afford to neglect the effect of ideas upon social development'.[73] Nevertheless, he seems to be groping for the correct diagnosis of the strong hold of the caste ideology. At places he attributes its survival to 'historical inertia' and expresses the view that the institution could be abolished 'only by fundamental alteration of the production mechanism – industrialization'.[74] Echoing Marx, he states[75] that when railways jumble people together and technical secrets of caste-guilds are no longer of any use owing to modern factories producing better and cheaper goods, the system is reduced to being 'least effective; and caste hierarchy is destroyed'.[76] But he cautions that caste may continue to persist as a 'set of political groupings' creating social tensions under the new bourgeois-democratic forms.[77]

The problem is that the ideology of caste legitimizes the socio-economic and cultural deprivation of not only the workers and primary producers who occupy the lower rungs of the caste ladder, but also of women in general. It is a highly gendered system which cannot survive without patriarchal control over female sexuality and her autonomy. No doubt certain aspects of the caste system such as the notion of hierarchy of castes and hereditary pursuit of occupations have withered or are withering away under the onslaught of the capitalist mode of production, but caste endogamy still persists as this feature of caste is not in contradiction with the capitalist mode of production. It survives on the custom of arranged marriages impregnated with capitalist values and provides fodder to identity politics in a highly competitive mode of production.[78] Marxist historiography of caste has yet to take full cognizance of its gendered role.

NOTES

1. D.D. Kosambi, *The Culture and Civilisation of Ancient India in Historical Outline* (hereafter *Culture*) Routledge and Kegan Paul, London, 1965, p. 10.
2. D.D. Kosambi, *Combined Methods in Indology and Other Writings*, edited by B.D. Chattopadhyaya (hereafter *CMI*), Oxford University Press, Delhi, 2002, p. 804.
3. *CMI*, p. 741.
4. D.D. Kosambi, *Exasperating Essays: Exercises in the Dialectical Method*, published by Shri R.P. Nene, Pune, 1957, reprint, 1986, p. 2.
5. Sheldon Pollock, 'Towards a Political Philology: D.D. Kosambi and Sanskrit', *Economic and Political Weekly* (hereafter *EPW*), July 26, 2008, p. 56.
6. 'Marxism and Ancient Indian Culture', *Annals of the Bhandarkar Oriental Research Institute*, XXIX, 1949, pp. 271-77.

7 Daniel H.H. Ingalls, 'My Friendship with D.D. Kosambi', in *Indian Society: Historical Probings. In Memory of D.D. Kosambi*, edited by R.S. Sharma and V. Jha, Peoples Publishing House, New Delhi, 1974, p. 26.

8 *CMI*, p. 804.

9 Ibid., p. 415.

10 S.V. Ketkar, *History of Caste in India: Evidence of the Laws of Manu on the social Condition in India and Examined with an Appendix on Radical Defects of Ethnology*, first published 1909, reprint, Rawat Publications, Jaipur, 1979.

11 A.M. Hocart, *Caste: A Comparative Study*, Methuen, London, 1950. Kosambi's comment on it is characteristic: 'A.M. Hocart's *Caste* (London, 1950) is pure theory undiluted with reality', CMI, p. 324, n. 3. He is more appreciative of Hocart's *Kingship* (London, 1927), but points out that Hocart's evidence comes from a much later period. CMI, p. 164, n. 33.

12 B.R. Ambedkar, *The Untouchables*, first edition 1948, reprinted in *Dr. Babasaheb Ambedkar: Writings and Speeches*, edited by Vasant Moon, Education Department, Government of Maharashtra, Bombay, Vol. 7, p. 239.

13 *An Introduction to the Study of Indian History* (hereafter *Introduction*), Popular Prakashan, Bombay, 1956, pp. 75-7, *Myth and Reality: Studies in the Formation of Indian Culture*, pp. 68, 76. Also see his article 'Indo-Aryan Nose Index' (translated from his Russian Article 'Indo-Ariiskii Nosovoi' *Sovetskaya Etnografia*, 1958, pp. 39-57), *CMI*, pp. 524-49.

14 *CMI*, p. 533.

15 *Introduction*, pp. 76-77.

16 *CMI*, pp. 62, 123f. Kosambi had developed the broad contours of his theory as early as 1938. In his 'The Emergence of National Characteristics Among Three Indo-European Peoples' published in *The Annals of Bhandarkar Oriental Institute*, Vol. XX, 1938-39, pp. 195-206 (*CMI*, pp. 753-63) he wrote 'The Caste system has a racial origin, as is clear from the theoretical ban on intermarriages and from name *Varna* (colour, complexion) for caste'. Later he refined his concept of 'race' and insisted on the distinct ethnic identities of the Aryans and pre-Aryans.

17 See his criticism of the views expressed in the *Oxford History of India*, and of Paul Rosa's *Caste and Class in India*, *CMI*, pp. 189, 773-89. For a critique of this view, Survira Jaiswal, *Caste: Origin Function and Dimensions of Change*, Manohar Publisher, Delhi, 1998, pp. 43-45.

18 *CMI*, p. 126. Also see ibid., pp. 117-8.

19 For an excellent review of the current research from the point of view of linguistics, Madhav M. Deshpande, 'Aryan Origins: Brief History of Linguistic Arguments', in *India: Historical Beginnings and the Concept of the Aryan*, National Book Trust, India, New Delhi, 2006, pp. 98-156.

20 *CMI*, p. 200.

21 Ibid., pp. 778-79.

22 Ibid., p. 106. Elsewhere he explains that by 'Brahmanism' he does not mean wholesale recruitment of pre-Aryan clans, but the formation of clan-groups by the adoption of some conquered priests. *CMI*, p. 426.

23 *CMI*, p. 317. Romila Thapar too in her *Lineage to State* regards the brahmana and the shudra as addenda to the initial structure of Aryan tribes and speaks of the earlier Arya-*dasa* dichotomy deriving from ethnic, linguistic and cultural differences being replaced by the Arya-shudra dichotomy in later Vedic times, *Ancient Indian Social History*, Orient Longman, Delhi, 1989, p. 47. For a critique of these views, see Suvira Jaiswal, *Caste*, pp. 188-204.

24 Jarl Charpentier, 'A Note on Prathama Saka Brahmanas', *Indian Antiquary*, Vol. 53 (1924), p. 124.

25 J.N. Bhattacharya, *Hindu Caste and Sects: An Exposition of the Origin of the Hindu Caste System and the Bearing of the Sects towards each other and towards other Religions systems* (1896), reprint Calcutta, 1968.

26 'Early Brahmins and Brahminism', *The Journal of the Bombay Branch of the Royal Asiatic Society*, Vol. 23 (1947), pp. 39-46.

27 Irfan Habib, *The Indus Civilization: A Peoples History of India*, Vol. 2, Aligarh Historian's Society, Tulika Books, Delhi, 2003, pp. 60-61.

28 Ibid., p. 49.

29 For a detailed critique of such views, Jaiswal, *Caste*, p. 43f. Interestingly Kosambi, while comparing them with parallel Mespotamian excavations, regards these as dwellings of slaves. *Introduction*, p. 55.

30 Michael Witzel, 'Early Indian History: Linguistic and Textual Parametres', in George Erdosy (ed.), *The Indo-Aryans of Ancient South Asia: Language, Material Culture and Ethnicity*, W.de Gruyter, New York, 1995, p. 108.

31 D.D. Kosambi, *CMI*, p. 320. For more such examples, S. Jaiswal, *Caste*, pp. 59-61.

32 M.M. Deshpande, 'Vedic Aryans, non-Vedic Aryans and non-Aryans: Judging the Linguistic Evidence of the Veda' in George Erdosy, *The Indo-Aryans of Ancient South Asia*, pp. 67-84.

33 *CMI*, p. 87f., *Introduction*, p. 127.

34 *Brihadaranyaka Upanisad*, IV 4.14-16. The text has prescriptions for the birth of a learned daughter too.

35 D.D. Kosambi, 'Combined Methods in Indology', *Indo-Iranian Journal*, VI (1963), p. 192. However a study of the types of ploughs used in India led Jaya Datta Gupta and B.N. Saraswati to suggest that 'the ploughs of India are likely to line up with east and south-east Asia in historical relationship', and philological investigations could provide useful clues. They draw attention to the work of Przyluski on *langala* in this regard. Nirmal Kumar Bose (ed.), *Peasant Life in India: A Study in Indian Unity and Diversity*, Anthropological Survey of India, Memoir No. 8, Calcutta, 1961, p. 29.

36 S. Jaiswal, 'Reconstructing History from the Rgveda: A Paradigm Shift?' *Social Science Probings*, Vol. 18 no.2, Dec. 2006, pp. 7-. Also see *Caste* pp. 136-37.

37 Louis Dumont, *Homo Hierarchicus: The Caste System and Its Implications* (1966), completely revised English edition, Oxford University Press, Delhi, 1988.

38 I have presented a critique of his views elsewhere. See S. Jaiswal, 'Caste in the Socio-Economic Framework of Early India' Presidential Address, Ancient India

Section, *Proceedings of the Indian History Congress*, 38th Session, Bhubaneswar, 1977, p. 25; Jaiswal, *Caste*, pp. 34-8.

39 For a detailed discussion, Suriva Jaiswal, 'Varna Ideology and Social Change', *Social Scientist*, Vol. 19, Nos. 3-4 (1991), pp. 41-48, Idem, *Caste*, pp. 147-8; 195-6; 226.

40 I have used *Rigveda Samhita*, edited (with Hindi Translation) by Pandit Ramgovind Trivedi, 9 Vols., Chowkhamba Vidya Bhavan, Varanasi, 1991.

41 *Manusmriti*, fifth edition, Chowkhamba Sanskrit Sansthan, Varanasi, 1997.

42 Shereen Ratnagar, 'Kosambi's Archaeology', *EPW*, July 26, 2008, p. 75.

43 Marshall D. Sahlins, *Tribesmen*, Prentice-Hall, Englewood Cliffs, New Jersey, 1968.

44 Ibid., p. 39. Italics added.

45 Andre Beteille, 'On the concept of Tribe', *International Social Science Journal*, Vol. 32, no. 4 ,1980, pp. 825-28. In his monograph on the Chenchus published in 1943 Furer-Haimendorf speaks of them as a tribe which is more or less non-agricultural. He mentions tribal societies of India representing every stage from hunting-gathering to primitive agriculture in his article 'Cultural Strata in the Deccan', *Man*, Vol. 48 (1948). Kunal Chakrabarti rightly remarks that Kosambi's occasional use of the term 'savage' for tribes is not judgmental and was possibly borrowed from contemporary anthroplogical usage (*EPW*, July 26, 2008, p. 69). Perhaps it was influenced by Engels' *The Origin of the Family, Private Property and the State*, wherein 'Savagery' constitutes a prehistoric stage.

46 *Introduction*, p. 25. Emphasis in the original.

47 S. Jaiswal, *Caste*, pp. 99-100.

48 *Introduction*, p. 11.

49 *CMI*, p. 310.

50 *Dr. Babasaheb Ambedkar: Writings and Speeches*, Vol. 5, pp. 9-18. Devaraj Chanana too pointed out that untouchable labour was cheaper than that of the slaves. *Slavery in Ancient India*, Peoples Publishing House, Delhi, 1960, reprint, 1990, p. 177.

51 Kathleen Gough, *Rural Society in South-East India*, Cambridge University Press, Cambridge, 1981; Robert Deliege, *The Untouchables of India*, translated from the French by Nora Scott, Berg Publishers, Oxford, 1999.

52 Gen'ichi Yamazaki, 'Social Discrimination in Ancient India and its Transition to the Medieval Period', in H. Kotani (ed.), *Caste System, Untouchability and the Depressed*, Manohar Publishers, New Delhi, 1997, p. 11.

53 For example the caste of Charmakara (Chamar). See Suvira Jaiswal, 'Caste, Gender and Ideology in the Making of India', General President's Address, *Proceedings of the Indian History Congress*, 68th Session, Delhi, 2007, p. 10f; Joan P. Mencher, 'The Caste System Upside Down, or the Not-so-Mysterious East', *Current Anthropology*, Vol. 15, no. 4, December, 1974. For Chamars working as agricultural labourers in medieval times, see Masanori Sato, 'The Chamars of South-Eastern Rajasthan, A.D. 1650-1800' in H. Kotani (ed.), *Caste System, Untouchability and the Depressed*, pp. 34-35; Irfan Habib, 'The Peasants in

Indian History' in *Social Change in India*, Marx Centenary Volume, *Social Scientist*, pp. 44-8.

[54] In a unique and outstanding autobiography written in a dispassionate manner, Dr Tulsi Ram of the Jawaharlal Nehru University, himself a dalit, recounts that his father, a *haravaha* (bonded ploughman) of a brahmana landlord left for Asansol to work in the collieries owing to some domestic problem. However, he soon returned home to work in the fields of the landlord owing to his blind belief that he would be guilty of committing *brahmahatya* (killing of a brahmana) if he abstained from his traditional duties. '*Murdahiya* V', *Tadbhav*, Vol. 20, July 2009, p. 157. Traditionally the 'untouchable' dependents even espoused the quarrels and factions of their upper-caste landlords practicing vertical solidarity rather than mobilizing horizontally to rebel against their exploitation. R. Deliege, *The Untouchables of India*, pp. 62-77.

[55] *Exasperating Essays*, p. 87.

[56] *CMI*, p. 332.

[57] *Introduction*, p. 266.

[58] Pollock, 'Towards a Political Philology'.

[59] For Mahayana Buddhism, see *Introduction*, p. 246; Suvira Jaiswal, 'Caste, Gender and Ideology in the Making of India', Section VII.

[60] U.N. Ghoshal, *A History of Indian Political Ideas*, Oxford University Press, Madras, 1966, pp. 456-62.

[61] Malini Adiga, *The Making of Southern Karknataka: Society, Polity and Culture in the Early Medieval Period, A.D. 400-1030*, Orient Longman, Hyderabad, 2006, p. 259.

[62] Ram Bhushan Prasad Singh, *Jainism in Early Medieval Karnataka* (c. A.D. 500-1200), Motilal Banarsidass, Delhi, 1975, pp. 73, 82, 138-39.

[63] In the *Nitivakyamrita* of Somadeva Suri the water from a tank used by Chandalas is described as unusable, quoted in J.P. Jain, *The Jaina Sources of the History of Ancient India* (100 B.C.-A.D. 900), Munshiram Manoharlal, Delhi, 1964, p. 215.

[64] D.N. Jha, 'Damodar Dharmanand Kosambi: A Scholar Extraordinaire', *The Marxist* (Theoretical Quarterly of the Communist Party of India (Marxists), Vol. XXIV. 4. (October-December, 2006), p. 8; reproduced in the present volume.

[65] *Amarakosha* II 10.19. The list is of lowly tribal peoples living beyond the edge of settlements.

[66] Hiroyuki Kotani, 'Ati Shudra Castes in the Medieval Deccan', in Kotani (ed.), *Caste System, Untouchability and the Depressed*, pp. 71-72.

[67] *Mahabharata*, XII 297, and XIII 35 (Vulgate), quoted by Kosambi, *CMI*, p. 223.

[68] *Introduction*, p. 150, *CMI*, p. 223-24.

[69] G.V. Devasthali in R.C. Majumdar (ed.), *The Classical Age, The History and Culture of the Indian People*, Vol. III, Bharatiya Vidya Bhavan, Bombay, 3rd Ed., 1970, p. 313.

[70] *CMI*, p. 208.

[71] *Culture*, p. 34.

[72] *CMI*, p. 774.

[73] *Culture*, p. 28.

[74] *Introduction*, p. 361.

[75] *CMI*, p. 415. On Louis Dumont's mistaken representation of Marx's views on the impact of industrialization on caste, see Suvira Jaiswal cited in note 38 above.

[76] *Culture*, p. 52.

[77] Ibid.

[78] S. Jaiswal, 'Caste, Gender and Ideology in the Making of India', section VIII.

Kosambi on Sanskrit

Kesavan Veluthat

D.D. Kosambi was doubtless among the finest representatives of the new tradition of Sanskrit scholarship in India which combined in it the best aspects of classical scholarship and the new disciplined method of philology and text criticism. While deeply rooted in the Indian tradition of scholarship, Kosambi brought to bear on the study of the language and its literature not only the modern scientific outlook which developed in the West but also a comprehensive philosophy of social development. He was the first to analyse the Sanskrit language and literature within the framework of historical materialism.

In 'Steps in Science', his famous essay which also traces his intellectual autobiography in some sense, Kosambi gives an account of how he came to the study of ancient Indian history and culture. He had taken up the analysis of coins to solve a problem in statistics and he used the famous Taxila hoards for this purpose. A question, outside the scope of his problem at hand, about who issued these coins and who used them, occurred to him. He saw that 'the written sources display a shocking discordance. The *Puranas*, Buddhist and Jaina records often give different names for the same king.' So he decided to go into the records himself, but

> [s]tudy of the records meant some mastery of Sanskrit, of which I had absorbed a little through the pores without regular study. Other preoccupations made it impossible to spend as much time as the average student on the classical idiom. So, the same method was adopted as for study of statistics: to take up a specific work, of which the simplest was Bhartrhari's epigrams (*Subhasitas*). The supposed

> philosophy of Bhartrhari, as glorified by the commentators, was at variance with his poetry of frustration and escape. By pointing this out in an essay, which made every god-fearing Sanskritist who read it shudder, I had fallen into Indology, as it were, through the roof.[1]

In the present paper, we examine Kosambi's engagement with Sanskrit – we ask whether he had really absorbed Sanskrit only through the pores, and go from there to an examination of what he had to say on the language and literature in the context of what he saw as the feudal society in India. On evidence of his own writings and reports of those who knew him, modesty does not appear to have been one of his weaknesses; yet there is reason to believe that his own statements about his facility in Sanskrit are most certainly an understatement. An assessment of his interpretations of Sanskrit passages in historical analyses and text-critical and other contributions directly on the language and literature is beyond my competence; I confine myself to his general proficiency in the language and insights about the literature. The uncharacteristic modesty that Kosambi has shown in the passage quoted above is all the more surprising because there are instances where his lack of modesty exposes his lack of mastery, as in the case of his unjustifiably devastating review of H.D. Sankalia's book.[2]

What then can we make of the modest claims that Kosambi makes of the immoderate command he had over the Sanskrit language and his thorough familiarity with its literature? It may be useful to look at some of his significant observations on Sanskrit – both the language and its literature. In one of his very first essays on Sanskrit literature, published as early as 1941, on the quality of renunciation in Bhartrihari's poetry, the one which is said to have catapulted Kosambi into the field of Indology, he shows a remarkable competence in the language, grammatically and in terms of the familiarity with the literary treasures available there.[3] Again, his discussion of the authorship of the *Shatakatrayi* (published in 1945) demonstrates, apart from his critical abilities, a sound scholarship of the language and even the intricacies of its grammar.[4] The detailed comparisons of the extant versions of the *Shatakatrayi* (published as early as 1942), particularly in the elaborate tables and charts, shows how systematic analysis coupled with a proficiency in the language can be superior to impressionistic statements based on a smattering of the language.[5] So also, his work on *Mahabharata*, especially the *parvasaügraha* (1946) shows a similar thoroughness.[6] The elaborate charts, prepared by E.D. Kulkarni at the instance of Kosambi, are a standing monument to the rigour and discipline shown in scientific analysis of texts, something which his training in mathematics and exposure to modern western text criticism must have inspired. So also, his work on fixing the text of the *Arthashastra* shows his mastery over the language.[7]

At another level, we see that Kosambi had gone into the problem of Sanskrit in its relation with Prakrit/Pali. In his masterly discussion of the Sanskrit equivalent of two Pali words, namely, *sammapasam* occurring in a *gatha* in the *Kosalasamyutta* and Vassakara, the name of the chief minister of Ajatashatru, Kosambi displays brilliant knowledge of both the languages.[8] This goes beyond just etymology and semantic jugglery; it carries with it rare historical insights gained through an erudite knowledge of the texts starting from the Vedic. His detailed introduction and the critical edition of the *Chintamanisaranika* of Dashabala is evidence of not only his scholarship in Sanskrit but his competence in Indian astronomy learned through Sanskrit.[9] The critical scholarship, apart from the social scientific insights, exhibited in his essay 'Introducing Vidyakara's *Subhasitaratnakosa*', is also evidence of his extraordinary mastery of the language.[10] All this would show that Kosambi's knowledge of Sanskrit went beyond what could have been 'acquired through the pores'.

Against this background, it is worthwhile to look at some of his significant observations about the Sanskrit language and literature in general and some texts in particular. It should be noted that his appreciation of Sanskrit language and literature was not done in a mood of idle literary interest, whatever that may mean. His analysis was informed by a firm commitment to a social and political ideology – what is called *littérature engagé.* He was sure that literature should be read within the material milieu which produced it. As he says in 'Steps in Science':

> No Marxist would claim that science can be independent of the social system within which the scientist must function. Much the same treatment may be given to literature. Disregarding oversimplification, can one say that Shakespeare's plays manifest the rise of the Elizabethan proto-bourgeoisie, when the said dramas are full of kings, lords and princes? The answer is yes. Compare Hamlet or Richard the Third with the leading characters in the *Chanson de Roland.* Not only Pistol, Nym and Bardolph but the fattest Shakespearean parts like Shylock and Falstaff are difficult to visualise in feudal literature. The characters in those plays have a 'modern' psychology, which accounts for their appeal to the succeeding bourgeoisie, and hence the survival value of the dramas themselves. Troilus and Cressida are not feudal characters any more than they are Homeric; Newton's Latin prose and archaic geometrical proofs in the *Principia* make that work unreadable, but do not make it Roman or Greek science.[11]

Kosambi, however, does not elaborate this point with reference to Indian literature in that essay.[12] Moreover, it can be seen that whatever he has written on literature in general and Sanskrit literature in particular is informed by the understanding that literature, like science, should be understood as a function of the age in which it is produced. Even his very first essay on the subject, on the quality of renunciation in Bhartrihari's poetry mentioned above, bears testimony to this. The concluding paragraphs in this essay try to answer a disturbing question: 'How is it that the new literature in those countries where such [socialist] revolutions have been completed does not yet show the same relative power in the way of new authors and impressive new literary forms that may be seen with the earlier changes?'[13] He suggests that in all previous cases, the new class had formed in the womb of the old and that it had begun to express its new ideals, needs and aspirations in literary form because political expression was not feasible in those early days. Obviously, this was not possible in a socialist revolution as the working class, the vast and illiterate majority, assumes power there. From here he goes on to say that 'the great poet in a class society must not only express the position and aspirations of an important class, but must also transcend the class barriers, whether explicitly or implicitly.'[14] It is here that he finds his poet lacking: Bhartrihari does not lay bare the structure of society, pointing the way to its future generation. And that is what Kosambi sees as responsible for making the poet's greatness fictitious, something of a facade erected by the members of his class, to mask their real use of his poetry. Elsewhere, Kosambi shows how there is an 'unquestionable note of frustration' in his poetry, with the *vairagya* desired by Bhartrihari being in future conditional – something which he did not actually experience. So also, his *shringara* smacked 'less of a voluptuary's practice than unsatisfied desire taken out in literary exercise of the imagination'. This is reading literature with a sense of history at its best.

This reading of literature with a sense of history is in evidence wherever Kosambi has used or commented on literature. A few instances will suffice to bear this out. One of the most celebrated instances of Kosambi's use of a famous theme figuring in the Sanskrit texts of various periods is his analysis of the Urvashi-Pururavas story.[15] Taking up the theme and its variations, he goes on to examine its very origins and sees in it veiled references to the forgotten practices of the sacrifice of the husband in certain ancient societies. This kind of anthropology may be outdated by today's standards; to be sure, Fraser's *Golden Bough* will not be accepted as current anthropology. But the point is that even in this, Kosambi showed a historical awareness in the reading of literary texts. As a text lends itself to a variety of readings, it enables the later observer to analyse the compulsions behind each reading. Thus, whether we accept Kosambi's anthropology in re-reading the various readings of the Urvashi-Pururavas story or not, it allows us to examine Kosambi's commitment to a particular philosophy of history. The way in which he analyses the myth of Vishvamitra's patronage of Shunahshepa and curse of his sons is another case in point in this direction. Equally important is his interpretation of the myth of Indra smiting Vctra, where he sees an allegoric representation of the invading Aryans destroying the embankments of the Harappans.[16] It is a different question whether the category of the Aryan has as much validity today as when Kosambi wrote; but the historical materialist argument there is hard to miss. In the same way, the *Shatapatha Brahmana* account of Videgha Mathava demonstrates the originality with which Kosambi interprets literary references within the framework of historical materialism. This story of Agni moving eastward from the Sarasvati, burning the forests *en route* till he reached the river Sadanira, is taken to show the eastward migration of the Aryan peoples, settling the heavily forested land for cultivation after clearing it by burning it down.[17] This shows how a reading of literature with a historical understanding can be useful in calibrating the changes in the means and relations of production, the one category that is central to Kosambi's understanding of history.

The use of historical materialism in reading literature and the attempt to bring a class analysis to bear on it is best demonstrated by Kosambi's important study of the working class in the *Amarakosha.*[18] He rejects the charge that the classification of words in the dictionary is haphazard, 'exceedingly imperfect and confused, especially in all that relates to abstract ideas and mental operations'. He stresses that Amarasimha is mnemonically superior to his competitors (such as the authors of *Medini*, *Vishva*, etc.) precisely because he gave more attention to objective reality than ideal categories, unlike the scholiasts who concentrated upon grammatical form and derivation. Following a general analysis of the *varga* sections labelled after the four classes of contemporary society as brahman, kshatriya, vaishya and shudra and bringing out some interesting features of these, Kosambi takes up for elaborate analysis the working class treated in the lexicon. He shows how the text-book understanding of *sankirnajati* or mixed caste, exhibited in the earlier sections, are implicitly contradicted by the exposition of the reality that they were in most cases shudra castes that had come to be accepted as such following the proliferation of occupations and transformation of tribes into castes. This leads him to the significant observation that 'the *Amarakosa* was written in feudal times' although he is conscious that 'the evidence is poor'. What he has done is not just a listing of the entries where the working class shows up in the dictionary but a class analysis of the text, bringing out its evolution and changes. Incidentally, it may also be emphasized that this treatment of one of the most famous dictionaries in Sanskrit demands a mastery of Sanskrit language and the vast literature in it as well as a sensitivity to the class reality of the times in which the text was produced.

Arguably one of the most provocative statements of Kosambi on Sanskrit language and literature, in the context in which it was made, is regarding its class character. He says that 'most of the surviving Sanskrit literature has been the creation of brahmins or in their possession'. He goes on to say that 'the class [of brahmins] adapted itself to various changes in the means and especially the relations of production, a good many of which can be discerned only through their ideological framework'. He considers these adaptations 'in their proper setting'. This forms the background against which we have to place his observations.

After observing that 'some form of Sanskrit was spoken by the Aryan invaders of the second millennium BC, Kosambi notes that the Prakrit tendencies present in the Vedic literature onwards got the better of it and Prakrit became something of a *lingua franca*. Asokan, Kushana and Satavahana inscriptions suggest this. It was in the 'inscriptions and literature of the succeeding period', that Sanskrit comes of its own regardless of the region of the inscription. Kosambi then asks a question about its causality: 'How did this change come about? How does it happen that the classical period of the language follows a period of the vulgar idiom, instead of a steady development from Vedic through classical into the vernaculars, parallel to the sequence: old Latin, classical Latin, medieval Latin to the Romance languages.' 'The answer', he tells us, 'cannot be given in purely cultural terms', because the 'question of Sanskrit language and culture is deeply rooted in the development of India's productive forces, in particular with the emergence of a special position for the brahmin caste'. While he admits that this answer may at best explain a mere survival of Sanskrit, like that of Sumerian in Assyrian priesthood or the continued use of hieroglyphics by Cleopatra, the full answer for the literary efflorescence will have to be sought in the new class relations that supported the economy of the period of this efflorescence. While the three upper castes had the right to sacraments, to instruction from the brahmin, etc., the shudra had no such rights. Some newcomers with the requisite power, wealth and arms could join the upper classes as new high castes, or marry into the higher castes. It is, says Kosambi, difficult to imagine Heliodoros of the Besnagar pillar as a shudra by those who had enrolled him into the Bhagavata cult of Krishna-Vasudeva. Sanskrit was, thus, 'a new instrument to mark the unity of the upper classes, to emphasise their distance above the rest'.

It should not, therefore, come as a surprise that the first *prashasti* in Sanskrit, arguably the very first use of Sanskrit for *kavya*-like literary expression, is the Junagarh inscription of Rudradaman, a Shaka Satrap. Rudradaman and his governor talk about, among other things, protecting the four *varnas* – something which gained them acceptability in the society of the higher castes. It may be noted particularly that the talk was all the more convincing as it was backed by gifts to brahmanas. 'The proper attitude to cows, Brahmins and Sanskrit', says Kosambi, 'mitigated the lamentable choice of parents on the part of both Satrap and governor.' The point he emphasizes is that Sanskrit literature, which is exquisite and intricate in the pattern of beauty, is not, even at its best, capable of giving depth, grandeur of spirit and the real greatness of humanity as found in the Pali *Dhammapada*. The explanation is that it is 'the literature of and for a class, not a people'. That is why, he argues, it did not produce 'books of any use to the blacksmith, potter, carpenter, weaver, ploughman. . . . Ritual, philosophy, theology and poetry take up the bulk of

Sanskrit writings'. Here he strikes a comparison between Sanskrit and Arabic: Arab works on medicine, geography, mathematics, astronomy, practical sciences were precise enough to be used in their day from Oxford to Malaya. Although Arabic, too, was tied up with a religion, the 'difference was that "Arab" literati were not a disdainful priest-caste'. 'Those who wrote were not ashamed to participate in trade, warfare and experimental science, nor to write annals.'

This somewhat harsh judgement on Sanskrit and its literature need not be thought of as coming from an inability to appreciate the creative, positive side of it. Kosambi is all too conscious of it and does appreciate it. He does not stop with appreciation; he continues to analyse it within the framework of historical materialism. 'The great period of classical Sanskrit literature', he says, 'is intimately bound (in its various localities) to the rise of feudalism from above.' The contrast of this situation with that of classical Greek and Latin, whose decline was completed with the onset of feudalism in Europe, is explained by the difference in historical background and the different function of feudalism in India. Similarly, a secondary, minor, Sanskrit efflorescence and the rise of vernacular literature are attributed to the first success of feudalism from below. He generalizes from these:

> Every great new literary form implies the unfolding of a new social form, headed by a new class. . . . Whenever the type of society crystallises, the class turns from the task of rallying the whole society behind its own leadership to its proper work of steady exploitation: the literary forms correspondingly harden and culture decays. If it did not speak at first in the name of the whole of mankind, the new literature would appeal neither to a wide contemporary public, nor to posterity; if it continued to speak for all humanity it would necessarily become offensive to the class whose interests it must serve, the class with which it came into being. This shows why in the literature of most class societies, the great names come at the beginning.

Then he goes on to show how, from the time of Ashvaghosha on, through the great stalwarts in creative Sanskrit literature in the earlier parts of the first millennium, there was a steady decline.

Kosambi's analysis of literature within the framework of historical materialism also helps him to offer a causal explanation for the spread of Sanskrit in the first millennium AD and its decline in the subsequent period. In his provocative introduction to the *Subhashitaratnakosha* of Vidyakara, Kosambi discusses two major points: the social function of literature and the basis of feudal Sanskrit literature.[19] Here he is able to offer a consistent, defensible, explanation of the phenomenon of Sanskrit: its development from a language of religion and rituals into one of literary expression. Linking its growth with the social and economic development of India, particularly in what has been described as the feudal phase, Kosambi sees that, like all literature in a class society, the productive period was over in the age of early feudalism. Hence the difference between the poetry of Kalidasa and his ilk on the one side and Vidyakara's and Bhartrihari's on the other.

In this context, one may look the recent formulation regarding the spread of Sanskrit literary forms in southern Asia in the first millennium CE. Sheldon Pollock has, in a masterly study of the way in which the language of Vedic liturgy and rituals became that of secular literary practices, shown that a Sanskrit cosmopolis came into existence by the Common Era all over the South Asian subcontinent and Southeast Asia, held sway for about a millennium, before bowing out to the emerging vernacular literary practices. Pollock takes up the literary expressions in both the inscriptional *prashasti*s and the *kavya* variety of texts.[20] However, his causality is somewhat weak, almost nonexistent. Kosambi had adumbrated the idea of a Sanskrit cosmopolis half a century ago, although he had not fleshed it out. What is more important than the details is the causality: he explains it within the framework of historical materialism. In this context, it will be interesting to see what Pollock has to say about Kosambi. He does not, of course, recognise or accept that Kosambi had almost hit upon the brilliant idea of Sanksrit being the language of literary practices from the second century onwards, short of using the expression 'Sanskrit Cosmopolis'. The causality of the spread of Sanskrit, which Kosambi has given, is trashed thus:

> Sanskrit, for Kosambi, was a language that had lost all contact with the sensuous world of 'real life' in ancient India (some lives being apparently more real than others); it was purely an instrument of elite power and 'legitimisation' of power.[21]

'Real life' is about the realities of life; not about the world of fantasy and phantasmagoria in which the elite in that feudal society lived; it is not the life of those living in cosy comforts unaware and unmindful of the suffering masses. Again, Pollock attempts to pick holes in Kosambi's argument that 'Sanskrit meant less to [the 'proletariat' of medieval India] than Greek to the soldiers of Marcus Aurelius', by saying that

> Fifty years after Kosambi wrote this we have still a long way to go in developing an even remotely adequate social history of Sanskrit literary culture. But it is becoming increasingly clear that brahmans were not alone in writing Sanskrit poetry; Buddhists and Jains wrote it, too, studied it, taught it, and cherished it. And the social spectrum of secular Sanskrit seems to have been far wider than that: How else are we to understand verses from a 13th-century literary anthology that praise the Sanskrit poetry of a simple potter named Ghrona ('Caste is no constraint for those rendered pure by the Goddess of Speech') or that of a chandala named Divakara ('Ah, what power does the Goddess of Speech possess, that Divakara should have been a member of the literary circle of King Harsha, and the equal of Bana and Mayura'). Manuscript colophons, a huge and (for social history) as yet almost untouched archive, give abundant evidence that the readership of Sanskrit far exceeded the bounds of Kosambi's 'miserable class'. . . . Brahmanas no

> doubt typically promoted themselves as the custodians of the language, but it is to swallow their ideology whole to equate Sanskrit and brahmanism, as Kosambi, to say nothing of other far less critical scholars, invariably does.[22]

It is not difficult to see that even these are exceptions which proverbially prove the rule. In fact, it can be seen that even the 'vernacular' literature that was produced in the period after the first millennium was permeated through and through with the ideology of this class. In the circumstances, it is only intolerance that can lead to this kind of a trashing.

The argument is not that Kosambi pronounced the *last* word in the matter. But it is important that he said the *first* word. Improving upon what he wrote is not to show disrespect to him; it is to rejoin him. This engagement is yet to happen.

NOTES

1 D.D. Kosambi, 'Steps in Science' reproduced in *Science and Human Progress: Prof. D.D. Kosambi Commemoration Volume*, Popular Prakashan, Bombay, 1974, pp. 199-200.

2 Kosambi, 'Archaeological Review 2', *The Times of India*, October 13, 1964. Reproduced in B.D. Chattopadhyaya, ed., *Combined Methods in Indology and Other Writings of D.D. Kosambi* (hereafter *CMI*), Oxford University Press, New Delhi, 2002, pp. 829-832.

3 Kosambi, 'The Quality of Renunciation in Bhartrhari's Poetry', reproduced in *CMI*, pp. 703-720. This was originally published under the pseudonym 'Vidyarthi'.

4 Kosambi, 'On the Authorship of the *Satakatryi*', reproduced in *CMI*, pp. 555-567.

5 Kosambi, 'Some Extant Versions of Bhartrhari's *Satakas*', reproduced in *CMI*, pp. 568-594. See, especially, the chart on pp. 580-593.

6 Kosambi, 'The Pravarasamgraha of the *Mahabharata*', *CMI*, pp. 595-660; 'The Pravarasamgraha for the Bhsmaparvan of the *Mahabharata*', in ibid., pp. 661-669. See the detailed charts on pp. 610-660 and 664-669.

7 Kosambi, 'The Text of the Arthasastra', *CMI*, pp. 677-684.

8 Kosambi, 'The Sanskrit Equivalent of Two Pali Words', *CMI*, pp. 670-676.

9 Kosambi, 'The *Cintamanisaranika* of Dasabala', *CMI*, pp. 685-702.

10 Kosambi, 'Introducing Vidyakara's *Subhasitaratnakosa*', *CMI*, pp. 721-749.

11 Kosambi, 'Steps in Science'.

12 He does it, however, in his essay 'Introducing Vidyakara's *Subhasitaratnakosa*', *CMI*, pp.721-749.

13 Kosambi, 'The Quality of Renunciation in Bhartrhari's Poetry', *CMI*, p. 718.

14 Ibid., p. 719.

15 D.D. Kosambi, *Myth and Reality*, Bombay, (1962) 2002, pp. 42-81.

16 D.D. Kosambi, *An Introduction to the Study of Indian History*, Bombay, 1956.

17 Ibid.

18 Kosambi, 'The Working Class in the *Amarkosa*', *CMI*, pp. 283-294.

19 Kosambi, 'Introducing Vidyàkara's *Subhasiitaratnakosa*', *CMI*, pp. 731-6 and 740-5.

20 Sheldon Pollock, *The Language of the Gods in the World of Men: Sanskrit, Culture, and Power in Premodern India*, New York, 2006.

21 Sheldon Pollock, 'Towards a Political Philology: D.D. Kosambi and Sanskrit', in *Economic & Political Weekly*, July 26, 2008.

22 Ibid.

Kosambi the Mathematician

C.K. Raju

D.D. Kosambi's entire mathematical career appears as one long clash of values. A rejection of the value of specialization saw him leave Harvard. The high value he placed on research saw his exit from Banaras Hindu University and Aligarh Muslim University. His attempt to impart real knowledge of mathematics saw him sacked from Fergusson College, Pune. His insistence on ethical and relevant research led to his exit from the Tata Institute of Fundamental Research where, too, the diversity of his interests was portrayed negatively, though he continued his mathematical research till the end of his life. His mathematical career raises a number of questions regarding science management in post-independence India. These questions are vital today when the state is again making huge investments in science and technology.

Apart from his more popular work on numismatics and genetics, Kosambi worked on path geometry, exploring the foundations of general relativity. He also worked on statistics in infinite dimensions, computing, and probabilistic number theory. He successfully applied mathematics (or rather statistics) to history (through numismatics).[1] Why not the other way around? Why did he not do anything on the history of Indian mathematics, asks Romila Thapar.[2]

Thapar might address a related question to her colleagues in history. Why have not the leading historians in India provided any space for the history of science in the last 60 years? Capitalism breeds specialization (which leads to higher profits): therefore a scientist's wider interests (in, for example, history) are viewed negatively, as a disqualification and may jeopardize his job – as happened with Kosambi. Consequently, neither historians nor scientists, in India, are willing to do the history of science, except as a post-retirement pursuit. (And there are no professional historians of science, for there is no university department for the history and philosophy of science in the country.)

Remarkably, even Marxist historians, who hold up Kosambi as a model,[3] have not bothered in these 40 years to study his main preoccupation (and means of sustenance), which was mathematics. I am no expert in the history of mathematics in that period. Moreover, Kosambi published also in French,[4] German,[5] Italian,[6] Japanese,[7] Chinese,[8] and Russian[9] journals, but I know only some of his publications in one language. If I have nevertheless written this essay, it is only to set the ball rolling and because consideration of Kosambi's scientific career highlights some key current issues, which need discussion. Science has become the new holy cow in Indian tradition on which a critical historical perspective is urgently needed at this juncture,[10] particularly when the state is again making enormous new investments in it.

Like economic poverty, capitalism also breeds information poverty – or scientific illiteracy. The capitalist welcomes new technology, as a source of profits, but is disinterested in educating the general populace. This is evident in the enormous disparity between well-funded high-end research institutions and ill-funded (or non-funded) ordinary schools and colleges. This disparity creates a huge knowledge gap between the high-end researcher and all others. Even the otherwise educated elite are scientifically illiterate – to the point that they cannot even discriminate between mathematics and statistics – and are not ashamed of it, as they would be if they spoke bad English. Widespread scientific illiteracy is especially true of India where people have simply transferred their *bhakti* from things like astrology to science. Science is today the dominant form of epistemic authority which people blindly accept without understanding, and without question. In practice, this amounts to uncritical reliance on a few persons in positions of authority ('experts') in the scientific community, howsoever that authority was obtained. This 'expert raj' suits the capitalist, who uses it to exploit scientific illiteracy just as ordinary illiteracy was exploited earlier. Kosambi was almost a solitary critical voice who could see through this uncritical belief in science and ask: 'Is it any less a superstition?'

For example, Kosambi mentions the case of an Indian solar cooker, which used a pot polished from the outside to improve its looks and make it more saleable.[11]

> We know that the cooker produced some years ago with such fanfare and self-congratulation is useless. Even a schoolboy should have known that the pot at the focus of the solar cooker, being nickelled and polished, would reflect away most of the heat. But our foremost physicists and research workers, who rushed to claim personal credit and publicity, did not realise this.

Not that this sort of thing happens only in India. For example, Stephen Hawking's singularity theory is a sophisticated discourse on creationism.[12] But few people, even among relativists, understand singularity theory. So, to decide scientific truth, they weigh social authority. Thus, millions can be persuaded about creationism simply by marketing Hawking as the new scientific messiah.

We need to situate Kosambi in the context of a historical transformation in the understanding of science in India. In the 19th century, the Indian elite had concluded, rightly or wrongly, that Indians were colonized because they were inferior, and that they were inferior because they lacked science and were steeped in superstition. This led to the well-known reform movements during which the elite demanded education in 'western science', not Sanskrit. Calcutta became a well-known centre for scientific activities, with key achievers such as J.C. Bose, S.N. Bose, K.S. Krishnan, and C.V. Raman. During the first part of the 20th century, science was pursued in mission-mode.

Post-independence, however, science became professionalized – a quest for funds, not truth. Post-independence scientists in India are people who control (or have controlled) vast funds and power. It is impossible to say how their scientific work, if any, has benefited the people in their everyday lives. There is a vast difference between J.C. Bose, inventor of the radio, and Raja Ramanna, Kosambi's junior colleague, and former chairman of the Atomic Energy Commission. On the other hand, scientific illiteracy ensures that scientific truth is decided purely by authority, making scientists even less accountable than bureaucrats, or businessmen, or the judiciary. Big funding with no accountability has led to the emergence of a veritable science mafia in the country, and Kosambi was one of the isolated few to resist it.

> [B]y research is not meant the writing of a few papers, sending favoured delegates to international conferences and pocketing of considerable research grants by those who can persuade complaisant politicians to sanction crores of the taxpayers' money. Our research has to be translated into use.[13]

Kosambi, therefore, needs to be celebrated as a symbol of dissent, and studied if only to understand what is wrong with Indian science today.

First, however, an account of Kosambi's career and achievements as a mathematician is in order. I will suppose that Kosambi's map function,[14] which replaced Haldane's, is well known, like his work on numismatics, and I will restrict myself to the neglected aspects of his work on path geometry, statistics in function space, and number theory. We will first focus on 'prehistory': or his career and work on path geometry (which, along with tensor analysis, he describes as his 'main field of work for 20 years'), and statistics in function space, which took place before the publication of his book on history. The latter part of this essay concerns his later years, where his work was on number theory, and also considers the contemporary lessons that can be drawn.

CAREER

Kosambi was initially weak in mathematics[15] in his early days of school in Poona. But he worked on it, and soon turned mathematics into a strength, just as he transformed his initially frail body into an impressive physique while at Harvard Grammar School and Cambridge High and Latin School in the early 1920s. He went on to study mathematics at Harvard University, under the famous G.D. Birkhoff, to become the 'strongest' mathematician, as he called himself (meaning physically strongest). Birkhoff spotted Kosambi's talent, and admitted him to a personalized student research course on the many-body problem. He also advised Kosambi to focus on mathematics.

Kosambi sensed that specialization was a disguised form of semi-literacy; he valued what he called the 'Renaissance type of versatility: wide range of knowledge without sacrificing depth'. He consulted his father who concurred that he should acquire knowledge as widely as possible. Thus encouraged, Kosambi used the freedom available in American universities to take 18 courses in a year. Though he excelled in his studies, and graduated summa cum laude in 1929, together with a Phi Beta Kappa, his refusal to specialize went against him, even at the very beginning of his career, for, on the capitalist value of specialisation, non-specialists are taken non-seriously. In any event, Birkhoff did not offer Kosambi a fellowship for further research in mathematics at Harvard. The Great Depression had just started, and Kosambi returned to India. On the way, he stopped by in France, to try (unsuccessfully) and meet T. Levi Civita (who later communicated some of his papers) and Eli Cartan (of Bourbaki fame,[16] who later commented on his work).

Shortly after his return, Kosambi took up a job at Banaras Hindu University. Despite a sympathetic vice chancellor (Madan Mohan Malaviya, Kosambi's senior friend), Kosambi did not find the atmosphere there conducive to knowledge. He shifted within a year to Aligarh Muslim University where the mathematics department was headed by André Weil, also of Bourbaki fame. Weil could not cope with the politics at Aligarh, and was soon sacked, and Kosambi followed in 1933. He had got married in 1931 and settled in Poona, in a house built for him off Bhandarkar Road. Eventually, like his illustrious father, Kosambi settled for a lower social position and presumably greater peace of mind. Like his father, he took up a low-paid job in the nearby Fergusson College, where he taught mathematics for many years. As recognition for his research in path geometry, he received the Ramanujan prize in 1934. He described this situation as 12 years *vanvas* (banishment to a forest), for he lived in Erandavane, and had no one with whom he could discuss his mathematical research. His students were only interested in passing examinations to secure a job.

The few mathematicians he could interact with in Poona included a person with the improbable name of Wrangler Paranjape, who carried his undergraduate achievements in Cambridge as a sort of British-conferred title all his life (and even beyond in that at least one building was named after him) though he never did any research in mathematics. The story goes that one day Paranjape arrived to meet Kosambi and was late by some 10 minutes. An annoyed Kosambi, who had imbibed the value of punctuality in the US, opened the door himself and said 'Professor Kosambi is not at home' and promptly shut it! (There are other, milder, versions of this anecdote.) One must recall that, as principal of Fergusson College, Paranjape had given jobs, even if only ill-paid ones, to both Bapu and Baba Kosambi.

Eventually, Fergusson College sacked Kosambi, on the alleged grounds that students did not understand the mathematics he taught. Mathematics is a difficult subject to teach, especially to exam-oriented students in India. If one tries to teach the subject in its proper spirit, as Kosambi did, one loses most of one's students whose aim is a job or a degree, and not knowledge. Forced out of his *vanvas*, Kosambi met Homi Bhabha who was then expanding the Tata Institute of Fundamental Research (TIFR) in Bombay. Bhabha offered Kosambi a lucrative job which involved pure research, and which paid him more than five times what he had got as a teacher in Fergusson College. Kosambi accepted this in June 1947,[17] the same year he was given a special Bhabha Prize.

As is well known, Kosambi commuted from Poona on the Deccan Queen, switching from daily commute to weekend commute and back to daily commute. The two-way train journey itself was seven hours. Additionally, in the morning, he trudged a few kilometres from his house to the Poona station with a haversack full of books to read on the journey. The countryside, which Kosambi loved, had great natural beauty. As J.D. Bernal perceptively commented,[18] for Kosambi, 'history was not only in the past but also in the present', so his thoughts on these journeys naturally turned to history. (His book on history was written on the Deccan Queen during these lengthy commutes. He is also known to have consumed three mystery novels in three hours, and donated hundreds of science fiction and mystery novels to the common room in TIFR.) Since he had a few kilometres to go on the Bombay side, first to Kenilworth, on Peddar Road, and then to the Old Yacht Club at Gateway of India, and finally to Holiday Camp (now Navy Nagar) beyond Afghan church, Kosambi naturally joked that TIFR was just a 'third-class waiting room', which he used between train journeys.

FIRST PAPER

The first time is always of great interest. Kosambi's first paper was on 'Precessions of an Elliptical Orbit'.[19] As one would suspect, it links planetary orbits to atomic orbits: 'The solar system is but a step away from the atomic model'. But the sweep is breathtaking. The paper starts unexpectedly with hydrodynamics, giving the simplified equations of motion for an infinite cylinder. It then points out that these equations could be used to describe 'an electron in a magnetic field, a Foucault pendulum, and even the restricted problem of three bodies'. It then moves on, via observations of the motion of banjo strings, to general relativity, and points out that 'relativity has still to account for the observed precession of planetary orbits'. He then focuses on Venus and just the effect of its direction of rotation on the direction of precession (recognizing the limitations of the simplified theory he is using). He then tries to link it to the Zeeman effect and the electron spin-orbit interaction in the Bohr model, and moves on to the Raman effect. He concludes with a passing mention that 'electro-dynamically unsound models have usually been employed for purposes of illustration' and refers to the notes of Birkhoff. The paper is dated 'Harvard, September 1927; Banaras Hindu University, April 1930'. It may not amount to much, but for a paper written by an undergraduate student just out of his teens, it is absolutely astounding.

PATH GEOMETRY

From the very beginning, Kosambi's mathematical research was where the action was: on the frontiers. Relativity was one of the most intellectually exciting and challenging developments of that period. One of the most dramatic scientific events of the time was the sensational newspaper reporting on the three empirical tests of general relativity in 1918, which made Albert Einstein into a celebrity. Arthur Eddington had then boasted that only three people understood relativity.[20] As a schoolboy in the US, during 1918-24, with a keen interest in science, Kosambi grew up with these stories, which must have had a deep impact on him. As he puts it, the theory 'aroused theological passions'. That is the theatre Kosambi's mathematics of path spaces[21] impinged upon, and on which he worked for 20 years.

The correct equations of general relativity theory (GRT) were first obtained by David Hilbert in 1916, as a sort of mathematical exercise during vacation, and accepted with great alacrity (within five days) by Einstein,[22] eager not to lose out on the credit. Possibly because of the haste in its formulation, GRT leaves many questions unanswered.

The broad agenda of GRT was to replace the Newtonian concept of force by geometry, and this idea had been around for some time. But which geometry? As currently formulated, GRT uses Riemannian geometry. (This is named after Bernhard Riemann, a famous 19th century mathematician, who speculated along the lines of a four-dimensional space-time continuum, but was unsuccessful, since he lacked the special theory of relativity, and was not clear how to handle the physical notion of time, so his time coordinate was no different from a space coordinate.)[23] But the reasons for this choice of Riemannian geometry in GRT are not entirely clear, and raise several questions. Should one use what are called Finsler spaces instead? (In Finsler geometry, the metric, or the measure of 'distance', need not involve a quadratic form, as it does in Riemannian geometry.) Kosambi's path geometry included both Riemannian and Finsler geometry as special cases.[24]

Another key dispute of the times was whether geometry should be metric at all. While devising new foundations for mathematics, around 1900, Hilbert (and Bertrand Russell) interpreted Euclidean geometry as synthetic or non-metric. This was contested by Birkhoff who advocated a metric interpretation of Euclidean geometry. (The difficulty was that the metric interpretation trivializes the *Elements*, attributed to 'Euclid', for the 'Pythagorean' theorem can be proved in one step.)[25] A similar dispute applied *a fortiori* to non-Euclidean geometry. Length measurement requires lengths to be picked and carried. But, in curved space-time, picking and carrying lengths can distort them, just as a shadow moving over an uneven surface gets distorted. Geometry, it was thought, should be concerned with invariants. So, should one drop the metric, and do non-metric geometry (purely with the affine connection, or some notion of parallel transport) as suggested by Cartan? The absence of a metric, or the strange idea of defining area without defining length, however, makes geometry useless for mathematical physics, as Kosambi noted. Kosambi explored the circumstances under which his path spaces admitted a metric.

Yet another question relates to geodesics. A geodesic is an extremal path, either the shortest or the longest path between two points; in flat space, geodesics are straight lines, but on a curved surface they may be curved lines. For example, on the surface of the earth (regarded as a sphere) the geodesics are great circles. Geodesics may be regarded as characterizing the surface or higher-dimensional geometry in question. A key idea of general relativity is that one can substitute the Newtonian force by a space-time geometry in which the geodesics are approximately the particle trajectories that would have been obtained with that force. Thus, instead of saying that the planets move in elliptical orbits around the sun because of the force exerted by the sun on the planets, one says that planets move in geodesics of the Schwarzschild geometry, due to the solar mass. The three famous tests of general relativity actually tested geodesics in Schwarzschild geometry. (The Schwarzschild geometry was obtained as the first solution of the equations of general relativity; it was obtained even before the equations were finalized. The solution corresponds to the 'field' of a point mass. Planets being at large distances from the sun, the difficulty that a point mass must be surrounded by a black hole is not relevant for planetary orbits.) But is it meaningful to speak of geodesics in the absence of a metric? The calculus of variations studies extremal paths, and Kosambi considers an affine (or non-metric) calculus of variations.[26]

The replacement of force by geometry also brings in aesthetic considerations. To see this we need to consider the relation of force to geometry in another way. In Newtonian physics, masses are usually treated as geometric points, and geometric curves arise naturally as the trajectories of these points. For example, if we throw a ball, its path is approximately a parabola. The exact trajectories are obtained by solving Newton's equations of motion (Newton's second 'law'), which are ordinary differential equations of the second order. In the Lagrangian reformulation of Newtonian physics, one can regard the very same curves as the extremal paths of the action (which is the integral of the Lagrangian with respect to time). These extremals are studied in the calculus of variations, where they are obtained as solutions of the Euler-Lagrange equations, which may be ordinary or partial differential equations. An interesting aspect of this Lagrangian reformulation is that the Lagrangian function can be decided largely or entirely by considerations of symmetry. Mathematically, these symmetries form a group, which helps characterize the geometry in question. From this perspective, the key difference between Newtonian gravitation and general relativity may be roughly stated thus: Newtonian physics is required to be the same for all observers moving with constant velocity (invariance under the Galilean group), while general relativity is required to be the same also for all accelerated observers (general covariance). In contrast, special relativity is restricted to the Lorentz group (observers moving with constant relative velocity, when time measurement depends upon relative velocity).

This awe-inspiring grand narrative that the nature of the cosmos is decided from purely aesthetic (and geometric) considerations was seen to have some flaws even in the 1930s when Kosambi started his research. In his theory of path geometry (a term which he coined himself),[27] Kosambi explored these ideas. He also took up an issue which seems not to have been much discussed in the literature. Newton's equations of motion are the same for all inertial observers (moving with constant velocity) because they are of the second order. (Since velocity is the first derivative, taking the second derivative kills any constant velocity term that one might add.) However, if one now demands general covariance (indifference to the acceleration of the observer as well), there is no longer any reason why the equations of motion should still remain of the second order – they might well be of higher order. In this situation, what sort of geometry would emerge? This was a question that Kosambi investigated in his theory of path spaces of higher order.[28]

Although Kosambi does not explicitly motivate the use of higher-order differential equations of motion (or perhaps he mentions it somewhere, for I have not seen all his papers), he could easily have stressed the following compelling point. When a charged particle accelerates, it radiates energy (the technology of the radio, television and microwave is based on harnessing electromagnetic radiation). Consequently, the motion of the charged particle is damped. However, the force of radiative damping involves the third order derivative in time. This upsets the stock scheme of Newtonian physics, and the issue of what to do with this third-order term has remained unclear practically to this day.[29] This issue is also closely related to the difficulty of the 'unified field theory' which fruitlessly occupied Einstein for the final decades of his life: whether and how one could include electromagnetic and other forces, apart from gravitation, into geometry, possibly in a higher dimensional space. Kosambi had, in 1934, already applied path geometry to this question of the 'unified electro-gravitational field theory', as he called it,[30] particularly what is today called the unified field theory of De Donder, Einstein and Mayer.

Apart from the very high level of abstraction involved (even by the standards of relativity) in the kind of non-Riemannian geometry involved in Kosambi's path geometry, these papers are remarkable for their breadth of vision and for their use of sophisticated mathematical concepts. Kosambi extensively uses the theory of Lie groups, then still in its infancy. He repeatedly cites Richard Courant and Hilbert's *Methods of Mathematical Physics* (in the original German) which banks heavily on variational principles. There is also a noticeable amount of explicit computation with tensors, suggesting that Kosambi enjoyed playing with them.

There were other philosophical questions such as those raised by Edward Athur Milne: whether science is inductive (beginning with observations and moving to principles) or whether it is 'hypothetico-deductive' (beginning with hypothesis and deducing consequences which are then compared with experimental data). These related to the 'cosmological principle', which was later turned into the 'perfect cosmological principle' by Hermann Bondi in the formulation of the steady-state theory in 1948 in association with Thomas Gold, and Fred Hoyle. Kosambi links his path geometry programme to Milne's cosmology.[31]

Through all this maze of mathematical sophistication, the persistent vision was to explore an alternative, less arbitrary and more general reformulation of the general theory of relativity. Kosambi eventually visited the Institute of Advanced Study, Princeton, as a guest, and discussed his work with Einstein in what he described as 'several long and highly involved private technical discussions'.[32]

It would be inappropriate for me to assess Kosambi's work, for my own point of view is somewhat different. I have opined that GRT is an incomplete theory since it lacks the notion of 'particle'.

(The simplest solution due to Schwarzschild gives rise to a black hole, so it is not easy to speak of even the 'test particles' needed to formulate the geodesic hypothesis. The geodesic hypothesis states that 'test particles' naturally follow geodesics.) An actual notion of particle (as distinct from the geodesic hypothesis) would bring in the equations of particle motion, which get coupled with the equations of the field.[33] Therefore, my opinion is that a purely geometric approach (which was Hilbert's forte, and which presumably led to his profound neglect of matter while formulating general relativity) is not likely to be ultimately productive for a physical theory of gravitation.

However, there are other indicators. As already noted, Kosambi received the Ramanujan prize for this work. Another way to assess Kosambi's work on path geometry is to note the difficulty of the questions he tackled, and that can be judged by the fact that the answers are not clear yet, even after seven decades. Then, one can look at the impact among his fellow mathematicians. Some Japanese mathematicians took great interest in his work, and translated it into Japanese. On what I have called the 'Indian scientific method', the value of science (especially mathematics) is judged solely by the reactions of prominent western scientists. From this perspective, Kosambi was very successful, for the foremost western mathematicians of the time (such as Levi Civita, Cartan and Weil) responded well to him. As already stated, Cartan wrote an extended response to Kosambi's paper.[34] Further, as described by M.S. Raghunathan, in conversation, Weil told him, 'Kosambi is one of the finest mathematicians in your country'.[35]

COMPUTING

Everyone has heard of how Kurt Gödel knocked down Hilbert's number-theoretic program in 1929. However, few seem to understand that Gödel's metamathematics involved, first, a whole-hearted acceptance of Hilbert's formalization of mathematics, which has had far-reaching consequences, extending far beyond his celebrated theorems. In the 1930s, there was extensive development of formal mathematics leading to the formalization of set theory by John von Neumann, Paul Bernays, Gödel, and others. This was followed by the reworking of all mathematics in formal terms by the Bourbaki group, whose books became the Bible of mathematicians. (Non-mathematicians can perhaps connect to this as the 'new math' using set theory, which was introduced in schools and colleges in India in the late 1960s and early 70s.)

One of the consequences of Hilbert's formal and mechanical vision of mathematics was its influence on the theory of computation, around which present-day digital computers are built. Like atomic energy, this technology emerged during the Second World War. The Tatas were interested in it, and Kosambi was awarded a Unesco fellowship in 1948-49 to tour the UK and the US to study this new technology of electronic calculating machines. He was probably the first Indian to study it. Curiously, in a paper,[36] in connection with an infinite dimensional stochastic integral (later related by others to Feynman path integrals, but still hard to formalize today in any context other than Brownian motion – such as Lévy motion), Kosambi proposes an elaborate and detailed design for an analogue computer. Note that Kosambi proposes an analogue rather than a digital technique of computation. The key relevant difference is this: the theory of digital computation was (and still is) based on formal mathematics, whereas analog computation is obviously based on physics. This attempt to bring in physical and empirical methods of computation into mathematics at this high level of abstraction is very interesting,[37] although it is not clear that Kosambi intended this as a direct challenge to the dominant philosophy of formalism in mathematics.

About his study tour, Kosambi said:[38]

> One of my theoretical papers deals with probability and statistics in infinitely many dimensions. There has been no effective use, because the attempts at getting a special electronic calculating machine to translate this theory into practice failed.[39]

However, that trip was productive in other ways. Kosambi revisited Harvard and renewed his links. He saw the changes that the war had brought about in American science. He also visited Chicago and gave a whole course of 36 lectures on tensor analysis there. He visited Einstein at the Institute of Advanced Study in Princeton (also to discuss path geometry) for a couple of months. He met with A.L. Basham in London. As regards computers, TIFR did later try to build its own computer (Oldap) which I do not recall ever having seen working beyond printing out coy statements like 'Oldap is a good boy'. Today, of course, Tata Consultancy Services is a corporate giant in the field of information technology outsourcing, and is now trying to do cutting edge research on its own.

STATISTICS IN INFINITE DIMENSIONS

Kosambi said he got into numismatics because he used coins to teach himself statistics, and his first paper on statistics[40] related to numismatics. However, he also combined statistics with his deep knowledge of differential geometry, and successfully applied the geometric approach[41] to statistics in (infinite-dimensional) function space.[42] The infinite-dimensional analogue of the multivariate normal distribution is today known, in the theory of stochastic processes, as the Wiener measure, and is related to the stochastic process known as Brownian motion. It should be recalled that Wiener senior was a colleague of Kosambi senior, also teaching languages at Harvard, and he taught Russian to Bapu Kosambi. He had some radical theories about the origin of the native American languages and their relation to African languages. Norbert Wiener, whom he reared into a child prodigy (based on his radical theories of parenting), was Kosambi's friend from an early age. Although Wiener was 12 years older, he had a similar temperament, and the two became good friends. When Kosambi revisited the Massachusetts Institute of Technology in 1949, Wiener greeted him, 'Welcome, wise man from the East', and Kosambi responded, 'No, a wise guy from Cambridge'.[43]

In the geometric approach to statistics, a random variable is regarded as an infinite-dimensional vector which can be expanded in an infinite basis in function space, somewhat in the way a finite-dimensional vector can be so expanded in a finite basis. While the meaning of a finite sum is unambiguous, there are issues of convergence in the infinite-dimensional case. Kosambi studied this first in a paper of 1942. This leads to an orthogonal decomposition, similar to the expansion in Fourier series, and known as Proper Orthogonal Decomposition. Today this is also known as the Karhunen-Loeve expansion after Kari Karhunen who seems to have picked up the idea five years later, in a 1947 publication. One wonders why G. Kallianpur[44] has attributed 'independent rediscovery' to Kosambi, for it was Kosambi who discovered it first, and Karhunen who 'independently rediscovered' it later.

Regarding this business of 'independent rediscovery', people seem unaware that Western scientists have been rather liberally and comically claiming the privilege of 'independent rediscovery' for centuries. This is not confined to isolated incidents such as Guglielmo Marconi 'independently rediscovering' the work of J.C. Bose (which piece of historical nonsense it took a century to correct) but applies also to purported scientific revolutionaries such as Copernicus and Newton. As such, this is a systematic phenomenon of appropriation. During the religious intolerance of the Inquisition, the claims of 'independent rediscovery' were understandable, for theological deviance spelt big trouble. (Copernicus, a priest, waited till he was on his deathbed, to avoid the fate of his colleague Scultetus who was arrested by the Inquisition. Acknowledging his Arabic-Islamic sources would not have helped Copernicus' case for theological correctness in the preface of his 'revolutionary' book. Similarly, Mercator was arrested by the Inquisition, and did not reveal the non-Christian sources for the projection and table of secants needed to construct his map.) Later day colonial historians built on these false claims. Such unethical claims by influential westerners of having 'independently rediscovered' the earlier published work of an Indian continue to this day, as happened more recently with this author.[45] Even if there is no dishonesty involved, there is, as Newton remarked, no reason why the 'second inventor' of an idea should get the credit for it. Therefore, the 'Karhunen-Loeve' expansion ought to be renamed Kosambi's expansion.

In 1954, Kosambi published his last paper on path geometry and tensor analysis.[46] The next year, his book on history was published, and he led the Indian peace delegation to Helsinki, and toured China and the USSR. Kosambi published nothing in mathematics or statistics during 1955 and 1956. Sumit Sarkar recalls that when he graduated in 1958, Kosambi was not so famous as a historian. Irfan Habib (whose father was Kosambi's colleague at Aligarh) concurs. However, Kosambi's fame had spread as a Marxist statistician. In May 1957, he gave a talk to the Mathematical Institute of the Chinese Academy of Sciences on probabilistic aspects of Tauberian theorems.[47] Later he published a paper in a Chinese journal on an extension of the least-squares method to abstract function spaces.[48] He visited China under an Indo-China exchange programme, and according to biographer C. Deshmukh,[49] was invited by the Chinese government to apply statistics to agricultural production. (His genetic mapping function is still widely cited in Chinese publications.) In any case, he subsequently began publishing in the *Indian Journal of Agricultural Statistics* on the applications of probability to number theory.

PROBABILITY AND NUMBER THEORY

By way of background, Norbert Wiener, Kosambi's childhood friend, also contributed to number theory. After his PhD at the young age of 18, Wiener went from Harvard to Cambridge, and, on Russell's advice, studied number theory with G.H. Hardy. Wiener obtained the prime number theorem by means of his famous Tauberian theorem of 1932 which used only the methods of real analysis, surprisingly contrary to Hardy's belief that complex variables were a must for its proof.

As regards the terminology 'Tauberian theorem', broadly speaking, there are two categories of theorems, Abelian and Tauberian. These theorems originally related to the notion of summability of a divergent series, which Abel stated to be the work of the devil. Abel's theorem asserted that if a series converged in the ordinary sense, then it also converged in the sense of Abel sums. The converse of an Abelian theorem is known as a Tauberian theorem: the original theorem by Tauber asserted that if the Abel sums of a series converge, then, under certain conditions, the series itself converges. This general idea of deducing the behaviour of a series from the behaviour of its weighted averages, such as Abel sums (or of a function from its integral transforms, such as Fourier transform) has come to be known as a Tauberian theorem. Towards the end of his life, Kosambi got drawn into the application of probability to number theory through the class of Tauberian theorems.[50]

The prime number theorem is also closely related to the Riemann zeta function. Taking off from his work on Tauberian theorems, Kosambi developed a statistical approach to the Riemann hypothesis. This was a bold and innovative step. However, what Kosambi did next was a bit strange: he published a purported proof of the Riemann hypothesis in the *Indian Journal of Agricultural Statistics.*[51] In his own annotated list of papers, however, he carefully noted that this only gave a conditional proof: he said that it 'shows that if the primes in suitably defined covering intervals behave like an unbiased random sample, then the Riemann hypothesis follows'.[52]

Possibly the unconditional statement was one of those jokes which needed to be explained,[53] as sometimes happens with even the simplest jokes.

Kosambi's possible joke about the Riemann hypothesis may be better understood if it is placed in the context of the dilemma faced by B. Bagchi, who did his PhD thesis on the Riemann hypothesis. He, too, applied statistical techniques to number theory, and subjected me to his 'endless ramblings' on it, as he acknowledges in that thesis.[54] The Riemann hypothesis is one of the most difficult unsolved problems in mathematics. Bagchi could neither prove nor disprove the Riemann hypothesis. But he obtained some results that he thought were of value. An issue that worried him then was this: would that research be judged adequate for a PhD? What was he to do with those results?

This dilemma brings out a central difficulty with formal mathematics: the object of research in formal mathematics is to prove theorems – a good (formal) mathematician is one who proves good theorems. While a mathematical proof (as enunciated by Hilbert) can be mechanically checked for *validity*, there is no objective way to ascertain *value*, for all theorems are tautologies, some less obvious, some more so. The empirical world does not intrude at all into formal mathematics, unlike the way it does even in a pseudoscience like astrology. Therefore, the value of a mathematical theorem, like the value of a piece of art, lies solely in the eyes of the beholder. Unlike a piece of art where the beholders can be many, only a few people may understand a piece of advanced formal mathematics well enough to assess it. Due to the combined effects of scientific illiteracy and semi-literacy (over-specialization) this number may sometimes be five or six people in the world – if one is lucky. Therefore, value is typically assessed by a few 'experts' who can be deeply influenced by various subjective considerations. Had the Riemann hypothesis been proved, the value of the theorem would have been demonstrated. But, for a partial result, no one can say for sure whether it is the right road or a blind alley; so, judging its value, like judging the value of most other research in formal mathematics, calls into play the subjective perceptions of those in positions of social authority. Since formal mathematics has no external empirical anchor, the dependence on authority is total. On the maxim that absolute power corrupts absolutely, those in positions of authority in mathematics tend to get corrupted, and to use this subjectivity in ways that are not always above board. This is especially true of formal mathematicians in a non-egalitarian society.

So what could Kosambi have done? He had some results that he thought were promising, but could not establish their value unambiguously, for the non-expert, since he could neither prove nor disprove the Riemann hypothesis. On the other hand, there were too few experts around. In the matter of Bhartrhari, Kosambi was concerned that his 'heavy labours' should not go to waste, and should at least provide guidance to future workers. So, the natural thing in this case too was to create a record of what he had done, and also explain its value to others – most of whom might otherwise miss the connection, for connecting probability to number theory was a radical idea at that time.

But doing something so unsubtle would have been contrary to Kosambi's academic upbringing at Harvard. On the other hand, Kosambi was well known from childhood for playing practical jokes.[55] Therefore, it is possible that he combined subtlety with wit, and as yet another prank, published a 'proof' of the Riemann hypothesis in the *Indian Journal of Agricultural Statistics*. The curious choice of journal in which so momentous a claim was made does suggest that he was perhaps not serious about the claim and well knew that the purported proof of the Riemann hypothesis was not unconditional, as he clearly recorded in his own list of papers.

Kosambi had played such a prank earlier in his second paper.[56] That was quite a historic prank, for it confirmed the christening of Bourbaki, the famous 'mathematician' whose works are the Bible of formal mathematicians.

> In later years, Weil was at a meeting in India and told his friend Kosambi the story of the incident at the Ecole [where a student donned a false beard and strange accent and gave a much advertised talk which was balderdash from start to finish]. Kosambi then used the name 'Bourbaki' in a parody that he passed off as a contribution to the proceedings of some provincial academy. Soon the still-nascent Bourbaki group determined that this would be its name. Weil's wife Eveline became Bourbaki's godmother and baptized him Nicolas.[57]

However, after Hilbert, a mathematical proof is required to

be addressed to a machine or a moron, so present-day mathematicians often have neither a sense of humour nor of ethics, but only a sense of quibble.

A young man asked me why Kosambi played such a rash prank about the Riemann hypothesis when he had so many enemies. My only answer is that he probably did not expect his enemies to be so undignified as to hit below the belt – that too at a joke. Inevitably, however, this possible attempt at subtlety and humour had a tragic consequence. The Riemann hypothesis is notorious for the numerous wrong proofs of it that have been published. Kosambi's prank was misconstrued by the humourless mathematicians in TIFR to portray him as a crank and to sack him by not renewing his contract. Typical of the culture of back-room gossip[58] which characterizes the TIFR mathematics school built by K. Chandrasekharan, Kosambi was not asked for his version nor given a chance to explain his side.

Kosambi remained active in mathematics, and continued his work on probability and number theory[59] even after his removal from TIFR. Characteristically, the same idiosyncratic sense of humour was again on display. Realising that the people at TIFR were petty enough to block his papers, he wrote papers under the pseudonym of S. Ducray, who thanks Kosambi.[60] The name Ducray sounds vaguely French (*a la* Ducré), but *dukkar* means 'pig' in Marathi (actually, rather more than 'pig' – closer to 'swine'). Sure enough the papers were published. Kosambi kept up his interest in this area. A few days after completing his first book on mathematics (the typescript of which has mysteriously disappeared[61]), Kosambi died in his sleep.

CONTEMPORARY LESSONS

As the late Ravinder Kumar used to say: history is futuristic. What contemporary lessons can we learn from Kosambi's history? Why did India have no room for talented and knowledgeable people like him? Instead of being honoured for his lifelong devotion to research, he was repeatedly sacked, and left in bad financial circumstances. Can something be done today to prevent this history from repeating itself?

These questions are particularly acute today when we again stand at the threshold of large-scale changes in the education system. Post-independence India happily continued with the educational system it blames on Thomas Macaulay. Education was seen as a passport to a scarce white-collar job, so the bulk of the country was deliberately kept illiterate. Money was available for almost anything except education. However, recent years have seen a boom in outsourcing IT, business processes (BPO) and knowledge processes (KPO) to India. The fear, now, is that the comparative advantage of lower labour costs may evaporate. So, the large illiterate population in India is now being seen as a resource. Accordingly, a serious attempt is now on to educate the masses, since the perceived future of corporate profit depends upon that. A National Knowledge Commission has been constituted to this end. The changes that it recommends may have as substantial and long-term an impact as the changes made by Macaulay and Nehru earlier. Under these circumstances, repeating history by not learning from past mistakes could be an unmitigated disaster.

Let us examine Kosambi's case in more detail. Kosambi was, by all accounts, an extremely erudite and creative person, and such people are needed for research. The systematic elimination of knowledgeable and creative persons has practically characterized science management in post-independence India – Kosambi was repeatedly eliminated by the system. The reasons are not hard to understand.

In the first place, like many knowledgeable and creative persons, Kosambi tended to be outspoken – what is the point in being knowledgeable if one cannot communicate this knowledge to others? According to a well-known anecdote, at a social gathering in TIFR, speaker after speaker got up to praise the Tatas for their benevolence in contributing their hard earned money for the noble causes of research and education in setting up TIFR. Kosambi, a Marxist, knew the real reasons why TIFR was set up.

However, he disagreed only with the description of the Tata money as 'hard earned'. He felt compelled to explain that capital often starts off as rogue capital before turning respectable. He illustrated this by pointing out that the Tatas had earned big during the opium wars. The truth, however, may not be spoken loudly in a hierarchical system of management – Kosambi's remarks naturally did not go down well with Bhabha, who was once seen as a potential successor to the Tata empire since his aunt was married to Dorab Tata, and the couple was childless.

POST-INDEPENDENCE SCIENCE MANAGEMENT

Those remarks might have been shrugged off, but there was a more fundamental reason: Bhabha's knowledge was insecure. Bhabha's initial training was in engineering, which was what was considered valuable for the family business. It is another matter that the youthful Bhabha, smarting under the intellectual snobbery of Cambridge, later switched to physics, like Paul Dirac, the idol of the times. Though Bhabha subsequently took the mathematics Tripos, it did not teach enough physics either. So, he hired a displaced Jew, Heitler, to teach him physics. Bhabha is known in physics primarily for the paper that he wrote jointly with Heitler. It is a common tactic among our science managers to use their personal or institutional wealth to exploit those (such as research scholars) who are financially insecure. As Kosambi put it:

> The Byzantine emperor Nikephoras Phokas assured himself of ample notice from superficial observers, at some else's expense, by setting up in his own name, at a strategic site in the Roman Forum, a column stolen from some grandiose temple. Many of our eminent intellectuals have mastered this technique. There is little point in discussing the personal experiences of the scum that naturally floats to the top . . .[62]

A hierarchical knowledge-management system does not allow the worker to be more knowledgeable than the manager, for this risks exposing the ignorance of the manager. To put

Kosambi in his place, Bhabha appointed Chandrasekharan, a junior and undistinguished mathematician, over his head as deputy director. It always seems a smart move for the manager to appoint a subservient deputy. To ensure constant dependence, sycophants are selected for incompetence. This can gravely damage the entire system through a chain reaction, leading to long lineages of sycophants of progressively degraded quality, institutionalizing incompetence.

As Kosambi put it:

> The greatest obstacles to research in any backward, underdeveloped country are often those needlessly created by the scientist's or scholar's fellow citizens . . . The meretricious ability to please the right people, a convincing pose, masterly charlatanism, and a clever press agent are indispensable for success.[63]

As pointed out earlier, widespread scientific illiteracy ensures that the scientific method, in practice, is reduced to mere reliance on scientific authority. On the 'Indian scientific method' this scientific authority is taken to reside in the west – western social approval (such as publication in *Nature*) is thus regarded as the ultimate test of scientific truth. Consequently, it was natural for Bhabha to conflate development in science and technology with mimesis of the west, as many people still do today. Bhabha made a clear distinction between an east canteen in TIFR (where ordinary folk ate, and which served Indian food), and a west canteen (where the scientists ate, which served western food). He always wore western clothes, and reportedly even went so far as to demand that scientists in TIFR do the same.[64]

Bhabha's affinity for the west suited Chandrasekharan who built strong linkages with the west on one side, and with people from his caste and college in Chennai on the other. (TIFR was and remains exempt from the purview of reservations, so this freedom was bound to be misused. Andre Weil, in his autobiography[65] mentions the dominance of 'brahmins of southern India' in the

TIFR math school, but gives a hopelessly naïve sociological explanation for it.) Chandrasekharan's strategy fetched the mathematics school of TIFR a good reputation in the west.

However, the TIFR mathematics school contributed nothing of value either for the people of India, or for the atomic energy programme, despite more than half a century of intensive public funding, and despite access to the very best talent in the country. On the contrary, it exerted a strong negative influence across mathematics departments in India, and systematically (and often unethically) eliminated those who could do something of practical value, Kosambi being just the first. (When it was my job to implement various applications of national importance on the first Param supercomputer, despite offering high salaries, I could find no competent mathematicians in the country for the practical tasks at hand. Kosambi, incidentally, did link his work on statistics to diffusion in atomic reactors.)[66] The stranglehold of the TIFR math school has led to the systematic failure of mathematical creativity across the country. Admittedly, salaries in the west are far higher than in India, but if western social approval is what the country wants to spend money on, in the name of research in mathematics, that should not be done under the misleading heading of expenditure on atomic energy.

NEHRUVIAN VISION

A little deeper enquiry would help to place the issue also in the surrounding economic and political circumstances. Briefly, the Tatas were then interested in diversifying in a big way into energy, especially in exploring the possibility of atomic energy, which could bring in super profits like any new technology. But they lacked the know-how. Moreover, as Kosambi pointed out, the whole project of atomic energy was 'fantastically costly' if one took into account the costs of the research involved in generating the know-how. The investment in research made the project unprofitable, unless the state was persuaded to underwrite the costs of research, while privatizing the profits. Though the plan was initiated by the Tatas, this policy suited Nehru.

Nehru had a vision of modern India where capitalists would replace the traditional rajas, and science would replace superstition. In this vision, both private capital and science needed to be built up in the country through the agency of the state. So he created large research enterprises: vast sums of money were pumped in by the state into the departments of atomic energy, space, and scientific and industrial research. Nehru appointed the scions of leading industrial families to the apex management of these enterprises: Bhabha for atomic energy, Vikram Sarabhai for space, and the Birlas for the Council of Scientific and Industrial Research (CSIR). The sole expected outcome from the vast investments in these research enterprises was knowledge – to which those in apex managerial positions naturally had unhindered access. Thus, these vast state investments in knowledge were intended also to act as an invisible subsidy to help accumulation of private capital in India.

It is routine to pass on the results of state-funded research to private capital, but Nehru built a unique system of science management in India, by going a step further and giving representatives of private capital managerial control over state-funded research. Therefore, he forced scientists to be subordinate to capital. Those whom Kosambi called 'official Marxists' happily went along, for they clung to the antiquated idea of science as a 'progressive' force regardless of how it is managed.

Nehru reinforced this policy of 'science for the capitalist' with two further profoundly anti-democratic measures. The first was to take the Department of Atomic Energy outside the purview of even Parliament – Bhabha accounted directly to Nehru. (Though it is also true that science and technology issues are rarely debated in Parliament, except for absurd things like the petrol-from-water case!) Second, the last vestiges of any resistance through the university system were crushed by sidelining the enterprising Meghnad Saha in favour of Bhabha.[67] Over the next 60 years, there was a concentration of funds and powers with science managers, who now virtually established a dictatorship, while the relatively more democratic universities were systematically starved of funds.

In line with the 'Indian scientific method' of relying on western social authority as the sole means of validating science, our science managers became mere brokers of western scientific knowledge. The huge funds available to science managers were mostly used to import outdated technology and assimilate scientific developments from abroad, establishing linkages with the west, and getting also their brokerage in this process. Since funds and power were ends in themselves (and not the means to an end) for key science managers in post-independence India, this created an oppressive atmosphere to escape which the really talented and knowledgeable people often emigrated to the west. Like the dependence on western authority to decide truth, or the dependence created by the import of outdated technology, the export of talent is a process most appropriate for a vassal state.

The importance of the last factor is not recognized: western dominance depends upon a lead in technology, which, in reality, is very fragile. Pumping large sums of money into research does not guarantee innovation; so, to maintain this lead, it is crucial to ensure that scientific and technological innovation does not take place outside of direct western control. Bad science management in India, by punishing innovators, and encouraging mediocrity, willy-nilly plays a supportive role in maintaining western hegemony – just as crucial as the supportive role of the Indian civil service in maintaining the British empire. In a word, post-independence science has become an instrument to maintain dependency.

Kosambi, however, had grown up in the US, and had seen the post-war situation there and had no illusions that it offered greater freedom to the scientist.[68] Having rejected the option of emigrating, he had opted out of the larger western scheme of things. There was no possibility of his being a sycophant, so he had no place in India. Therefore, he had nowhere to go.

Mimesis of the west hardly suits the requirements of the people of this country. Contrary to the Nehruvian vision of mega projects, suited to transfer of capital, Kosambi argued in vain for technology better adapted to the needs of the Indian people, such as solar energy or small dams (even small atomic reactors) – and we are still having those debates.

ATOMIC ENERGY

The immediate cause of Kosambi's elimination has been described as his opposition to the atomic energy programme,[69] funding for which was the *raison d'être* for the Tatas to have set up the TIFR. It is quite true that Kosambi was an active campaigner for peace from the early 1950s. He participated in many public meetings in Bombay and led the mammoth 90-member Indian delegation to the World Peace Conference in Helsinki in 1955. It is also true that shortly before his exit from TIFR he gave a talk to the Rotary Club, in 1960, outlining the dangers of atomic energy.[70] (One of the arguments he advanced in this connection was that, since radioactivity brings about genetic changes, it might make everyone too stupid to be able to reverse the changes!)

However, championing peace or solar energy, or opposing large atomic energy plants in urban areas, could hardly have been the official cause of discontinuing Kosambi's contract, especially so soon after independence when democracy was linked to free speech and Tata's unwavering support for the British was still fresh in everyone's mind. I was unable to get hold of the papers at either the Bhabha or Nehru end when I first investigated the matter, long before the Right to Information Act. I regard it as likely, as stated by Deshmukh,[71] that a case was made out on the basis that Kosambi had published a wrong proof of the Riemann hypothesis, and that this had damaged the reputation of the institute. If this is correct, it suggests a clear intention to manipulate: even supposing Kosambi had made a mistake, why should one mistake in a long and distinguished career invite such retribution? In a subsequent letter that Bhabha wrote to Kosambi,[72] he snidely commented that Kosambi would now have more time for his other interests (namely history), indirectly suggesting that Kosambi had ceased to be a mathematician because of his interest in history.[73]

Of course, we have seen that Kosambi kept doing research in mathematics till the very end of his life. However, in the logic of specialization, a mathematician who did no serious research (and there were many such in TIFR) was preferable to one who did some mathematics but also did history, for by doing history he ceased to be a mathematician. Who says there is no identity politics in science! Also, Kosambi erred in being innovative in his mathematical research, for innovative ideas are very often initially socially disreputable, and what is required in the 'Indian scientific method' is respectability.

All this is not to deny that the system of keeping people on contract has been instituted just to silence criticism. People are rarely removed for non-performance, but quickly removed for defiance. Kosambi, of course, had ample strength of character and would not be cowed down in his criticism of Bhabha or the atomic energy programme, though he was well aware that his contract could be discontinued.

> In one matter it was necessary to speak out though it meant considerable damage to finances, health and research. Atomic war and the testing of nuclear weapons must stop. A flimsy 'Indian Report' on the effects of atomic radiation shows our moral and scientific bankruptcy by ignoring the extensive data compiled since 1945.[74]

Just about the time Kosambi's contract was discontinued, there was the Panshet dam disaster. A dam burst in July 1961, inundating large parts of Pune, especially the heart of the old city on the banks of the Mutha river. Kosambi, known to be extremely generous in helping people, helped in the relief effort, giving succour to people and offering them food and money.[75] According to an unconfirmed report, Kosambi donated his entire savings for the relief effort; although this is denied by other sources.[76] Anyway, his dismissal from TIFR created difficult financial circumstances, as Kosambi himself noted in the above quote (apart from depriving him of a library and other facilities he needed for research). According to A. Rahman, when he visited Kosambi in this period, instead of the usual hearty Goan meal of fish, all he got was tea and biscuits. Bhabha's influence with Nehru prevented any alternative appointment for Kosambi.[77] He could get an Emeritus position in CSIR only after Nehru's death in 1964, and had some difficulty even getting affiliated to the Maharashtra Association for Cultivation of Science.

To summarize: Nehru's method of building modern India imposed a culture of managing science hierarchically, and the knowledge insecurity of the top managers generated a culture of sycophancy. The resulting situation suited western hegemony, but was fatal both to knowledge development and to knowledgeable people like Kosambi who refused to turn into sycophants, and also refused to emigrate to the direct control of the west. In an atmosphere of widespread scientific illiteracy, it is the subservient sycophants who later become top science managers, and are often conflated with top scientists. Through a process of the 'survival of the unfittest', over time, these lineages of sycophants lead to a noticeable deterioration in quality. The only way to prevent perpetual recurrence of this state of affairs is to disband 'expert raj' and ensure accountability, by subjecting our science managers to sustained public scrutiny, and by making them personally accountable for the grants they sanction, and the people they promote, compared to those they reject. Such accountability will help dismantle the huge empires they have built through lifelong science management.

FINAL RESPONSE

Finally, it is interesting to consider Kosambi's response, as a mathematician, to his dismissal. In 1964 he again published a proof of the Riemann hypothesis in the *Indian Journal of Agricultural Statistics.*[78] Kosambi was not repeating the same joke a second time, so the viewpoint this time was different. As he explained it, the method of proof for deductions based upon probability differ radically from those of pure mathematics. Conclusions cannot be 'true or false' without qualification.[79]

He thought the 'modern statistical method can be an excellent guide to action'. What he meant was that the truth of statements must be understood 'only in the sense of unit probability', a point he had made in his earlier paper, but not emphasized. Anyway, in the above quote he was clearly drawing a distinction between 'statistical proof' (with probability one, which is 'almost sure', and an excellent guide to action) and formal mathematical proof (which is purportedly certain).

For a proper understanding of these remarks about mathematical proof, we should place them in their appropriate historical context. At about this time, three influential Indian academics, P.C. Mahalanobis,[80] J.B.S. Haldane,[81] and D.S. Kothari,[82] had taken up the issue of the Jain logic of *syadavada*. Haldane (a non-official Marxist, and Kosambi's friend) was willing to engage with Indian tradition, and interpreted Jain logic as a three-valued logic, while Mahalanobis sought a new foundation for probability theory based on this, and Kothari thought of explaining quantum physics on this basis.[83] Although Jains and Buddhists started off as contemporary (though rival) groups, the Jain ethic of non-violence has made them the richest community in India.[84] Buddhists were eliminated, and revived Buddhism still remains associated with dalits. Therefore, while Jain logic found a supporter in Kothari (a Jain and Chairman of the University Grants Commission), the Buddhist position on the matter was left unarticulated until recently, by this author.[85] Kosambi, however, should certainly have known of the Buddha's use of *catuskoti* (or the logic of four alternatives) in the *Brahmajala sutta* (Bapu Kosambi knew the *Tripitaka* by heart).

The other part of the historical context is the rise in the 1930s of a group of mathematicians known as the intuitionists, who challenged Hilbert's notion of formal mathematical proof. Though the intuitionists, led by L.E.J. Brouwer and Arend Heyting, did not go so far as to suggest the use of a non-two-valued logic, they rejected proof by contradiction (or the 'law' of the excluded middle), and this changed notion of proof radically altered the theorems of mathematics. (Proof by contradiction certainly fails with Buddhist *catuskoti*, which I have explained[86] as a quasi truth-functional system, though the situation is more complex with Haldane's interpretation of *syadavada*, as a three-valued logic.) It is irrelevant that the intuitionists lost the subsequent battle for social acceptance among mathematicians.

This historical context also enables us to counterfactually answer Thapar's question with which we started. Had Kosambi seriously applied himself to the history (and philosophy) of Indian mathematics, he could hardly have failed to notice that traditional Indian mathematics accepted the *pratyaksa* or empirical as a means of proof – as indeed did all systems of Indian philosophy,[87] without exception. This is in striking contrast to the western understanding of mathematics, which has deep religious roots,[88] and led to a formal mathematics that is divorced from the empirical, and admits only purely metaphysical means of proof. This metaphysics, being divorced from the empirical, is naturally a pure social construct. What has not been noticed is that this social construct has a religious bias, for it declares two-valued logic to be 'universal', while we have seen that it is not (Buddhist and Jain logics are not two-valued, and the debates between Buddhists and the Naiyayikas dragged on for a thousand years for this reason). Therefore, mathematical proof offers no certainty to the non-believer.

As for the practical applications of mathematics, they all relate to calculation, where formal mathematical proof is more of a hindrance (which has made it difficult to teach mathematics). Therefore, if Kosambi had indeed taken up the study of traditional Indian mathematics, he would have noticed its focal concerns with practical calculations, which linked it to the key means of production in India (monsoon-driven agriculture and navigation needed for overseas trade).[89] He would also have uncovered and attacked the key western superstition underlying the taboo against empirical means of proof in mathematics, and the belief that certainty can be found only through metaphysics of a certain religious sort. So, had Kosambi taken up the study of traditional Indian mathematics, it might have significantly altered the entire mathematics scene in the country, and perhaps the world, by now.

NOTES

1 D.D. Kosambi, 'A Statistical Study of the Weights of Old Indian Punch-Marked Coins', *Current Science*, 9 (1940), pp. 312-14. There was a long series of subsequent papers. A popular summary is in 'Scientific Numismatics', *Scientific American*, February 1966, pp. 102-11. Also, *Indian Numismatics*, Hyderabad: Orient Longman, 1984.

2 R. Thapar, 'Early Indian History and the Legacy of D.D. Kosambi', *Economic & Political Weekly*, 43(30), 26 July 2006, pp. 43-50, 47.

3 K.N. Panikkar, 'Culture as a Site for Struggle', *The Hindu*, 27 January 2009, p. 11.

4 D.D. Kosambi, 'Les metriques homogenes dans les espaces cosmogoniques', *Comptes rendus*, 206 (1938), 1086-88. 'Les espaces des paths generalises qu'on peut associer avec un espace de Finsler', *Comptes rendus*, 206 (1938), pp. 1538-41. 'Sur la differentiation covariante', *Comptes rendus*, 222 (1946), pp. 211-13.

5 D.D. Kosambi, 'Affin-geometrische grundlagen der einheitlichen feld-theorie', *Sitzungsberichte der Preuss B Akademie der Wissenschaften, Physikalisch-mathematische klasse*, 28 (1932), pp. 342-45.

6 D.D. Kosambi, 'Geometric differentiale et calcul des variations', *Rendiconti della R Accademia Nazionale dei Lincei*, 16(6) (1932), pp. 410-15.

7 D.D. Kosambi, *Tensor* (old series) No 2 (1939), pp. 36-39.

8 D.D. Kosambi, 'The Method of Least Squares', *Acta Sinica* (1957).

9 D.D. Kosambi, 'Indo-Ariiskii Nosovoi Ukazatel', *Sovetskaya Einografia* (Ak Nauk USSR) 1 (1958), 39-57.

10 C.K. Raju, 'Indian Science at the Crossroads', plenary talk at the 32nd Indian Social Science Congress, Delhi, December 2008. Also, 'Swaraj in Science', International conference on the centenary of Hind Swaraj, Delhi, February 2009.

11 D.D. Kosambi, *Atomic Energy for India*, Poona: People's Book House, 1960, p. 10. Transcript of talk given to Rotary Club, Poona on 25 July 1960.

12 Hawking's serious book ends, 'The actual point of *creation*, the singularity, is outside the presently known laws of physics'. S.W. Hawking and G.F.R. Ellis, *The Large Scale Structure of Space-Time*, Cambridge University Press, p. 364 (emphasis added). This linkage was made even more explicit by Tipler who uses Hawking's authority, and the authority of the journal *Nature* in which he has published on related issues, to begin his book with this startling assertion: 'Theology is a branch of physics'. F.J. Tipler, *The Physics of Immortality*, London: MacMillan, 1995. A more detailed analysis is in C.K. Raju, *The Eleven Pictures of Time*, Sage, 2003.

13 D.D. Kosambi, *Atomic Energy for India*, p. 9.

14 D.D. Kosambi, 'The Estimation of Map Distance from Recombination Values', *Annals of Eugenics*, 12(3) (1944), pp. 172-75. This formula appears in the stamp issued in honour of Kosambi. What Kosambi himself said about it seems not widely known: 'It seems to have given a new lease of life to genetical theories which I, personally, should like to see revised; so that I am accused at times of not

appreciating my own formula'. 'Steps in Science', in *Science and Human Progress* (D.D. Kosambi Commemoration Volume), Bombay: Popular Prakashan, 1974. p. 198.

15 Chintamani Deshmukh, *Damodar Dharmanand Kosambi: Life and Works* (Mumbai: Granthghar), 1993. Anon Eng trans. from Marathi. Deshmukh mentions Kosambi's poor marks in mathematics in school.

16 For the uninitiated, Bourbaki is a romantic figure in the history of mathematics. This name was used by a group of the foremost French mathematicians, and Bourbaki's books remain the Bible of formal mathematicians today.

17 There is a discrepancy in my secondary sources on this point. Deshmukh's biography gives the date as 1945 (51), while the Kosambi commemoration volume gives the date as 1947 (310). R.P. Nene confirms that Kosambi left Fergusson College only in 1946, and joined TIFR in 1947. However, the date in Deshmukh's book is not a typo, for he again states on 84 that Kosambi spent 17 years in TIFR.

18 J.D. Bernal, 'D.D. Kosambi' in *D.D. Kosambi Commemoration Volume*, p. 331.

19 D.D. Kosambi, 'Precessions of an Elliptical Orbit. Notes on: Vibrating Strings; Planetary Orbits; The Raman Effect', *Indian J. Phys.* 5 (1930), pp. 359-64.

20 One is not sure today whether Einstein was among the three. Einstein made a mistake regarding the general relativistic many-body problem, which exposed his lack of understanding of even special relativity vis-a-vis Poincaré. For an elucidation of the mistake (and its correction), see, C.K. Raju, *Time: Towards a Consistent Theory*, Dordrecht: Kluwer Academic, 1994, p. 122.

21 D.D. Kosambi, 'Geometric differentiale et calcul des variations', *Rend R Ac dei Lincei*, 16(6) (1932), 410-15; 'Parallelism and Path-spaces', *Math Zeit*, 37 (1933), pp. 608-18; 'Systems of Differential Equations of the Second Order', *Quart J Math*, 6 (1935) 1-12; 'Homogeneous Metrics', *Proc Ind Acad Sci*, 1 (1935),pp. 952-54.

22 See, for example, Jagidish Mehra, *Einstein, Hilbert, and the Theory of Gravitation*, Dordrecht, D. Reidel, 1974.

23 That is, his space-time was locally Euclidean rather than locally Lorentzian.

24 For example, D.D. Kosambi, 'Path-Spaces of Higher Order', *Quart J Math*, 7 (1936), pp. 97-104.

25 On the other hand, the difficulty with Hilbert's interpretation of the *Elements* was that it either fails after *Elements* 1.35 or else requires us to define area, while declaring the notion of length to be meaningless. See C.K. Raju, 'Euclid and Hilbert', chapter 1 in *Cultural Foundations of Mathematics*, Pearson Longman, 2007.

26 D.D. Kosambi, 'An Affine Calculus of Variations', *Proc Indian Acad Sci*, 2 (1935), pp. 333-35.

27 D.D. Kosambi, 'Steps in Science', p. 195.

28 D.D. Kosambi, 'Path-Spaces of Higher Order', *Quart J Math*, 7 (1936), pp. 97-104.

29 See, for example, C.K. Raju, *Time: Towards a Consistent Theory*, for a detailed

list of references.

[30] D.D. Kosambi, 'Systems of Differential Equations of the Second Order', *Quart J Math*, 6 (1935) 1-12.

[31] D.D. Kosambi, 'Path-geometry and Cosmogony', *Quart J Math*, 7 (1936) 290-93.

[32] D.D. Kosambi, 'Steps in Science', p. 195.

[33] This coupling leads to functional differential equations. This point, which has caused considerable confusion, is explained in detail in C.K. Raju, 'The Electrodynamic 2-body Problem and the Origin of Quantum Mechanics', *Found Phys*, 34 (2004), pp. 937-62.

[34] Eli Cartan, *Math Zeit*, 37 (1933), 619-22.

[35] M.S. Raghunathan, *Current Science*, 85(4) (2003), 526-36 (531), 'Young man, I find that people who know nothing about Kosambi want to talk about him! Let me tell you this: he was one of the finest intellects to come out of your country'. However, the word I recorded in conversation with Raghunathan, eight years before this publication, was 'finest mathematician' and not 'finest intellect', and that would also better fit the context of Raghunathan's question to Weil, which Raghunathan stated was Kosambi's publications on the Riemann hypothesis, considered later.

[36] D.D. Kosambi, 'Statistics in Function Space', *J Ind Math Soc*, 7 (1943), pp. 76-88.

[37] A key difference between the Indian and the European philosophy of mathematics is that Indian mathematics permitted empirical methods of proof, on which Western mathematics has placed a taboo. C.K. Raju, *Philosophy East and West*, 51(3) (2001), pp. 325-62. Draft at http://ckraju.net/papers/Hawaii.pdf.

[38] D.D. Kosambi, 'Steps in Science',p. 198.

[39] Today, of course, this is possible, and in 1994, this author implemented a package 'Stochode', which solves stochastic differential equations driven by Brownian or Lévy motion, as his last piece of work in C-DAC. Some details were reported several years later in C.K. Raju, 'Supercomputing in Finance', *Pranjana*, 3 (1&2) (2000), 11-36.

[40] Note 1.

[41] D.D. Kosambi, 'The Geometric Method in Mathematical Statistics', *Amer Math Monthly*, 51 (1944),pp. 383-89.

[42] D.D. Kosambi, 'Zeros and Closure of Orthogonal Functions', *J Indian Math Soc*, 6 (1942), pp. 16-24. 'A Test of Significance for Multiple Observations', *Current Science*, 11 (1942), pp. 271-74. 'Statistics in Function Space', *J Ind Math Soc*, 7 (1943), 76-88.

[43] L.B. Arguimbau, '"Baba" of Harvard Days' in *D.D. Kosambi Commemoration Volume*, p. 321.

[44] G. Kallianpur, *Bull Amer Math Soc*, 24(1) (1997), p. 46. 'Incidentally, as long as we are mentioning authors, the original K-L theorem should be properly called the Karhunen-Kosambi-Loeve theorem. The result was independently discovered during World War II by the Indian mathematician and Marxist historian D.D.

Kosambi.'

45 M.E. Walker, 'Retarded Differential Equations and Quantum Mechanics', *Notices of the American Mathematical Society,* 54(4) 2007,p. 473, belatedly acknowledges my earlier work. G.W. Johnson and Walker had in a 2006 article in the *Notices,* reported on Michael Atiyah's 2005 Einstein lecture, and renamed my ideas as 'Atiyah's hypothesis'. My theory correcting Einstein's error was already published in ref 14, and the Johnson and Walker article was published well after Atiyah was informed of my prior works – within a few days of his 2005 Einstein lecture.

46 Why did Kosambi suddenly lose interest in pathgeometry? There could have been many reasons, and one can only speculate. The atom bomb surely was not the only reason, for Kosambi did publish on pathgeometry even after Hiroshima and Nagasaki. Perhaps Kosambi's demotivation had something to do with Edmund Whittaker's 1952 book which accused Einstein of having plagiarized the special theory of relativity from Poincaré and Lorentz. E.T. Whittaker, *A History of the Theories of Aether and Electricity,* Vol II: *The Modern Theories* [1951-53], New York: American Institute of Physics, 1987.

47 D.D. Kosambi, 'Classical Tauberian Theorems', *J Ind Soc Agricultural Stats,* 10 (1958), pp. 141-49.

48 Bibliography in the Commemoration volume, entry at 105, says the Chinese text was published in *Ac Sinica* 1957, of unknown date, and later published in English as D.D. Kosambi, *J Ind Soc Agricultural Stats,* 11 (1959), 49-57.

49 Deshmukh, *D.D. Kosambi: Life and Works,* p. 72.

50 D.D. Kosambi, 'Classical Tauberian Theorems', *J Ind Soc Agricultural Stats,* 10 (1958), pp. 141-49.

51 D.D. Kosambi, 'An Application of Stochastic Convergence', *J Ind Soc Agricultural Stats,* 11 (1959), pp. 58-72.

52 (D.D. Kosambi), 'Bibliography of Kosambi's Writings', compiled from Kosambi's notes by R.P. Nene. In *Science and Human Progress* (Prof D.D. Kosambi Commemoration Volume) Popular Prakashan, Bombay, 1974, entry number 119, 373.

53 Martin Gardner, in *The Annotated Alice,* explains various jokes in *Alice in Wonderland.* That many people would otherwise miss the joke is clear from the fate of Swift's satire against formal mathematics in *Gulliver's Travels,* which has sunk into oblivion.

54 B. Bagchi, 'The Statistical Behaviour and Universality Properties of the Riemann Zeta-Function and Other Allied Dirichlet Series', PhD thesis, Calcutta: Indian Statistical Institute, 1981.

55 Deshmukh, *D.D. Kosambi: Life and Works,* p. 17, points to the doggerel which described Baba Kosambi as a school student at Cambridge High: 'The rest to some faint meaning make pretense/but Baba never deviates to sense'.

56 D.D. Kosambi, 'On a Generalization of the Second Theorem of Bourbaki', *Proc Acad Sciences UP,* 1 (1931) (3 pages).

57 S.G. Krantz, *Mathematical Apocrypha,* Mathematical Association of America, 2002, 144.

[58] The systematic use of malicious gossip by the TIFR math school to mislead the unwary is clear from the way R.S. Anderson, who researched in TIFR for his PhD thesis, was planted with the information that Kosambi was 'just a college teacher from a Bombay [Poona] college', while Chandrasekharan was from Princeton. This information is in Anderson's PhD thesis, though not in the subsequent book. R.S. Anderson, 'Life of Science in India: Comparative Ethnography of Two Research Institutes', PhD thesis, University of Chicago, 1971, Ann Arbor, Michigan, and *Building Scientific Institutions in India: Saha and Bhabha*, McGill University, Centre for Developing Area Studies, 1975.

[59] D.D. Kosambi, 'The Sampling Distribution of Primes', *Proc Nat Acad Sci* (USA), 49 (1963), pp. 20-23; 'Statistical Methods in Number Theory', *J Ind Soc Agricultural Stats*, 16 (1964), pp. 126-35.

[60] S. Ducray (D.D. Kosambi), 'Normal Sequences', *J Univ Bombay*, 31 (1962), pp. 1-4; 'Probability and Prime Numbers', *Proc Ind Acad Soc*, A 60 (1964), 159-64; 'The Sequence of Primes', *Proc Nat Acad Sci*, A 62 (1965), pp. 145-39.

[61] R.P. Nene recalls that he posted a copy of the typescript of the book to the publisher. Kosambi had apparently discussed number theory with Paul Erdos, who visited him in Pune. Nene also recalls that John Irwin, the curator of a London museum, was interested in the book, and was trying to get it published by Routledge (who do not normally publish mathematics). But Routledge seems to have lost the typescript. Nene also recalls that Kosambi was very meticulous about keeping copies of all his papers. But copies of the typescript of this book no longer seem to be available.

[62] D.D. Kosambi, 'Steps in Science' p. 201.

[63] Ibid.

[64] Bhabha's sartorial proclivities were reportedly the cause of M.L. Mehta leaving TIFR. I interviewed some people about this in 1995. Yashpal, former Chairperson of the University Grants Commission, whose kurta is his sartorial trademark, denies that there was any such demand. According to N.R. Puthran, Bhabha's registrar, Bhabha said: 'The answer to a shirt is a tie'. 'Those were his exact words', Puthran added. A contemporary of Chandrasekharan was K.G. Ramanathan; the only occasion I saw him without a tie, he offered an explanation for it.

[65] André Weil, *The Apprenticeship of a Mathematician*, trans Jennifer Gage, Basel: Birkhauser Verlag, 1992, p. 80.

[66] D.D. Kosambi, *J Ind Soc Agricultural Stats*, 11 (1959), pp. 49-57. The paper mentions that the solutions it obtains are 'of considerable importance for diffusion theory and the integral equations for atomic energy piles'. This is repeated in his annotated bibliography in the Commemoration volume in the entry at 105 which notes that this paper 'solves abstract equations, including integral equations for atomic piles (diffusion)'.

[67] Some details are in R.S. Anderson, *Building Scientific Institutions in India: Saha and Bhabha.*

[68] D.D. Kosambi, 'Science and Freedom', *Monthly Review*, 4 (1952), pp. 45-49.

[69] Dhirendra Sharma, *India's Nuclear Estate*, New Delhi: Lancers Publishers, 1983,

p. 120. I discussed this with Dhirendra Sharma in Hawaii, January 2000, but he had no recollection as to the source of this information.

70 D.D. Kosambi, *Atomic Energy for India.*

71 C. Deshmukh, *D.D. Kosambi: Life and Works,* p. 82. Deshmukh did not put down his sources, and died before he could do so.

72 My information about this letter comes from R.P. Nene, Kosambi's friend, who saw the letter. His account is corroborated by Deshmukh, ibid.

73 Ibid. Interestingly, M.S. Raghunathan also describes Kosambi as a 'mathematician turned historian' thereby suggesting that Kosambi had ceased to be a mathematician. Now, it is a simple empirical fact that Kosambi remained active in mathematics right until his death, although, of course, empirical facts are of no concern to formal mathematicians or postmodernists. M.S. Raghunathan, *Current Science,* 85(4) (2003), pp. 526-36 (531).

74 D.D. Kosambi, 'Steps in Science', p. 265.

75 Deshmukh, *D.D. Kosambi: Life and Works,* p. 86.

76 The source is A. Rahman. R.P. Nene, who was close to Kosambi in his last years, denies this. He however points out that Kosambi did donate the royalties from his book on the *Culture and Civilisation of Ancient India* to Cuba for hurricane relief. Deshmukh, *D.D. Kosambi: Life and Works,* pp. 85-86, cites some of Kosambi's petty extravagances on chocolates, travel, and the like, which would be 'profligacy' only from a strict Gandhian perspective, which Kosambi, a Marxist, obviously did not accept. On the other hand, Deshmukh also points out that Kosambi was excessively generous, and always ready to help others, and hence had little savings.

77 Deshmukh, *D.D. Kosambi: Life and Works,* pp. 96-97, goes into elaborate detail. This was corroborated by A. Rahman.

78 D.D. Kosambi, 'Statistical Methods in Number Theory', *J Ind Soc Agricultural Stats,* 16 (1964), pp. 126-35. This is not mentioned in the bibliography in the commemoration volume.

79 D.D. Kosambi, 'Steps in Science', p. 197.

80 P.C. Mahalanobis, 'The Foundations of Statistics (A Study in Jaina Logic)', *Dialectica,* 8 (1954),pp. 95-111; reproduced in *Sankhya, Indian Journal of Statistics,* 18, 1957, 183-94; reproduced as Appendix IV B in *Formation of the Theoretical Fundamentals of Natural Science,* vol 2 of *History of Science and Technology in Ancient India,* by D.P. Chattopadhyaya, Calcutta: Firma KLM, 1991, pp. 417-32.

81 J.B.S. Haldane, 'The *Syadavada* system of Predication', *Sankhya, Indian Journal of Statistics,* 18 (1957), pp. 195-200; reproduced as Appendix IV C in D.P. Chattopadhyaya, *Theoretical Fundamentals of Natural Science,* pp. 433-40. This account, together with Bhadrabahu's syllogism, is discussed at the level of the layperson in C.K. Raju, *The Eleven Pictures of Time,* Sage, 2003, chapter 10.

82 D.S. Kothari, 'Modern Physics and Syadavada', Appendix IV D in D.P. Chattopadhyaya, *Theoretical Fundamentals of Natural Science,* pp. 441-48.

83 Unfortunately, Kothari (or perhaps his student adviser, Kishan Lal) overlooked

the similar unsuccessful explanation of quantum mechanics in terms of three-valued logic advanced two decades earlier by Reichenbach.

[84] There is a simple causal nexus between wealth and the ethic of extreme non-violence: the Jain ethic compelled them to become traders and moneylenders, which most of them still are. According to the *Census of India 2001*, only 3.2% of Jains were into agriculture, compared to an all-India figure of 31.65%, and similarly for cultivators. The reason is this activity may involve the incidental killing of living beings while ploughing, etc. For more details, see *The Eleven Pictures of Time.*

[85] C.K. Raju, *Philosophy East and West*, 51(3) (2001), pp. 325-62; draft available from http://ckraju.net/papers/Hawaii.pdf.

[86] For an exposition of the different logics, see my article 'Logic' *Springer Encyclopedia of Nonwestern Science, Technology, and Medicine* 2008, a draft of which is available from http://ckraju.net/papers/Non_western_logic.pdf.

[87] C.K. Raju, 'Proof vs Pramana', chapter 2 in *Cultural Foundations of Mathematics*, Pearson Longman, 2007. This is an elaboration of the argument in my paper in *Philosophy East and West*, 51(3) (2001), pp. 325-62, a draft of which is available from http://ckraju.net/papers/Hawaii.pdf.

[88] This point perhaps needs to be explained. The word 'mathematics' derives from *mathesis*, meaning learning, and Plato opined, in *Meno*, that all learning is recollection of knowledge of past lives by the soul. Proclus explains that mathematics, 'the science of learning', is particularly suited for this purpose since mathematics concerns eternal truths which sympathetically move the eternal soul. Accordingly, Plato, in his *Republic*, recommended teaching mathematics for the good of the soul, and expressly not for any practical purpose. This theme was picked up by the Neoplatonists who used mathematics to contest changes to Christian theology in the 4th century, and then got incorporated into Islamic rational theology (*aql-i-kalam*) and from that (with some key changes) into post-Crusade Christian rational theology, the beliefs of which are reflected in present-day formal mathematics. C.K. Raju, 'The Religious Roots of Mathematics', *Theory, Culture, and Society*, 23(1-2), 2006, pp. 95-97. For the current *political* uses of rational theology, see C.K. Raju, 'Benedict's Maledicts', *Indian Journal of Secularism*, 10(3) (2006), pp. 79-90.

[89] *Ghadar Jari Hai*, 2(1) (2007), pp. 26-29. http://ckraju.net/IndianCalculus/Cultural-Foundations-Mathematics-review-from-GJH.pdf. C.K. Raju, *Cultural Foundations of Mathematics*, Pearson Longman, 2007.

Contributors

IRFAN HABIB is Professor Emeritus of History, Aligarh Muslim University. He is the author of numerous books, including the seminal *The Agrarian System of Mughal India 1556-1707* (1963/1999).

SUVIRA JAISWAL is a former professor of history, Jawaharlal Nehru University, New Delhi. She is the author of *Caste: Origin, Function and Dimensions of Change* (1998).

D.N. JHA is a former professor of history, University of Delhi, Delhi. He is the author, most recently, of *Early India: A Concise History* (2004).

PRABHAT PATNAIK is a former professor of economics, Jawaharlal Nehru University, New Delhi. He is the author of several books, including *The Value of Money* (2008).

C.K. RAJU is a computer scientist, mathematician, educator, physicist, and polymath researcher. He is affiliated with the Centre for Studies in Civilizations in New Delhi. He is the author of *Cultural Foundations of Mathematics* (2007).

KRISHNA MOHAN SHRIMALI is professor of history, University of Delhi, Delhi. He is the editor of *Reason and Archaeology* (1998).

EUGENIA VANINA is Head, Centre for Indian Studies, Institute of Oriental Studies, Moscow.

KESAVAN VELUTHAT is professor of history, University of Delhi, Delhi. He is the author of *The Early Medieval in South India,* (2009).